# TEAMING FOR QUALITY

# TEAMING FOR QUALITY

## The Right Way
## for the Right Reasons

H. David Shuster

Project Management Institute

## Library of Congress Cataloging-in-Publication Data

Shuster, David, 1934–
    Teaming for quality : the right way for the right reasons / by
David Shuster.
        p.     cm.
    Includes bibliographical references and index.
    ISBN: 1-880410-63-X (pbk. : alk. paper)
       1. Total quality management.   2. Teams in the workplace.
3. Industrial project management—Quality control.   I. Title.
HD62.15.S565   1999
658.4'013 – – dc21                             99–41751
                                                 CIP

ISBN: 1-880410-63-X

Published by: Project Management Institute, Inc.
               Four Campus Boulevard
               Newtown Square, Pennsylvania 19073-3299  USA
               Phone: 610-356-4600 or Visit our website: www.pmi.org

PMI® books are available at special quantity discounts to use as premiums and sales promotions, or for use in corporate training programs. For more information, please write to the Business Manager, PMI Publishing Division, Forty Colonial Square, Sylva, NC 28779  USA. Or contact your local bookstore.

The paper used in this book complies with the Permanent Paper Standard issued by the National Information Standards Organization (Z39.48—1984).

10  9  8  7  6  5  4  3  2  1

# Dedication

For Erin, Matthew and Tyler …
    my immortality

And for Suzi, Scott, Mark, Cory, and Heather …
    my paths to them

# Contents

# Figures

# Tables

You just don't get it, do you Jean Luc! The Trial never ends. We wanted to see if you have the ability to expand your mind and your horizons. For that one fraction of a second, you were open to options you had never considered. That is the exploration that awaits you. Not mapping stars and studying nebula, but charting the unknown possibilities of existence. See you "out there!"

"Q" to Captain Jean Luc Picard
*Star Trek, The Next Generation*
Final episode; All Good Things

# Introduction
## Escaping Management Fads

Seek the unpredictable ... yearn for surprise.

Author

## PURPOSE

Have you sometimes wondered why people become cynical about new management theories and view them as fads? Promising permanent revolutionary change, they seem to ignite and extinguish like fireworks—e.g., management by objectives, zero defects, total quality management, quality circles, and all manner and styles of process and quality improvement teams. What amazes me is how many employees (I call them healthy skeptics) seem ready, in spite of being burned more than once, to try the next management revolution coming along. They are rightfully skeptical but healthy in their optimistic expressions that 1) they like the ideas, 2) they do not think that they will work here, and 3) they will give it a try if they are only allowed to give it a try.

Why, if these designs have merit, do they so regularly die? The answer, I believe, rests on a kind of round peg-square hole phenomenon. Having observed it for over two decades—as private- and public-sector manager, consultant, trainer, speaker, and author—I believe that most organization personnel fail to realize 1) what they are getting into, 2) how conditioned and addicted they really are to

1

things as they are, 3) what they must do to succeed, 4) the impact of human resistance to change and how to overcome it, and 5) how much their change efforts depend on management philosophy. I have watched countless numbers of people attempt to use new management techniques (brainstorming, team building, network analysis, nominal group technique, fishbone and Pareto diagramming, and so on) without comprehending their larger purposes and the kind of cultural atmosphere they require to breathe and survive. It is like attempting to use hammers and screwdrivers without ever having heard of wood, nails, or screws or envisioned what you want to build.

This book addresses these issues and offers a principle-focused teaming process that helps good change happen. You will see how it works—from abstract philosophical grounding, through strategic design (theory), to concrete tactical implementing tools and techniques (technology). We shall compare and contrast pertinent quality and project management mindsets, principles, and practices, learn how to implement effective corporate cultural change, and learn how to overcome resistance to that change. Chapter 6 guides you through every teaming step required to implement the abstract but vital principles and strategies offered in Chapters 1–5. The book is, therefore, both text and handbook and has four specific purposes:

1. Present a complete and tested teaming philosophy, theory, and process, ensuring that people who choose to work together will experience exceptionally high levels of bonding, individual creative expression (innovation), and collective agreement (consensus). Teaming is represented as an act (verb) conducted in specially designed corporate environments by cooperating individuals in both formal groups and informal transactions. All of the concepts, rules, procedures, and steps required to conduct user-friendly teaming (Process for Innovation and Consensus [PIC]) are defined in Chapters 5 and 6.

2. Compare and contrast teaming-supportive and teaming-inhibiting corporate cultures, and learn how to turn the latter into the former, a critically necessary prerequisite for effective teaming.

3. Examine the root causes of resistance to change so often preventing creation of teaming-friendly corporate cultures, and offer recommendations for overcoming them.

4. Unite common, but often separately expressed, quality management and project management teaming principles and practices.

## PERSPECTIVE

Good management philosophical principles are generic and invariant. If they apply in one management area, then they pertain to all others. I shall show that they can be expressed through many varied implementing practices, techniques, methods, and exercises.

The invariant principle, for example, that moral leadership demands acting in the interest of constituents, rather than in one's own self-interest, can be internalized through virtually infinite varieties of simulations, discussions, stories, confrontations, and life experiences. Constant management principles, hence, wear multiple situational costumes. Ends are absolute! Means are not! Teaming, as a discipline, is no exception.

Those who think that people either cannot or do not sense these philosophical connections deny five decades of collapsing corporate teamwork histories. Given the challenge, even highly cynical employees and managers will try a new management-improvement technique. But the minute that they spot it as yet another gimmick lacking substance or direction, they bury it in the fast-growing cemetery of broken management fads. Be assured that those who rote-memorize PIC steps without internalizing and following its internal values might just as well forget it. Effective teaming practices depend on a firm grasp and acceptance of fundamental teaming philosophy: no principles—no results!

This book illuminates philosophy-to-practices teaming linkages by 1) specifying realistic generic teaming principles, and 2) defining consistent theory-based implementing teaming tools and techniques. Being simultaneously a text, reference guide, and handbook, it therefore addresses both what and how-to teaming questions and answers. Constructed around the two distinct but closely interrelated quality management and project management disciplines, the work thereby extends, enhances, and unifies several decades of accumulating teaming experience.

## MERGING TWO MANAGEMENT DISCIPLINES

Both quality management and project management gurus tend to offer adherents somewhat exclusive toolboxes, overlapping at their edges but essentially separate and unique. This essay dissolves that boundary and weds the two disciplines. We shall, in effect, "join together" what practitioners have unintentionally "put asunder." Readers will find interdisciplinary methodological linkages that at once blend quality and project perspectives, illuminate possibilities, and extend horizons. An entirely new holistic quality/project management child emerges, clearly greater than the sum of its parents' parts and ready to grow.

## AUTHOR'S APPROACH

Four critical points: First, I shall write in the first, second, or third person using narratives, outlines, quotations, and stories, as necessity dictates. I want to reach you at all levels—intellectual, emotional, imaginative, and moral. We must therefore establish a warm personal rapport if the spirit, as well as the letter, of our teaming message is to enjoy successful delivery.

Second, I am not objective! I have a distinct viewpoint to promote and an agenda to fulfill, both of which will emerge in the process. The words "ought" and "should" join "is," "what," "why," and "how" throughout these pages. This does not mean that I lack conceptual rigor; it simply means that I have, for good or ill, a moral compass directing me toward what I believe and hope to demonstrate are valued ends. Teaming requires moral direction. It binds participants into functional and dysfunctional intimacies not unlike those defining families. People risk much in accepting such intrusive partnerships. The rewards can (but not always do) outweigh those risks. Our task is to ensure that they do.

Third, we must immediately replace the word *team* (noun) with the word *teaming* (verb). Teaming is an act, performed in concert with individuals, sometimes in formal groups but mostly in informal conversations with others. Groups (call them teams, committees, task forces, and the like) cannot and do not act. Only living, breathing human beings can and do act. This distinction involves far more than mere semantics. I shall argue that it explains why quality management organizational change efforts so often fail, and why project team-member relationships sometimes erode. We shall examine basic group theory assumptions, realign our thinking about joint behavior, and create a consistent principles-to-practices image of effective human cooperation.

Fourth, I am a management theorist, not a physicist, psychologist chaos expert, or cosmologist. Even so, I adopt and adapt broad insights, as imagination and opportunity allow. Although I encourage you to judge my accuracy for yourself, such cross-disciplinary borrowing is common and legitimate practice. Compressing (reducing) ideas into tiny isolated academic boxes and locking people into rigidly defined disciplines is a peculiarly modern and unfortunate Western tradition that can deny us much of life's richly varied experiences. We, as complex human beings, are more than our job descriptions and more than what we do. Different philosophies of knowledge, whatever their other faults, appreciate this bonding of ideas and nature into holistic ecosystems. This reductionism trend is finally reversing under the onslaught of undeniable globally integrating corporate realities. Remember:

*Actions anywhere have consequences everywhere.*

## TOPICS

Our study begins at the top with management philosophy and ends with the complete PIC presentation. We shall:

- Define invariant generic management principles, and explain why they can be expressed through many effective practices (Chapter 1).
- Examine the nature of corporate culture and how to change it into a *teaming-friendly* environment (Chapter 2).
- Offer an original approach for overcoming resistance to organizational change without which effective teaming cannot and will not occur (Chapter 3).

- Merge quality and project management principles regarding teaming and the nature of process (Chapter 4).
- Construct the PIC teaming model (Chapter 5).
- Present complete, step-by-step PIC actions, derived from the model, and implement PIC's underlying philosophy, i.e., teaming mechanics (Chapter 6).
- Describe informal teaming, and set a vision for the future (Chapter 7).
- Provide supporting definitions, ideas, and references (appendices).

Built on these foundations, teaming philosophy, theory, and technology gain a firm and user-friendly operational context. That is why four crucial preparatory chapters pass before the teaming model and mechanics, themselves, are addressed. The PIC design bears directly on both quality management and project management principles.

You may, in the press of events, choose to jump directly to Chapter 6 on teaming mechanics. Remember, however, that we are asking people to leave their comfort zones and behave in strange new ways under conflicting daily personal and work-related pressures. When obstacles impede teaming progress in seemingly irresolvable conflicts, as they most surely will, correctives will not be found in unending reviews of teaming mechanics. They rest instead in comprehension and appreciation of the philosophical principles underlying those mechanics. Decide for yourselves, then, when you will address the first four chapters—sooner or later. Do not doubt, however, that if you are really serious about teaming (and not just mouthing words to suit the boss, or find some quick fix), then you will address them.

# The Romance of Management

And what is it to work with love? It is to charge all things you fashion with a breath of your own spirit.

Kahlil Gibran, The Prophet

Then join your hands, and with your hands your hearts, that dissonance not hinder governance.

Shakespeare, King Henry VI

DOES IT SEEM strange to associate management with romance? Not to me! Passion and excitement drive our total absorption in both work and play. Real teaming depends on such ardor. We shall examine this connection, and learn how to use it to advantage.

Think back to some exhilarating work-related program that consumed you, offering challenge, creativity, possibilities, awe, joy, a sense of rightness, belonging, acceptance, sharing, and contribution—in other words, total professional fulfillment. I surmise that you could hardly wait to get to work each day and found it difficult to tear yourself away from it. I loved those times and remain captured by their memories. Cast sometimes in lesser circumstances, we naturally recall those magic years and use their memory to bolster sagging morale.

Nothing, in my experience, promises recharging one's sense of professional fulfillment than real teaming—i.e., a social "joining of hands and hearts … " (Shakespeare) in an individual charging "all things [we] fashion with a breath of [our] own spirit" (Gibran). We shall approach teaming from this highly abstract but vital foundation, recognizing from the start that its principles and practices seek both of these crucial social and individual virtues. Very practical and concrete management rules emerge from this heady source. Management philosophy provides, therefore, a moral compass, steering management theory and techniques in clear directions. Ordinary people warmed in these environments will surely perform extraordinarily.

## PROFESSIONAL FULFILLMENT HIERARCHY

Professional fulfillment means different things to different people. One seeks wealth while others seek position, recognition, control, self-esteem, challenge, creativity, and so on. These factors are captured in the following four career satisfactions, which, together, comprise one's sense of professional fulfillment:

1. Moral: Working in an environment in which the things one must do conform to one's belief about what he should do.

2. Emotional: Feeling good about one's career position and prospects.

3. Intellectual: Enjoying analytical and imaginative challenge.

4. Material: Acquiring some desired level of physical comfort.

Moral satisfaction is the most important element, ensuring one's long-term sense of professional fulfillment. Nothing erodes morale or sense of self-worth faster than forcing people to act against their personal values. No amount of material, intellectual, or emotional satisfactions can compensate for this loss. And, guaranteed such spiritual satisfaction, employees will accept substantial sacrifices in the other three categories. The familiar comment, "Yes, I know I can make more elsewhere, but I like it here … I feel good here, so I'm staying," reflects this attitude.

Emotional satisfaction, the second most influential fulfillment element, pertains to the belief that one's career is on track. Overall senses of joy and statements such as "Work is fun" and "The future looks bright" usually accompany this perception. While not compensating for moral dissatisfaction, emotional contentment often balances less than fully optimized intellectual and material satisfactions.

Intellectual satisfaction reflects excitement; i.e., "This job is interesting." Stimulated reasoning and imagination activate early-in/late-out behavior and arouse a desire to "be involved in everything." Joy and fun also permeate this category. High intellectual satisfaction might even, in the short run, arrest emotional satisfaction career considerations—not, however, in the long run. Hurt as it might to leave "that great program," career interests eventually dominate choice.

Material satisfaction refers to acquisition of physical goods, services, and social position determining lifestyle comforts for ourselves and significant others. Once achieving some minimal material comfort and potential material growth levels, people tend to sacrifice further incremental-compensation-increase opportunities for current or expected satisfactions in the other three categories.

## WORK, COMMON PERSPECTIVES, AND CHANGE

How many people find substantial, sustained, and prolonged professional fulfillment throughout their careers? Relatively few, I suspect. Some never feel it. Most probably enjoy intervals and bursts, while operating at generally low lifetime fulfillment levels. Naturalist and philosopher Henry David Thoreau said, "The mass of men lead lives of quiet desperation." How sad! Minute by minute, hour upon hour, days building into weeks, weeks into months, months stretching across years, and years consuming decades—for some, an entire lifetime of slow agony, compromised dreams, and lingering sorrow. For others, less despair, but only in degree. Some people find peace of mind, personal solace, reward, and fulfillment outside of work—e.g., in family, personal, social, and religious pleasures.

## Complimentarity

Must work fulfillment elude us? No! Not most of the time at least. And surprisingly, as we shall see, personal (individual) career fulfillment and organizational (collective) goals, although different, are not necessarily antagonistic. In other words, individual employee interests correlate positively with collective corporate success. They go together. They are compliments, not tradeoffs. We hold ourselves captive to the view that they are incompatible because of the mutually exclusive attitudes and convenient symbols that we use to describe them—for example, us versus them, labor versus management, workers versus bosses. We must, as James N. Powell states in *The Tao of Symbols*, break through this bewitching "dialogue [that] holds us captive. ... ," and seek the essential nature (Tao) of these truly compatible associations.

Compatibility and synthesis of apparently antagonistic opposites permeates life, relationships, and history. For instance, Niels Bohr, the great quantum theorist, in addressing the apparent contradiction of photon wave-particle duality (light sometimes behaving as a particle, other times as a wave) showed (as did Powell) that this seeming contradiction rests in our perceptions and symbols rather than in nature. Bohr's *Principle of Complimentarity* explains that light, in some experiments, behaves and displays as particles and, in other experiments, as waves—that it indeed does retain both qualities. And, to fully comprehend light, we must appreciate its total character and experimental contexts. Complimentarity emerges in many other contexts, e.g., the Korean Yin/Yang, the popular idea that opposites attract—indeed, that reproduction requires the joining of compatible opposites: sperm and egg.

## Change and Resistance to Change

Our journey from general, quality, and project management philosophy to teaming theory and techniques begins with the idea of change, that bugaboo on everyone's lips but seldom in their actions. Change is traumatic. It can also be exhilarating. People contemplating change in their organizations must eventually determine their pain/thrill ratio—i.e., how much suffering they are willing to endure to achieve so much ecstasy. Cultural differences do not affect this dynamic. People everywhere must eventually face their willingness and ability to overcome resistance to change. Niccolo Machiavelli, in *The Prince*, cited the familiar resistance to change complaint five hundred years ago, observing that there is "nothing more difficult to take in hand, more perilous to conduct, or more uncertain in its success, than to take the lead in the introduction of a new order of things."

Intervening centuries have only amplified this truth. My consulting clients always cite "resistance to change" and "lack of communication" as their two most aggravating organizational ills. Change management demands, therefore, clear and specific processes for overcoming this resistance. Addressing resistance to change in Chapter 3, we shall identify its roots in current behavioral approaches to addiction withdrawal and grief resolution. Chapters 5–6 will show that teaming principles and practices offer a reliable, sensitive, and user-friendly solution to this problem. All of this depends, however, upon clarifying invariant philosophical management principles supporting teaming, quality management, and project management theories and practices.

## A USEFUL PHILOSOPHY VOCABULARY

If management philosophy drives all else, then a common simplified (perhaps oversimplified) vocabulary of philosophical terms will ease communication and shared comprehension of ideas, claims, and approaches presented throughout these chapters. Table 1.1 provides that vocabulary. Become familiar with these seemingly cloud-nine concepts, because their direct link to management and teaming will emerge as we progress. These terms appear throughout the book, so take a moment now to review them.

Philosophy leads to what quality management guru Dr. W. Edwards Deming called "Profound Knowledge" (management knowledge based on theory, prediction, integrated systems, and human interactions), or what I call comprehension of the highest metaphysical meaning of ideas and existence. This search for ultimate universal meaning drives human quests for moral philosophy's ultimate perfections, presented in Table 1.1. It also underlies questions that managers ask every day.

### Moral Philosophy and Management

Consider for a moment that organizational vision statements are aesthetic and teleological, mission statements are ontological, charters and policy manuals are epistemological, standards of conduct are ethical (based on shared axiological values), and strategic plans include all of these elements. Managers awakening to these connections soon appreciate the very direct practical significance of heretofore-utopian abstractions to decisions, performance, productivity, and competitive success—especially in change-driven, global, and cross-cultural environments. Disabuse yourself now of any lingering doubts concerning this matter, or do not be surprised when (regardless of how many fishbone diagrams, brainstorming sessions, Pareto charts, critical path diagrams, Gantt charts, or responsibility matrix tables that you use), your teaming process falters for reasons you cannot fathom.

## MANAGEMENT AS A DISCIPLINE

Management is a discipline! Disciplines arise from fundamental issues, i.e., circumstances that somehow impede our ability to easily understand or do something we deem important enough to comprehend or do. Disciplines are, in other words, carefully studied and learned responses to difficult situations. Some things come easily. Walking, for instance, is quite natural and easy for most people two years or older; they simply stand up and do it. For some disabled people, however, walking presents an almost insurmountable obstacle, achievable only through intense efforts of will, concentration, and effort. Walking for them is a fundamental issue, the successful performance of which requires discipline in both its academic and personal contexts.

# Table 1.1
## Philosophical Terms

| Term | Topic |
|---|---|
| Philosophy | Love of wisdom—inquiry into abstract first principles as foundation of all other knowledge—critical examination of standards that other disciplines simply take for granted—the only area of study beginning with no limiting boundaries or assumptions |
| Metaphysics | Transcending physical experience—*meta* meaning *above* or *beyond* the senses, i.e., suprasensible |
| Moral Philosophy | Study of *ultimates* and perfection, including the following subtopics: |

Moral Philosophy subtopics:

- **Ontology** — Reality and existence—what it means to *be*
- **Epistemology** — Knowledge and truth—what it means to know or verify something
- **Aesthetics** — Beauty—the essence of that which delights our senses and imagination
- **Teleology** — Beginning, end, and meaning—from where do we come (origins)—where are we going (destinations)—and why
- **Axiology** — Values—highest standard(s) of good and bad—right and wrong—should and should not—comprehensive self-evident commanding criteria of ultimate worth and merit; includes the following subtopic:
  - **Ethics** — Rules (norms based on values) defining and regulating good, right, and proper conduct (behavior)

**Fact/Value Dichotomy: Critical Axiological/Ethics Question**

Can we *know* whether a value is *true* or *false*, in the same way that we can know that a fact is true or false; i.e., are values strictly subjective, or can they be objectively ranked in terms of one being *better* than another?

## The Fundamental Issue of Management

I suggest that the fundamental issue, giving rise to the discipline of management, is:

> tension arising out of conflicting organizational needs for both disordered (turbulent, chaotic, unpredictable) entrepreneurial creativity, and ordered (smooth, regulated, predictable) product and service delivery.

This tension begins the first moment that an organization exists, changing its character through development to full maturity. Organization textbooks usually define three or more development stages through which companies progress as they grow to bureaucratic maturity:

1. Entrepreneurial (opening in a garage), involving a few loosely coordinated familiar and friendly people throwing out suggestions—lots of ideas, no structure.

2. Prioritization, which requires some order because ideas must be jointly sorted, refined, and ranked—fewer ideas, some structure. Tension already emerges, but probably below most everyone's recognition threshold.

3. Marketing, sales, and production planning, which usually means more (unfamiliar) people (who see themselves as workers and the founders as managers), schedules, policies, payroll, government regulations, and so forth—big drop in ideas, expanding structure.

This trend continues until a full-blown self-perpetuating bureaucracy eventually joins the crowd, creators insisting that they be heard, butting heads with bottom-line delivery and financial types (with competitive pressures requiring satisfaction of both interests). Both the story and the tensions are generally familiar to most of us.

## Management as a Responding Discipline

Management responds to the tension arising from conflict between organizational demands for both creative chaos and performance order, but not to the conflict or demands, themselves. The demands and their attendant conflicts properly remain inherent organizational elements, defining the very nature of corporate reality.

Following the principle of complimentarity, discussed earlier, we discover that although organizational disorder and order are different, they are not necessarily competing. We traditionally choose to see them as competing. We can, thus, just as easily choose to view them as perfectly natural and complimentary corporate elements. Alone, each describes only one incomplete organizational priority, but together they illuminate the comprehensive organic wholeness of the complete creature.

### Management Definition

Management, then, pertains to the way we deal with that tension and is accordingly defined as:

> the *act* of determining the way we do the things we do. (Shuster's Laws of Management and Teaming (S/L), Definition 1; see Appendix I)

Management, according to this definition, is 1) an act, depicted by verbs rather than nouns, and 2) about the *way* we do what we do, rather than *what we do itself*; i.e., management is about process. And, therein rests one of the intimate links uniting quality management, project management, and teaming. All three topics focus on process.

# THE NATURE OF PROCESS

A process is a conversion device, i.e., a set of integrated acts combined and blended to convert the property, form, or function of something into something else. For example, a motor is a process that converts electrical energy into mechanical torque (energy becomes torque). A generator reverses the alteration, converting mechanical torque into electrical energy (torque becomes energy). Therefore, motors and generators are processes.

Essentially, A becomes B through a process. A process is, hence, a becoming, a pathway, for metamorphosing things that are into things yet to be (a directed journey of expectations, exploration, anticipation, newness, strangeness, and difference). Managers define the nature and character of that journey.

Informal (unplanned) processes, rooted in habitual attitudes and behaviors, might or might not add value to an enterprise. Formal (planned) processes, designed to add value, also might or might not do so. Chapter 6 includes my original Process for Innovation and Consensus (PIC) teaming technique, called process internalization, that helps identify the root causes of process events under investigation.

## Management Processes

Management processes involve human interactions and are, therefore, substantially more complex than their purely mechanical counterparts. Similar to biological systems, they are organic life histories, blending mixed streams of intended and unintended visions, ideas, feelings, attitudes, events, habits, relationships, biases, values, agendas, and skills characterizing purposeful and survival-interdependent human activities. People working together for even a short time recognize the swirling bath of influences within which corporate events occur.

## Control Systems Models (Input-Process-Output-Feedback)

Typical control systems (input-process-output-feedback) models show input demands entering a box (conversion process) and output responses exiting the box with feedback signals (output-to-input) moving under the box. *A Guide to the Project Management Body of Knowledge* (PMBOK® *Guide*) indeed connects its individual project management knowledge areas in this control systems input-output format. The basic idea is that if appropriate inputs exist and the boxed process is operational, then outputs and feedback occur; i.e., demand inputs convert into response outputs. But, this presentation, valid as far as it goes, remains vastly oversimplified. A familiar example explains why.

Imagine you are driving fifty miles per hour along an interstate highway. Deciding to accelerate to seventy miles per hour (you are in a state allowing such speeds), you press the accelerator (input) sending an increase speed input signal into the engine/transmission/differential/axle/wheel system (process box). The car's speed increases (output), and you adjust accelerator pressure accordingly (feedback)—simple enough? Certainly, except that we assume that sufficient energy (air and gasoline) to fuel (support or sustain) the process exists. Anyone who has either run out of gasoline or driven at thin-air altitudes knows that such assumptions entail risk.

> The lesson here is that processes will not convert inputs into outputs without sufficient supporting energy to fuel the system.

Management processes also require such support—not gasoline and air, but human sustenance. We saw earlier that human processes involve all sorts of attitudes, agendas, and behaviors that can, and (unintentionally or intentionally) often do, undermine, redirect, or prevent designed process operations. Again, anyone with even the slightest organizational experience recognizes familiar cries of "What's happening here? Why isn't it working? They did it (or did not do it). Doesn't anyone care around here?" Search yourself. You have up days and down days. Personal grievances and outside problems, labor-management disputes, interpersonal conflicts, low morale, and all of the other ills that "flesh is heir to" can render processes, however well designed, impotent.

About forty-five years ago, University of Chicago political scientist, Dr. David Easton, presented a landmark reinterpretation of control systems process models that included the influence of support and sustaining factors in human process operations. Looking at political processes (highly relevant in management arenas), he provided explicit insights into how we can 1) recognize, and 2) deal with these energy factors. Appendix II offers a teaming-focused control-systems adaptation of Easton's process ideas, which are crucial to diagnosis, treatment, and improvement of teaming, quality management, and project management processes. The discussion is quite technical but worth your concerted effort to read and contemplate. Project managers will especially find the approach useful when trying to reconcile PMBOK® *Guide* theory against real-world events.

## PHILOSOPHICAL DEFINITIONS OF QUALITY AND PROJECT MANAGEMENT

Keeping in mind that philosophy provides a moral compass directing teaming, quality management, and project management theory and technology, our initial quality management and project management definitions must, simply stated, reflect those ultimate motivating qualities. Philosophers seek universals—i.e., truths that transcend all of the conditional and situational events that alter and adapt daily experiences. When all of the exceptions, detours, and complexities of events peel away, what invariant essentials remain? Such propositions must, of necessity, stay abstract; that is their great strength. They remain applicable in all circumstances, and lead the way to more testable definitions at the theory and application levels of analysis.

## PHILOSOPHICAL QUALITY MANAGEMENT DEFINITION

I define quality management, philosophically, as:

> a never-ending journey toward ever-rising and receding horizons of something better.

Note the teleological emphasis of this definition, i.e., continuous movement toward unimaginably better ends—a quest for the unexpected aboard a vessel of dreams. Horizons are not just reached; they are breached, themselves rising to ever-new heights of possibilities. Here, then, resides the romance of quality management.

Quite unlike finite duration projects, quality management opens to infinite futures. The very act of discovering finality condemns the effort. Quality management history overflows with stories of organizational revolutions destroyed by self-satisfied protestations of "enough already." In management, as in politics, nothing destroys a revolution like success. Revolutionaries both create and prosper under change, but, whither in the status quo, often during postrevolutionary stability.

Be warned, those of you contemplating or engaged in quality management: Change and finality are oxymorons! You have chosen a way of life, not a project. Figure 1.1 illustrates the benefits and risks

## Figure 1.1
## Organizational Disposition for
## Management Change

| | | Ready to Change? | |
|---|---|---|---|
| | | **Yes** | **No** |
| **Initiating Change?** | **Yes** | 1       *Healthy* <br><br> • Testing Commitment <br> • Facing Pain <br> • Achieving Improvement <br><br><br> Watch out for sense of self-satisfaction. | 4       *Potentially Unhealthy* <br><br> • Avoiding Honest Self-Assessment <br> • Raising False Expectations <br> • Generating Cynicism <br><br><br> Watch out for major morale problems. |
| | **No** | 2       *Potentially Unhealthy* <br><br> • Avoiding Desired Action <br> • Promoting Personal Guilt <br> • Encouraging Adversarial Relationships <br><br> Watch out for increased turf wars. | 3       *Healthy* <br><br> • Allowing Time for Self-Assessment to Develop <br> • Encouraging Continuity <br> • Containing Expectations <br><br> Watch out for serious deterioration of organizational health. |

Alternatives ranking: 1=Best; 4=Worst

attending quality management initiation by comparing organizational readiness to change against change initiation. Chapter 4 examines these forces in some detail and suggests relevant issues requiring close consideration.

## Philosophical Project Management Definition

I define project management, philosophically, as:

the act of creating something beautiful.

Aesthetics, a quest for beauty, drives project management. Recall those relatively few products and performances that, in your experience, rose above mere technical excellence and contractual conformance. They shone brightly as works of art, delighting your senses and imagination. Here were exceptional and rare inspirations, lofty standards against which all else might be compared. In this resides the romance of project management.

### Joining Quality and Project Management

Complimentarity again links two different management enterprises initially displaying quite different characteristics—one temporary and aesthetically directed, the other endless and teleological.

Discipline comparisons presented in Chapter 4 will show that unique quality management/project management operating principles, processes, and tools and techniques are quite compatible and interchangeable. Be aware, however, that quality management, as presented here, involves much more than that presented in the *PMBOK® Guide* Chapter 8 (Quality). More than simply a project management subprocess, quality management represents an independent, freestanding, comprehensive management discipline. Quality, as legitimately presented in the *PMBOK® Guide*, reflects engineering quality assurance and quality control activities, rather than the much broader field discussed here (and often, regrettably, identified as total quality management).

## FIRST PRINCIPLES AND SHUSTER'S LAWS OF MANAGEMENT

Our journey from management philosophy to teaming theory and techniques rests on thirty-two propositions and six definitions that I dare to name Shuster's Laws of Management and Teaming (see Appendix I). I believe that they contain those invariant transcendent principles without which the essential spirit of true teaming cannot be realized. They define the right reasons supporting both my teaming philosophy and this book's subtitle, *The Right Way for the Right Reasons*.

Although viable teaming theories and techniques other than the PIC certainly exist, I assert that they too must (in one manner or another) trace back to these core principles. Purposeful human actions, moving without a moral compass, achieve their stated ends only through dumb luck—and then, only temporarily.

I began with approximately five laws twenty years ago. Thought, experience, other people's ideas, and imagination brought me slowly to the current number. Some were dropped or amended along the way. New laws will, no doubt, expand the list. Take a moment to review them. You will find references to them sprinkled throughout the book.

## THE NEXT STEP

We turn now to two critical topics that set the environment within which teaming operates: corporate cultural change (Chapter 2) and resistance to change (Chapter 3). They explain, I believe, much about why quality management and project management teaming enterprises often whither and collapse. Even the most inspired techniques perish in and around hostile environments and rigid attitudes. Fine castles built on sand eventually sink of their own weight. I designed PIC teaming with this in mind. As well as offering an innovative and consensus-building way to address issues, it helps create, nurture, and sustain the very supports within which it prospers.

Principles are, by definition, more abstract than practices. Be prepared, therefore, to float a while at intangible altitudes before we ground ourselves in the tangible PIC.

# 2

# Corporate Culture: The Alien's Garden

> If you inquire what the people are like here, I must answer, "the same as everywhere."
>
> Johann Wolfgang von Goethe

Effective teaming requires, and helps create, a friendly environment or corporate culture. The two virtues go hand in hand. Teaming cannot prosper in rigidly structured, command/obedience, top-down, fear-inducing hierarchical cultures. Virtually all organization personnel must change—indeed, literally reverse their entrenched historical character—if teaming is to prosper. But, changing such deeply ingrained habitual attitudes and behaviors requires persistent and total dedication, approaching almost heroic proportions.

Habitual behavior is addictive behavior. Changing embedded corporate culture means breaking addictions, a painful journey fraught with pitfalls, risks, doubts, and uncertainty. We shall see (in this and the next chapter) that psychological readiness to suffer the pain of withdrawal from habitual addictive behaviors is the single most critical step, which each individual employee must take, before culture can change. The old ways, although imperfect, are known ways, offering perceived security, comfort, and predictability.

Change causes some people to feel a profound sense of personal loss (not unlike loss of a loved one) and accompanying grief. We shall examine how working through that grief determines each individual employee's willingness and ability to adapt to, and adopt, change. The pace of total corporate cultural change depends, in large measure, upon how fast and completely those individuals work through and come to terms with their sense of loss and grief (see Appendix III).

Those looking for easy answers should consider keeping things the way they are, and forget about teaming. The good news is, however, that well-planned and sustained change processes reap early and increasing results that encourage and reinforce those willing and able to persevere. The battle never ends, but its uphill character does eventually reverse.

This chapter probes into the character of corporate culture and offers insights about how it might be changed. The following chapter topics construct a mechanics of corporate cultural change aimed at facilitating management transformation and effective teaming:

- Relating Culture to Management
- Culture and Cultural Change as Abstract Ideas and as Operational Entities
- Definitions of Management, Management Transformation, Culture, and Cultural Change
- The Key to Operationalizing the Concept of Culture
- The Logic of Management Transformation
- Organic versus Mechanical Systems
- A Pincer Envelopment Strategy for Cultural and Management Change
- Pincer Strategy Components
- Explaining the Levels of Analysis
- Explaining the Disciplines of Knowledge
- Resistance to Change: "There Be Devils!"

## RELATING CULTURE TO MANAGEMENT

Imagine that culture is to a corporation what soil and environment are to a garden. Sterile soil and inhospitable environments do not nurture healthy plants. Soil must be nourished and the environment protected. Soil and environment act together in complex, interdependent, and integrated patterns that are compounded of more than the simple arithmetic sum of their constituent elements.

Smart gardeners always dream of better crops and forever look for better ways to enrich the soil and environment in which to grow them. They find joy in, and are uplifted by, nature and the privilege of being allowed to participate in a universe-centered, rather than a self-centered, enterprise.

The connection between the gardener metaphor and the dynamics of corporate management transformation is quite direct. This book makes that association and offers a design for initiating and sustaining desired changes in corporate culture (the corporate soil, climate, and environment) leading to management transformation (the new improved corporate plant).

## CULTURE AND CULTURAL CHANGE AS ABSTRACT IDEAS AND OPERATIONAL ENTITIES

The assumption that cultural change is at the heart of quality management and project management has become one of the mantras chanted in management literature, seminars, classrooms, conferences, and symposia. The ideas of corporate culture and cultural change are well appreciated and accepted. If, however, quality management and project management practitioners are ever to act with consistent theoretical rigor to predictably change corporate culture, they must first define it as more than an abstract idea. They must define the term culture operationally—that is, in concrete, physically observable change-process terms that are analogous to the abstract idea and can be measured, manipulated (or operated upon), and evaluated.

Returning to the gardening metaphor, a creature living in outer space might accept the idea of the word soil but would hardly be able to appreciate or comprehend it in operational terms. Therefore, the alien would be ill prepared to understand, experience, or conduct the mechanics of gardening. Like our terrestrial friend, we have come to appreciate the ideas of corporate culture and cultural change but have much to learn about their operational mechanics.

This chapter offers an operational definition of culture and a consequent mechanics for conducting and evaluating its teaming-friendly change. The mechanics relies on a rather simple logic, backed by a set of philosophical assumptions concerning human relationships and from successful applications in public, private, civilian, and military sectors.

## DEFINITIONS OF MANAGEMENT, MANAGEMENT TRANSFORMATION, CULTURE, AND CULTURAL CHANGE

If the ultimate purpose of corporate cultural change is to transform management, then it is necessary to define these terms, in ends-to-means order—that is, management first, then culture. Each definition is worded to help us both conceptualize the abstract terms and learn how to empirically operate upon them.

- Management, defined in Chapter 1 (also see Shuster's Laws (S/L) Definition #1, Appendix I), is "the *act* of determining the way we do the things we do."
- Management transformation concerns *the way we improve management.*
- Culture is *the holistic summation of individual community members' habitual attitudes and behaviors.*
- Cultural change is *cultural metamorphosis or mutation*, accomplished through purposeful alteration of individual habitual attitudes and behavior.

Management, as discussed in Chapter 1, focuses less on the things that people are doing technologically and more on the processes (conversions) through which they are doing them. Purposeful cultural change cannot occur, therefore, without visible, persistent, dedicated, and driving commitment.

Management transformation pertains to improving management, which means continuously critiquing and changing the way we do the things we do (S/L #21, Appendix I). Feeling comfortable with this sense of chaos, disturbance, uncertainty, risk, turbulence, loss of comfort zones, and movement into unknown realms is crucial for people if they are to appreciate and accept their transforming journey. For those inclined toward the status quo and grieving for the loss of "things the way they were," this prospect can be quite discomfiting.

Those who fear projecting themselves into a future beyond experience must (as discussed in Chapter 3) become psychologically ready to suffer the pain of withdrawal from their addictive habitual ways, question their own preconceptions, and be comfortable in a turbulent environment (S/L #3, Appendix I).

They must learn to treat experience as a conditional data point (defined as one factor among many factors), but not as an absolute and inviolate rule for defining or circumscribing future possibilities (S/L #23, #25, #27, Appendix I). Nonetheless, their painful sense of loss over things as they were is honestly felt, and its effects can be crippling if it either goes unattended, is ridiculed by managers and peers, or is absent as a variable in the theory that guides change.

Numerous conceptual and abstract definitions of culture populate the social sciences, offering little in the way of measurable rigor. Although highly abstract, they provide important insights into the effect of culture on management.

Typical conceptual definitions include the following:

> Culture is the way of living developed and transmitted by a group of human beings, consciously or unconsciously, to subsequent generations. ... [It is] ideas, habits, attitudes, customs, and traditions. ... [It is] overt and covert coping ways of mechanisms that make a people unique in their adaptation to their environment and its changing conditions. (Harris and Moran 1990, 134)

> Culture is the integrated pattern of human behavior that includes thought, speech, action, and artifacts and depends on mans' capacity for learning and transmitting knowledge to succeeding generations. (Deal and Kennedy 1982, 4)

Insights derived from such definitions include, first, the refreshing ideas of integration, system, pattern, and holism. Western scientific thinking has driven too many of us to extreme reductionism—i.e., the idea that if we break complex systems into separate and isolated parts, then all we have to do is tie the individual items together again, and we shall understand the whole. How often, for instance, do we hear statements such as, "You do your part, I'll do my part. We'll keep out of each other's way, and things will be just fine." Or, "It worked on the test bench; why is it failing when we put it into the system?" Fortunately, systems analysis and systems integration are becoming staples of the physical, natural, and behavioral sciences.

Consistent with this integrating cultural perspective, W. Edwards Deming asserts the holistic prescription for optimizing the system as the cornerstone of his management philosophy (see Chapter 3). Stephen Covey elevates interdependence over independence in human relationships. Psychologist M. Scott Peck recommends that inclusive mutually bonding communities replace their exclusive restrictive counterparts. I combine their perspectives in my principle of optimizing the organic community (described later in this chapter) as the foundation supporting teaming-friendly cultural and management transformation.

These conceptual definitions of culture properly disabuse us of this reductionist fallacy. They suggest the idea of holistic culture, i.e., a complex web of bound-up and survival interdependent elements.

Second, these definitions effectively communicate appreciation of the learning environment that culture provides for teaching and socializing new generations. They target the social capacity for transmitting knowledge to succeeding generations.

What these typical conceptual definitions of culture do not do, however, is provide a basis for operationalizing that concept in the sense that management transformation requires. The terms in the definitions are so loosely constructed, broad in scope, group focused, abstract, and boundless that they make comparison and measurement virtually impossible.

## THE KEY TO OPERATIONALIZING THE CONCEPT OF CULTURE

The key to overcoming this definitional weakness, and finding a valid and reliable operational definition of culture, grew out of a 1960s revolution in strategic thinking and group theory. It centered upon a new way of thinking about individual attitudes and behavior, as modified by group association.

Culture implies the idea of group—that is, a defining set of relationships and expectations shared by two or more individuals that sets them off from other people. Although almost everyone knows that a group is a concept, and not a living person, some of us have allowed ourselves to reason with the hidden but implied assumption that groups are behaviorally the same as individuals. That seemingly innocent slip in exactness too often results in misleading conclusions. For instance, we sometimes pigeonhole people by political, economic, social, sexual, ethnic, racial, national, religious, and other preconceived categories. Then we presume to act as if we understand the qualities of those individuals according to the categories into which we have arbitrarily placed them.

How often, for example, do we hear someone say something to the effect that "Joe is a Republican, therefore, he thinks that. ... " And, political pundits think nothing of declaring that "the administration [or the White House] stated today that its policy is. ... ," taking no discomfort in attributing to the executive branch of the federal government (a conceptual group) the same qualities of existence, thought, and speech normally reserved for living individuals. Our individuality is too often submerged into the particular box (subgroup) on the organizational chart into which we have been placed, where we acquire the habit of speaking freely about "this division's" conformity to "company" policy. We too easily forget that only people can make and respond to policies. One negative result of this viewpoint is the tendency to avoid individual accountability for action. When the organization is accountable, no one person is accountable.

The breakthrough in group theory that serves our purpose came when its practitioners acknowledged that trying to operationally define the thinking and behavior of a group—an entity that exists only as a concept—required recognition of the distinction between a physically existing individual and a conceptual collection of individuals. Their new underlying axiom of group theory (S/L #4, Appendix I) became:

Groups do not act; people do!

Simple truths simply stated are very powerful. What this fundamental principle asserts is that the way to behaviorally comprehend, predict, and control group behavior is to approach it through analysis of the living, acting individuals of which a group is composed. Individual attitudes and behavior can be observed, measured, and changed. Group behavior—even the uniform swarming of bees, flocking of geese, or schooling of fish—can only be observed by seeing individual creatures within the context of their collective action. In other words, the sense of pattern that we perceptually impose on the swarm, flock, or school obscures the fact that we are actually physically sensing the actions of individual animals who happen to be acting together. Therefore, the critical modifier to the proposition that only living individuals can act is that the pattern of their collective behavior is more than the simple arithmetic sum of their individual behaviors. It includes the invisible interrelationships bonding them together.

The lesson to be learned here is that individual members of a group do not act independently, as they do when they are alone. They act interdependently, and, the complex, ever-changing mixtures of factors defining the character of their association are as much a result of the interwoven relationships existing between the people as they are a part of the personal character of each individual. Stated again, interrelationships make the whole more than the simple arithmetic sum of its parts.

There exist, fortunately, many reliable psychological instruments available to measure, classify, and evaluate individual attitudes and behavior. The chances are that each person reading this book has taken intelligence, interest, attitude, and psychomotor batteries during her lifetime—and therein lies the secret to operationalizing cultural change. First, measure individual attitudes and behavior and, second, ascertain how the holistic pattern of interdependent collective forces modifies that behavior within group associations; i.e., compare how they operate alone and together. Using this methodology, the abstract concept of culture can be restated and measured in concrete empirical terms.

## THE LOGIC OF MANAGEMENT TRANSFORMATION

Changing corporate culture to transform management requires a logically constructed plan, which includes the following propositions:

■ The ultimately desired end of management transformation is to build a vibrant organization that simultaneously becomes a leader in the new globalized competitive market, prepares for continuing leadership into the near and far future, and provides a healthy, self-actualizing, and fulfilling environment for every individual within its employ. The key to this haven is achieving and maintaining total customer satisfaction.

■ The secret to totally satisfying customers is to always give them more than they expect.

■ The secret to giving them more than they expect is to practice empathic management, meaning viewing things from your customers' perspectives and enabling them to totally satisfy their customers (S/L Definition #6, Appendix I).

■ The surest way to totally satisfy external customers and practice empathic management is to totally satisfy internal customers (all company personnel).

■ The surest way to totally satisfy internal customers is to unify the organic community.

■ The surest way to unify the organic community is to create, nurture, and sustain an enabling environment, in which people feel safe enough to lower their protective shields and make themselves vulnerable, and free enough to express (and act in accordance with) their own ideas, rather than simply reacting to external management directives.

■ An enabling environment (S/L Definition #4, Appendix I):
  ◆ Liberates intellect.
  ◆ Generates consensus.
  ◆ Empowers people to act in accordance with their own ideas.
  ◆ Eliminates fear of failure (failure acceptance prevents disasters).
  ◆ Loves, nurtures, and embraces risk, change, and failure.
  ◆ Celebrates diversity.
  ◆ Cements unity.
  ◆ Inspires joy.
  ◆ Ensures fulfillment.
  ◆ Recognizes dignity.

- The surest way to create an enabling environment is to devise a strategy for changing the corporate culture. This requires universal participation.
- A fruitful way to change corporate culture is to base the process on 1) principles of addiction withdrawal, and 2) working through the grief caused by the profound sense of loss accompanying change.

# ORGANIC VERSUS MECHANICAL SYSTEMS

## Organic Community

The concept of the organic community grows out of literature in the behavioral sciences and philosophy. Three authors who have had significant impact on my thinking are psychoanalyst Peck, chaos theorist James Gleick, and social dissenter Saul D. Alinsky. Also, as noted earlier, transforming management consultant Deming stressed the idea that the single most important requirement for successful management change is the associated idea of optimizing the management system.

Organic systems are best viewed as biological entities that display the behavioral qualities of a living organism. The survival of a body's parts and the whole body are inextricably bound up in each other. They cannot be separated; they are totally survival interdependent. Ensuring, for example, the health of one's stomach to the total exclusion of caring for the rest of the body is an exercise in futility. A sick spleen and a corrupted liver will eventually cause the stomach to suffer. To paraphrase Abraham Lincoln, a body divided against itself will not survive.

Therefore, in an organic system, it is both difficult and unwise to view the parts and the whole separately. They must be seen as merged into a symbiotic oneness, each contributing a unique quality that ensures the survival of all. They are, in effect, survival interdependent.

## Mechanical Systems

These systems, quite oppositely, are composed of parts that work together but are not survival interdependent. For example, a broken trigger housing might render a rifle inoperable but does not threaten the health or survival of the stock or barrel. Simply replacing the housing repairs the rifle; its parts are survival independent.

Organizations that encourage people to focus their interests, perspective, duties, and accountabilities exclusively within their particular boxes on the organization chart tend to view the company as a mechanical system. This parochialism creates the all-too-familiar barriers to communication so evident in bureaucracies. Transformed organizations reverse this tendency.

People in changed cultures learn to view their organizations and their parts in them as organic systems. In this environment, the interests of the parts are indistinct from the interests of the whole. One's personal interests are defined within the context of the general interest, and the general interest is always circumscribed within the context of individual interests. This idea is not utopian. Anthropologists have recorded long-surviving societies so organized; for example, the ancient city-state of Athens rested on this premise. Communities form in this way in the face of natural disasters, and organizations throughout the United States are transforming in just this manner under the banner of the quality revolution.

Members of organic communities soon learn to admire differences in people, instead of fearing them. They learn to be accepting and inclusive with others, rather than rejecting and exclusive. Their sense of personal wholeness grows, nurtured by their satisfied need to associate with others, and by others accepting their need for independent liberty of thought and action. Expectations and accountability are given and taken in consensual mutual accord. You will see in Chapter 6 how such mutuality and consensus are captured and mobilized through specialized voting procedures.

# A PINCER ENVELOPMENT STRATEGY FOR CULTURAL AND MANAGEMENT CHANGE

Changing mechanical into organic communities, and thereby transforming corporate cultures and management systems, requires a grand strategy. I developed a two-pronged pincer envelopment strategy that invades and engulfs the target organization in change, and I have successfully employed it in public, private, military, and civilian contexts. The invasion plan involves simultaneously approaching selected people at every corporate vertical level and every horizontal unit. The aims are to:

- Promote psychological readiness to withdrawal from addictive behavior, regardless of associated pain.
- Stimulate executive commitment to change.
- Generate early process and customer product/service delivery improvement through application of selected specialized performance enhancement methods and tools and techniques.

A military pincer movement surrounds its target with two flanking thrusts, or arms, simultaneously invading from opposite sides and enveloping (enfolding amoebae-like) the object (the organization, in our case) in victorious embrace. The goal is total absorption of psychological readiness to bear the pain of change throughout the organization.

Management transformation conventional wisdom states that change must begin at the top, rather than at the bottom of organizations. The pincer strategy simultaneously initiates change at both ends, which offers both managers and workers opportunities to direct and control transformation.

The upper (executive) pincer arm penetrates the organization through the CEO and immediately reporting executives (vice presidents and senior managers). Endorsement, readiness to commit, and, eventually, full commitment to change are its principle aims. Increasing levels of executive endorsement and commitment are its milestones. Executive endorsement (words) must, at some time, metamorphose into executive commitment (action). No arbitrary time for reaching this critical juncture exists. Organisms develop at their own paces, each unique unto itself.

## Figure 2.1
## Management Transformation Pincer
## Envelopment Strategy

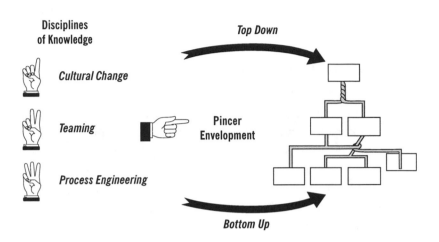

The lower (worker/supervisor) pincer arm invades at the laborer level, penetrating quickly through first-line supervisors and middle managers. The immediate purpose is to stimulate readiness for implementing fundamental changes in daily work processes. The idea is to have them experience numerous small successes (and some failures) in visibly improving self-selected aspects of their daily work lives and customer deliveries to:

- Make them feel good about themselves.
- Make them aware that they can control their lives.
- Open their minds to possibilities earlier deemed impossible or impractical. Formal and informal teaming processes, such as the Process for Innovation and Consensus (PIC), are superbly designed for this task.

Successes are immediately observed by workers creating their own real process and outcome improvements, lessons learned, shared trust, lowered shields, safe vulnerability, and enriched individual senses of personal fulfillment. Typical change activities should be short, incremental, concrete, and pertinent to people's work.

Both pincer arms eventually penetrate up, down, and sideways through the entire organization, overlapping and engaging virtually everyone in stimulating universal commitment and participation. Performance improvements and commitment symbiotically reinforce each other. Action, purposefully directed by philosophy and theory, defines the effort.

## Comparing Pincer Arm Results

Lower-arm progress typically outpaces upper-arm advances. Leaping from executive endorsement to commitment is the toughest nut to crack. Executives reach pinnacles of success within operating hierarchical cultures with values, norms, and standards they naturally respect and appreciate. They do not easily discard them for anyone. As Deming used to quip, "Why should they?" After all, they gained their elevated positions, status, and income in the very systems about to be changed.

Repeatedly demonstrated new and improved ways become, however, harder and harder for opponents to deny and ignore. Dedicated, persistent, philosophically directed, and well-designed change processes eventually turn everyone except those few who, for their own reasons, choose not to move under any circumstances. Lacking such perseverance, those who simply mouth the symbols of change, while denying the spirit of the change and fooling themselves into believing their vacuous rhetoric, slide quietly back into their womb-like comfort zones. I found that they tend to voluntarily leave or fade into the background.

Remember that attempting to change without sufficient readiness to bear pain and opposition is fraught with danger (see Figure 1.1, cell 4). For everyone's sake, and for your own peace of mind, (except in the most extreme circumstances) leave opponents of change alone (S/L #15, Appendix I). Their ability to withdraw from addictive behavior and accept the loss of old ways is different, and they need more time. Give them some space; they are grieving over loss of the old ways and must work through that grief to acceptance (see Appendix III). I find that serious opponents, as shown in Chapter 1, typically comprise only 10–15 percent of the population, and most of them come around with demonstrable improvements. Concentrate instead on the 85–90 percent who are either change champions or healthy skeptics.

## PINCER STRATEGY COMPONENTS

Of what, exactly, are the pincer arms composed? What specific theories and tools for change do they employ? Three disciplines of knowledge contain both the elements of commitment and the tools required to transform organizations. Each of these disciplines must be understood, and acted on, at three levels of analysis.

The three disciplines of knowledge are:

1. Cultural Change—altering individual habitual attitudes and behavior.

2. Teaming—enabling individual innovation and collective consensus.

3. Process Engineering—ensuring output uniformity and improvement by controlling process variation and by employing specialized statistical, mathematical, and engineering technologies.

The three levels of analysis, at which each of the three disciplines of knowledge must be understood and applied, include:

1. Philosophy—a set of coherent, universal, and transcendent normative (moral) management principles directing all change efforts.

2. Theory—a set of rigorous, empirically verifiable management concepts.

3. Technology—a collection of tools and techniques and methods for verifying and conducting theory-driven management practices.

## EXPLAINING THE LEVELS OF ANALYSIS

Philosophy embodies the highest moral ends to which any enterprise may aspire (see Chapter 1). Normative statements inquire into what one should or should not do. They rest upon a system of ethics that prescribes, in absolute universal terms, what constitutes good, right, and proper behavior.

Theory, here, as in any scientific discipline, provides the rigorous logic driving the transforming strategies and processes. It opens a window into reality that allows us to order, explain, control, and predict events that might otherwise be inexplicable. Theory helps us arrive at otherwise nonobvious conclusions and provides intellectual and imaginative vision and direction. It is our road map to discovery. Theories include logically derived models that predict certain outcomes under specified conditions. Some models are mathematically stated—e.g., $e = mc2$—while others, such as Chapter 5's PIC teaming model, take diagrammatic form.

Theories also provide empirical (pertaining to our five physical senses: sight, hearing, touch, smell, and taste) tests for verifying the model's predictions as observably true or false under specified conditions. Verification of the PIC model's predictions rests in the outcomes experienced by those properly and accurately performing the teaming techniques offered in Chapter 6.

Technology involves the application of specially designed, theory-consistent, methods and tools and techniques to manipulate specified events and conditions in the world of experience. These are the verification devices, specified earlier, that test the accuracy and completeness of the model's predictions. The PIC model asserts that teaming innovation and consensus will occur if people use appropriate technological instruments in prescribed ways under certain conditions. The test of the pie is, however, in the eating—no less so for teaming. Results matter!

These three levels of analysis, although analytically distinct, form an overlapping set of perspectives through which the three disciplines of knowledge are analyzed and employed. Figure 2.2 shows that:

- Fully transforming an organization requires nine separate, but integrated, areas of consideration (three disciplines at three levels).
- Techniques depend on theories that, in turn, need philosophical direction.
- Teaming, if attempted without attention to process engineering and cultural change, will produce only truncated satisfactions (explaining why so many teaming efforts evaporate).

## Figure 2.2
### Pincer Envelopment Strategy Components

| | | Disciplines of Knowledge | | |
|---|---|---|---|---|
| | | **Cultural Change (1)** | **Teaming (2)** | **Process Engineering (3)** |
| **Levels of Analysis** | **Philosophy (A)** | Universal Moral Directives<br>• Reality/Being<br>• Values<br>• Beauty<br>• Truth/Knowledge<br>• Beginnings/Ends<br>• Interdependence<br>• Spirituality<br>• Community<br>• Enabling<br>• Order/Chaos | Universal Moral Directives<br>• Individual Dignity<br>• Collective Unity<br>• Social Contract<br>• Enabling<br>• Interdependence<br>• Community<br>• Bonding<br>• Order/Chaos | Universal Moral Directives<br>• Knowledge (Truth/Validity)<br>• Facts/Values<br>  Is vs. Ought<br>• Authority vs. Accountability<br>• Reason vs. Intuition |
| | **Theory (B)** | Principles/Processes<br>• Organic Community<br>• Psychological Readiness<br>• Empathic Management<br>• Enabling Environment<br>• Grief Resolution<br>• Pincer Strategy | Principles/Processes<br>• Teaming (Verb)<br>• Team (Noun)<br>• Individual Innovation<br>• Collective Satisficing Consensus<br>• PIC Model (Phases/Stages/Steps) | Principles/Processes<br>• Process Variation<br>• Taguchi Methods<br>• Six Sigma<br>• Holistic Systems<br>• Chaos/Order |
| | **Technology (C)** | Applications<br>• Consensus Driven Strategic Flow Charting<br>• Addiction Withdrawal<br>• Kübler-Ross Grief Stages<br>• Personality Profiles<br>• I/O Systems Analysis | Applications<br>• Divergent Thinking<br>• Convergent Thinking<br>• Symptoms/Causes Analysis<br>• Recommendations/Consequences Presentation<br>• Creativity/Visualization Stimulation | Applications<br>• Control Charts<br>• Cost of Quality Calculation<br>• Quality Function Deployment<br>• Six Sigma<br>• Experimental Design<br>• Taguchi Tolerance Calculation |

# EXPLAINING THE DISCIPLINES OF KNOWLEDGE

Process engineering is the most fully developed discipline of knowledge. Current literature is replete with statistical, mathematical, and experimental process models and techniques. The most familiar tools in the arsenal are statistical process control charts, first introduced by statistician Walter Shewhart and later interpreted by Deming. Control charts are prime examples of theory-driven (the theory of process variation) management improvement tools.

The theory of process variation explains a condition that anyone working for even a few years has experienced, i.e., the feeling that you are trapped in a system that prevents you from succeeding, no matter what you do.

Briefly, the theory says that 85–90 percent of all system breakdowns (including management systems) are caused by the initial conception and design of the system, rather than by some event or individual action taken at a particular work station. In other words, "Good parts fail in bad systems" (S/L #16, Appendix I).

Consider an example in which widgets moving on an assembly line tend to jam at Charley's workstation through no fault of, or action by, Charley. Or remember Lucille Ball's famous *I Love Lucy* television chocolate-assembly line skit in which the accelerating line speed makes it impossible for either Ethel or Lucy to pick up the chocolate pieces and put them in boxes? Line speed was programmed to increase faster than any human being could possibly accommodate. No amount of finger pointing, training, rewarding, or punishing could help Charley, Ethel, or Lucy succeed. Yet, that fact did not stop their panic over what the boss would say; he would blame them and scream at them, regardless of reality.

Serious consequences, even disasters, can flow from this simple principle. The underprovisioning of the Titanic's lifeboats, for example, followed from design assumptions that the ship was virtually unsinkable and could, in the event of any accident, easily stay afloat until rescue arrived. Therefore, crew members were helpless, trapped in a system not of their making but destined to kill them nonetheless. Nothing they did could possibly prevent the loss of fifteen hundred lives in the two to three hours from hit to sink. System design destroyed them.

Problems aside, no natural, mechanical, electronic, or human process operates with perfect consistency. Barring major traffic problems, for instance, daily driving times from home to work vary by seconds and minutes, depending on how we design our travel arrangements. Daily travel durations randomly vary, according to chance occurrences along the way—i.e., red lights one day, green the next. Process variation, then, measures operating consistency of processes varying under randomly occurring influences. Persistent late arrivals at work require rethinking the overall process rather than blaming Tuesday's driver. These randomly occurring, design-provoked causes of process variation (and failures) are called common causes.

The theory of process variation also states that special causes account for the other 10–15 percent of process variations and failures and can be traced to specific events or individual actions. If Charley, for instance, fails to properly maintain his equipment, or someone else inadvertently does something to affect the line at Charley's station, then that special cause can be isolated, tracked, and corrected at the appropriate location without design considerations. Properly maintained control charts clearly separate and identify common and special causes of process variation and failure.

Imagine, for a moment, the implications of this theory. Jargon removed, it declares that the vast majority of failing office and plant processes cannot be legitimately traced to individuals working within the system—finger pointers beware! They are instead traceable to system-design errors. And, who controls the system? Managers, of course! Workers work within the system; managers control it. Hence, managers bear the burden of correcting most performance variations and failures. Those clinging to traditional bureaucratic blame-the-worker ways choke on such ideas.

This in no way implies less worker accountability. It simply means that workers cannot legitimately be held accountable for events over which they have no control—even when symptoms of the failure inadvertently appear at their workstations. One must,

41

therefore, ask executives the following question: "Since statistical process control charts accurately isolate and identify common and special causes of variation and potential failures, why are they not strewn all over the place?

The answer is, of course, culture. Hierarchical command/obedience attitudes and behaviors simply do not accept process variation's manager/worker relationship assumptions. These are the kinds of embedded habitual addictive human propensities that change demands be reversed. No wonder change is so painful—and so rare. Smoking addictions are probably easier to overcome.

Teaming, the second discipline of knowledge, is an act that occurs whenever two or more people communicate with each other, formally or informally, in an enabling environment characterized by individual innovation and collective consensus (S/L Definition #7, Appendix I). It now enjoys increasing interest, literature, and sophistication, especially in quality management and project management circles. Too often, however, the noun *team*—equated with groups, formal meetings, and institutionalized problem solving—restricts and distorts its operating values and outcomes. You know by now that I view the verb *teaming* in a far broader context, one within which groups, formal meetings, and problem-solving activities are merely restricted applications. Chapters 5, 6, and 7 present all of the theory and practices you need to conduct the widest possible number of philosophically driven teaming associations.

Individual innovation, in this context, means that all participants are (and feel) equally free to both say whatever they think and to listen to what others are saying. Consensus means that a 100 percent working (satisficing) agreement occurs on all collective decisions. This is not a utopian goal; it happens regularly in properly conducted teaming ventures. A complete step-by-step mechanics for achieving satisficing consensus is provided in Chapter 6, while the concept is fully explained in Chapter 5.

Cultural change, the third discipline of knowledge, takes us far afield from pure management theory into the realm of psychology, anthropology, and other behavioral disciplines. Although, as stated earlier, I am neither a psychologist nor an anthropologist, I can tread carefully through pertinent literature, and suggest lines of common association that might provide insights into the dynamics of corporate culture and resistance to change.

As previously noted, the most fruitful approaches to cultural change at the theory and technology levels of analysis involve addiction, addiction withdrawal, the tendency to cling to even unpleasant known ways of doing things over strange unknown ways, and working through the grief that accompanies the loss of old familiar ways.

One critical, relevant, and driving psychological principle of cultural change is that people must engage, face, and work through their deepest hidden feelings if they are ever to withdraw and recover from addictive behavior. This means that they must become psychologically ready to challenge the underlying fears that prevent them from acknowledging submerged feelings, and be willing to suffer the pain of withdrawal. Here is a well-developed theory explaining the source of behavioral inertia and how to overcome its grip on people—a way to engage, challenge, and overcome another mantra typically chanted in management transformation seminars, the all-encompassing resistance to change (discussed in Chapter 3).

Cultural anthropology offers significant insights into the analysis of adaptation and survival in human communities. Comparative politics contrasts how various peoples authoritatively allocate competing individual and collective values and interests—the very heart of those agonizing parochial barriers to communication raised across bureaucratic boundaries, which erode risk taking and accountability. Economics directly addresses the familiar cries of, "We don't have enough," by examining the production, distribution, and consumption of scarce material resources.

Engineering control-systems theory provides precise models for analyzing the feedback principles driving both systems that run amok and systems that self-correct. Political theory applies these same principles to the analysis of human systems with substantial success. The science of chaos provides profound insight into the study of turbulence, discontinuity, randomness, unpredictability, simplicity versus complexity, and the nature of ephemeral patterns of order—all direct descriptors of organizational behavior and environment. And, these bring us back to management philosophy.

Ontology, for example, the field of moral philosophy that examines the nature of being, provides direct assistance to those contemplating the mission and vision of their organizations. Epistemology, the study of knowledge and the nature of truth, provides a foundation for understanding the meaning, character, and use of verification and measurement. The contribution of ethics to the field has already been discussed. Aesthetics looks at the nature of beauty, which probes the roots of joy, wonder, spiritual uplifting, inspiration, and awe—characteristics so vital to personal work fulfillment.

These factors have led me to approach client organizations from the viewpoint of first ascertaining whether substantial and sufficient numbers of their populations are psychologically ready to challenge their addictive habitual attitudes and behavior. The developing theory suggests that the reasons many people, who are attempting to change their organizations, face frustration and despair is that they are attempting that which they are not ready to do.

Therefore, the first job is to enable people to become psychologically ready to suffer the pain of withdrawing from their addictions. This is done in a carefully measured process through application of various mixtures of the disciplines of knowledge at diverse levels of analysis, targeted at selected regions of the organization, through application of the pincer envelopment strategy.

Experience has shown that the best way to enable people to choose to address their addictions is to enlighten by example. The idea is to place them in an environment conducive to promoting behavior based on new attitudes; the PIC does this. Participants must arrive at a state of enabling, such that they choose, themselves, to change—easier said than done. It works only when they understand what is being attempted, when the facilitator is sufficiently skilled in the application of the theory-based techniques being employed, and when a sense of mutual trust, respect, and dignity pervades the atmosphere. Repeated experiences begin to erode individual and collective walls imprisoning people in their old ways. Perceived threats to survival and prosperity are chipped away by repeated positive reinforcement.

The change process is stressful. People are not being asked to simply learn new ideas. They are being asked to unlearn and suffer the loss of comfortable old habits of attitude and behavior and to adopt new, strange, uncertain, and risky new habits of attitude and behavior. You must remember that they cannot be directed into this change; they can only choose for themselves to change themselves.

The facilitator's role is to create an environment that puts people at enough ease to so choose. The word facile refers to making something easy. Cultural change, however, is not easy. Facile, as applied here, means putting people at ease and then giving them the skills, knowledge, and ability to create their own changes.

## RESISTANCE TO CHANGE: "THERE BE DEVILS!"

Early European mariners, believing that the world was flat, looked westward over the Atlantic Ocean with great longing and anxiety. They wanted to explore but feared falling over the edge of the world into hell or something worse—the unknown. Some contemporary maps of the ocean contained the statement, "There Be Devils." I sense that some of those who intensely resist organizational change anticipate the same thing: an unknown void at the edge of their work world, to be devoutly feared. "There Be Devils." Let us turn, then, to that old monster in the closet—resistance to change—and see what we can do about it.

# 3

# The Agony
# of Change

The fault, dear Brutus, lies not in the stars, but in ourselves,
that we are underlings.

Shakespeare, *Julius Caesar*

A great empire and little minds go ill together.

Edmund Burke

"Resistance to change!" This clarion call, heard throughout organizations attempting to change the way they do the things they do,
too often impedes (and even stops) teaming, quality management,
and project management enterprises. I often hear such comments
as the following from clients: "We are different." "Our problems are
unique." Our service company cannot respond like manufac-
turers." "As a government bureaucracy, we cannot act like private
sector people." "Our military unit must obey stricter hierarchical
rules than civilian counterparts." Excuses for giving up on sound
and proven management change processes are virtually infinite.
And, the most pervasive belief expressed in all sectors is that "our
unique situation dictates that everyone else's rules of change do
not similarly apply to us."

Wrong! Good management principles are, philosophically, generic and apply everywhere. Applied management theories and implementing mechanics (tools and techniques) are certainly situational. But, the highest transcendent management values, giving direction and meaning to lower-order applied principles and practices, are universal and absolute. That is what my subtitle, *The Right Way for the Right Reasons*, means. Using philosophically directionless management theories and tools and techniques is equivalent to flailing the air with a hammer.

Resistance to change is certainly real, but it impedes and stops organizational change if and only if managers and workers choose to allow it to do so. Opposition to change is a human choice, and overcoming it is an equal choice! We shall, in this chapter, explore the roots of resistance to management change, and how to successfully overcome it in the interest of revolutionary management improvement, employee fulfillment, customer exhilaration, and competitive success.

Let us begin with a detailed look at the concepts of profound knowledge and system optimization, ideas I suggest bear directly on why people resist change.

## DEMING'S SYSTEM OF PROFOUND KNOWLEDGE AND OPTIMIZATION

W. Edwards Deming, best known for his fourteen points of quality management, insisted that the key to real and sustained management improvement requires full comprehension of what he called a system of profound knowledge, i.e., knowledge based on theory. This system integrates four interdependent parts:

1. Appreciation of a system—management of a system requires action based on prediction to achieve organizational goals.

2. Theory of variation—vital for measuring operational consistency.

3. Theory of knowledge—all management involves verifying by interpretation of experimental and test data.

4. Psychology (add all social sciences and humanities)—vital for understanding purpose, attitudes, behavior, interactions, circumstances, and culture.

I do not intend to elevate Deming's quality management approach above those of other recognized experts. But his profound knowledge and optimization concepts do, I believe, strike a fundamental (but generally overlooked) theme undergirding all quality management and project management improvement approaches. Also, I believe that they illuminate how people can overcome resistance to organizational change.

### Interpreting the Four Parts of Deming's System of Profound Knowledge

The phrase, "profound knowledge," suggests insight into the transcendent moral ultimate meaning of ideas, perceptions, and events, as outlined in Table 1.1. Deming's definition, although less elevated, touches this philosophical plateau. He argues that the aim of every organization is optimization, meaning an environment in which everyone gains. Suboptimized organizations house losers, and when one loses, everyone loses.

Deming's joining of the terms optimization and environment parallels my core principles of the organic community and enabling environment (see Chapter 2), upon which the entire structure of my teaming philosophy, theory, and technology rests. Deming wondered why substantial numbers of people apparently misinterpreted his message that good management practices rest on sound management theory, stubbornly resisting the call to change from suboptimized to optimized organizations.

The answer to this dilemma, as we shall soon see, is that while learning (intellectualizing) new ways is relatively easy, unlearning old ways and actually adopting new habits (internalizing) remains a monumentally challenging feat, more often than not stretching beyond the willingness or ability of many people to accept. It is one thing to intellectualize with words about such matters but quite another to internalize and act upon them. To deny and change the principles upon which one has conducted a major segment of his life and replace them with new designs is an enterprise approaching heroic proportions. It is akin to asking people to change their religion, the central value system upon which they (consciously or unconsciously) direct their lives. The challenge of change is not merely to learn something new and different, but to act in new and ultimately unfamiliar ways.

> Habits, however ill advised, are not easily dropped for principles, however reasonably demonstrated.

> Habitual behavior is addictive behavior!

# PROFOUND KNOWLEDGE, MORAL DIRECTION, THEORY, AND EDUCATION

Thomas Jefferson wrote, in the Declaration of Independence, that "all experience hath shewn, that mankind are more disposed to suffer, while evils are sufferable, than to right themselves by abolishing the forms to which they are accustomed" (S/L #18, Appendix I). Most of us might say, "Better the devil you know." Rationality theory aside, we tend, therefore, to addictively cling to our familiar habitual ways, misery included, as long as known evils are sufferable. Revolutionary change occurs only when 1) pain and suffering become unbearable, and 2) possible alternatives exist. These truths apply equally to corporate, social, and political communities. Pain and hope together are powerful change motivators.

Hence, any theory purporting to overcome mankind's inherent resistance to change must address human irrational, as well as rational, qualities. We must reach beyond (in Freud's terms) the individual ego and delve into the id, and (like Jung) tap the collective consciousness imbued into us by our history, philosophy, and culture.

## Theory and Modern Education

Building on the concept of addictive attitudes and behavior, I suggest that some people have trouble internalizing profound knowledge as knowledge based on theory and as a foundation for necessary corporate change, because they do not understand the nature of theory, itself.

Further, I suggest that many people are not psychologically ready to suffer the pain of withdrawal from their addictive behaviors, or to trust apparently threatening theory and begin the act of changing. They are not ready precisely because probing into the nature of theory is an exercise in metaphysics, an arena of some discomfort for many people. Metaphysical study leads to questioning and critical examination of the first principles upon which we construct our lives—that is, our world view. Scary stuff!

Our discomfort with metaphysics typically comes from lack of education in moral philosophy, theory, and scientific methodology. How many of us, after all, studied philosophy in secondary school, or even in college? Metaphysical exercises must, therefore, seem necessarily strange and discomfiting when we lack experience, vocabulary, and methodological tools (not the intellect) to conduct such studies.

The ultimate root of our educational and psychological unpreparedness rests, I believe, in our historical tendency to devalue humanizing liberal arts education. The almost universal elevation of quantitative over qualitative studies and hard over soft disciplines runs rampant through academic and industrial halls. And yet, only those of us totally isolated from world events could deny that the great issues arising from technology's triumphs concern not what we can do, but what we should do. From abuses of atomic, chemical, and biological energy that might fry the planet to genocide, crime, cloning, abortion, human rights, justice versus law, nerds injecting viruses into personal computers, sex and gender, medical care, parenting, social rights and obligations, and, of course, work, our most pressing problems concern more our personal and social maturity and less our inventiveness (cultural lag in sociological jargon).

## Psychological Readiness to Withdraw from Addictive Habitual Behavior

The social sciences provide a rich source of knowledge concerning the dynamics of human attitudes and behavior. Disciplines including cultural anthropology, political culture, socialization, and psychotherapy offer tested mechanisms to guide and direct behavior and attitude changes. Some people are not, however, psychologically ready to withdraw from and alter their addicted behavior. Why? Because fear of the unknown, risk, and uncertainty outweigh expected benefits, and the suffering, to paraphrase Jefferson, remains bearable.

What, then, do we do to stimulate peoples' psychological readiness to change? I suggest that the single most crucial act creating psychological readiness to suffer change is the deeply personal (but not so simple) act of declaring one's choice for such readiness. This intensely private act can neither be delegated nor shared. Each individual must do it for herself; no one can do it for anyone else. The root of the decision rests in asking oneself questions such as, "Who am I?," "What matters to me?," "Where am I going?," and "What do I want?" Sound familiar?

Such seminal questions reach far beyond the boundaries of behavioral or physical sciences. They transcend our earthly experiences, directing us into those too often murky and discomfiting regions of metaphysics mentioned earlier. But, it is only here that one can adopt a change-motivating philosophy and find the sources of profound knowledge and psychological readiness to change. Knowledge is profound, therefore, when it transcends the boundaries of our physical existence and offers insight into the ultimate meaning, beauty, value, truth, source, or ends (see Table 1.1) of that existence. We must venture into metaphysical regions to fully internalize change, and all subsequent management principles, practices, theories, technologies, and tools and techniques must derive from, and remain true to, these root moral axioms.

## EDUCATION AND CHANGE

One might initially think that everyone who hears about theory translates it into common understanding. Not so! Remember that most college programs require neither moral philosophy nor scientific methodology courses. Lack of a common disciplinary vocabulary, therefore, virtually guarantees wide perception, comprehension, and opinion differences. I contend that these personal worldviews influence our willingness and ability to change. Let us examine how education and personal philosophy shape our capacity for change.

Regardless of educational inattention, histories of metatheory and human relationships play major roles in the story of Western thought and development. This influence continues today and into the future. Well into young adulthood, for instance, Albert Einstein's methodological hero was Earnst Mach, whose name defines the speed of sound. Mach was a strict empiricist, believing that all useful knowledge comes from individual direct observation through our five physical senses; modeled theory was of little consequence to him. Einstein eventually rejected Mach's theory of knowledge, maturing into a theorist who left us an invaluable epistemological legacy.

One's ultimate worldview concerning the nature of reality (ontology) and knowledge will screen and shape one's interpretation of received theory. Idealists, for instance, see reality as images originating and residing in the mind. Some of them believe that reason and faith are separate and that theory can guide our journey into indeterminate futures. Others assert that truth is found only through faith and that theory can only substantiate that preexisting reality.

Realists, such as Einstein, believe that reality is outside of the mind, existing independently in nature. Unlike idealists, reality to them is in what is out there. The meaning that one attaches to the word theory is significantly influenced by these differing prior assumptions.

Our views about appropriate and inappropriate learning methods also shape our understanding of the nature and value of theory. When Sir Francis Bacon, for example, offered us the inductive method of experimental verification, he suspected that inanimate objects kind of "perceived" other objects and kind of "reacted" to them. Inanimate objects, therefore, behaved in some mysterious animate way. Newton's concept of totally inanimate forces acting at a distance was yet to come. And now Newton's deterministic clockwork universe, operating independently of observer behavior, falls victim to quantum theorists Max Planck, Werner Heisenberg, and Niels Bohr's turbulent chaotic cosmos that forever 1) links observer to event, 2) denies determinism, and 3) declares that the apparent order perceived at our level of existence rests on a sea of subatomic disorder. What commonality of understanding and opinion can we find between competing protagonists (Einstein versus Bohr, for instance) for these seemingly incompatible positions? What does theory and what it teaches us mean to them?

We also sift our perspectives on theory through metaphysical screens concerning our own origin and place in the universe. Some people, for instance, assert that ideas and meaning precede existence; i.e., "I think, therefore I am." Existentialists claim the reverse;

i.e., "I am, therefore I think" (that existence is prior to ideas and all else). They state (somewhat, but not totally akin to quantum theorists) that there are no answers but only a stream of never-ending questions about reality. Some existentialists like it that way, enjoying virtually unlimited choices, while others see only misery and despair in such uncertainty. Proponents of the analytic school assert that philosophy offers us nothing substantial and that all we have to discuss is words and what they might mean.

These multiple beliefs concerning moral philosophy's profound issues dictate that individuals must probe their personal worldviews and sift their ideas about theory-based knowledge and optimization—directed management through their perceptual screens. Is it any wonder that so many techniques, laden corporate management change efforts, die under the weight of their own philosophically empty and morally directionless platforms? Tools and techniques, however ingenious, cannot promote change without clear philosophical prescriptions. And, we all must choose for ourselves to seek those directives.

Internalized collective change requires individual introspection!

If industry is afflicted with the disease of unfulfilling but hotly defended management practices, so too is our educational system. Rigid, uncompromising, and dehumanizing numerical performance and evaluation standards, remolding people into interchangeable numbers, defeat both corporate and individual worker interests. I am not arguing against performance standards; I am remonstrating against dehumanization. Organizational standards and humanization are not, as some people apparently believe, incompatible trade-offs. They are in fact compliments, offering benefits to everyone, i.e., optimization.

Companies promote dehumanizing practices, for instance, by paying only for those continuing education courses that apply directly to an employee's work. Failing to appreciate the full range of qualities and character workers bring to their jobs, they remunerate technical courses while rejecting appreciation classes that widen and enrich a person's creative horizons or self-esteem. Somehow the concept of investment to overcome resource depreciation makes sense for facilities and equipment but loses meaning when applied to the most important resource of all—people. Joy and work become separate facets of one's life, fulfillment and self-actualization being found elsewhere—alienation of the worst sort.

Wiser educational designs have existed for millennia. Plato, for example, defined the "Polity" as a vast educational system. Although his Republic was undemocratic and elitist (judged from quite different perspectives than ours), the scope of its learning process was universal, enriching, and comprehensive. Its ultimate values were justice, functional enlightenment, service to citizens, beauty, and social and individual integration.

Good education is humanizing and enabling, placing people in a safe environment where they can allow their own innate qualities of imagination, creativity, and intellect to flower and prosper. They need not react to debilitating external (Theory X) directives. Humanizing education prepares us to ask questions about first principles and to find harmony in the midst of imponderable disorder, risks, and uncertainties inherent in our globally interdependent world. It thereby lays the groundwork for that appreciation of philosophy and theory so necessary to effective change. Out of this brew comes the psychological readiness to comprehend profound knowledge and act out required management transformation.

Education is not a function of society; it is the society!

## THE WAY OUT

The question now is what can we do to inspire psychological readiness for transformation where neither top management commitment nor readiness currently exists. Uncommitted people, executives included, seldom recognize their states of mind. Many of them respond quite positively to readiness exercises once given opportunities to ponder the message. That initial acceptance typically remains, however, purely intellectual. They linger far from internalizing it.

## Beginning

The first step, therefore, is to enable them to make themselves ready for commitment. Note these words carefully. Committing oneself is a personal choice. All anyone else can do is create an environment within which individuals choose for themselves to commit. Remember the popular (and oversimplified) wisdom, "You can lead a horse to water, but you cannot make him drink?" What you can do is create an environment within which the horse chooses for itself to respond, "I think I'll take a drink." Choice stays personal and private.

## Initial Internalizing Propositions

Deming argued that preexisting top-executive commitment is necessary for change internalization and repeatedly said that he had no time for those lacking immediate precommitment. I contend, however, that this punitive rule obviates helping those who most need help. It seems like ordering physicians to treat only those who are already healing. Lacking prereadiness is a condition of the illness and a symptom requiring concern and attention.

I replace Deming's dismissive executive commitment rule with the following four propositions:

- Proposition 1: Although executive commitment (action) is necessary to achieve an advanced state of transformation, executive endorsement (words) is sufficient to start.
- Proposition 2: Approximately 10–15 percent of a typical firm's people adamantly reject any change. Another 10–15 percent champion change. The rest (70–80 percent) are *healthy skeptics*, meaning that they doubt that change will *work here*, but they are willing to try—if they are allowed to try. Rising like a Phoenix from the ashes of previous doomed management *fads*, they display an essential optimism too often unappreciated by top managers. Hope, for them, springs eternal.
- Proposition 3: Never try to convince those who will not be convinced. People have a right to their own ideas, and it is both rude and impractical to attempt arguing them out of it. Besides, they might be right. And why spend time with so few

change opponents when 85–90 percent of the population remain either eager or willing to act.

■ Proposition 4: People learn best by doing.

These four propositions allow me to jumpstart the firm. Proposition 2 identifies 85–90 percent of the population as fertile soil—those who cannot wait to begin. Proposition 1 allows them to try, because essentially indifferent executives provide sufficient lip service to crack open the door. Proposition 3 relieves everyone of the stress of dragging along the naysayers. Proposition 4 lays the groundwork for action vice lecturing. Although I suggest that the root of our psychological unreadiness is lack of humanizing education, I do not mean that a consultant's job is to conduct philosophy lessons. Appropriate actions will drive the point home.

I do recommend that consultants must place clients in environments allowing them to act as if they are ready. Such experiences, repeated many times, breed readiness. The rules of appropriate individual and collective behavior in these enabling environments reflect humanizing principles. Transcendent metaphysical questions are not directly raised, but people begin asking about them within the context of practicing new management experiences. Once they actually begin the act of changing habitual attitudes and behaviors, hard questions start cropping up, such as, "This is ok, but what about my real work?," "How do we do the things we do, and why?," "If I let my people make those decisions, then what's my job?," and "If we are doing it wrong, then what are the rules and principles for doing it right?"

Here are all of the metaphysical issues bound up in the context of the job, no longer cloudy abstractions divorced from everyday interest and relevance.

Context drives abstractions home.

What were once merely cloudy ideas relegated to bookshelves, while one's real work was driven by real practicality, now become internalized motivators. Awareness that theory is the window to reality seeps into people's sinews and consciousness, and repeated experiences erode denial, except for those few whose emotional barriers protect fragile psyches. Repetition induces readiness internalization.

Consultants must, therefore, 1) expose clients to those enabling environments, 2) ensure them a secure sense of safety to allow them to risk open self-expression, and 3) expose them to sufficient theories, methods, and tools and techniques to gain confidence and make change happen.

> It is not enough to *want* to change. One must know *how* to change!

## Vulnerability, Optimization, and the Organic Community

The link tying one's sense of safety to flowering of free and open expression is vulnerability. In diseased firms, where fear is prevalent, people are robbed of pride and joy in workmanship, and dehumanizing management by the numbers prevails—any sense of safety is a stranger. Trapped individuals naturally raise protective shields in these disabling environments; to risk opening oneself to others is to invite stinging arrows of hurt and retribution. One's survival is proportional to one's invulnerability. New ideas, derived from joy and love of enterprise are, therefore, considered dangerous. Their expression requires trust that punishment of some sort will not follow. But, such trust remains a rare commodity in diseased environments.

Therefore, an initial step is to employ techniques promoting a sense of safety that, in turn, instills sufficient mutual trust to allow people to lower their shields and risk vulnerability. Nothing I have yet found succeeds in this task like sound, philosophically based, and rigorously constructed teaming. Chapters 5 and 6 offer just that: a device creating the win-win optimizing universe demanded by Deming's optimization and found in the organic community.

The idea that each wins most only when all win is intellectually pleasing. But it makes little operational sense to those whose entire work history exemplifies suboptimization, zero sum survival, raised shields, and shared alienation. Happily, however, the lessons of change are denied only by those whose souls are imprisoned in constricted psychological dungeons. Acting as white blood cells, they sense new ideas as foreign, invading bacteria infecting and threatening the corporate organism's very survival. They inject defensive antibiotics into the body, bent on returning the patient to health—i.e., the old days. An apt metaphor would be change agents as infecting invading bacteria and change opponents as rescuing antibodies. It certainly describes the essential character of opposition to organizational change. The PIC reverses this behavior.

PIC voting techniques (multivoting, nominal group technique, and discrete summation) produce change, innovation, and satisficing win-win consensus. People originally doubting the feasibility of 100 percent agreement change their minds when, time after time, they achieve it themselves (see Appendix IV). But, before addressing the PIC, we need to compare and contrast quality management and project management similarities and differences. These disciplines vigorously promote, indeed require, genuine teaming to survive. The terms unteamed quality management and unteamed project management are, without doubt, oxymorons.

# 4

# Quality and Project Management: Sibling Rivalry

The rote mind solicits data, the analytic mind pursues knowledge, the profound mind envisions meaning.

Author

Projects can be done without hardware and software ... but not without people.

Kim Webb

Teaming is an essential element of both project and quality management disciplines. Chapters 2 and 3 showed that effective management transformation and teaming require 1) radical corporate cultural change, from command/obedience-centered to participative enabling-focused environments, and 2) overcoming resistance to that change. This chapter compares common quality management/project management traits, offering insights into how they can jointly meet these two demands and ensure successful teaming efforts. The next two chapters present the Process for Innovation and Consensus (PIC), a teaming theory and set of implementing tools/techniques designed to accomplish that transformation and establish a teaming-friendly environment. We shall see that the PIC, itself, is a powerful tool for helping to create quality/project management cultures in which widespread teaming prospers.

# PRIMARY QUALITY/PROJECT MANAGEMENT REFERENCES

I shall employ *A Guide to the Project Management Body of Knowledge* (*PMBOK® Guide*), prepared by the Project Management Institute (PMI®) Standards Committee, as my primary project management reference. Selected secondary references (including illuminating presentations by Aspen Group founders Dennis Lane, PMP, and David Maynard, PMP) are also introduced.

### Note, History, and Caution

*PMBOK® Guide* Chapter 8, Project Quality Management, should, I suggest, be renamed Project Quality Assurance Management. The reason, pertaining to more than semantics, is that quality management is not an element or subprocess of project management. Project management and quality management are, in fact, coequal management disciplines. Quality assurance (QA), including planning and control, as discussed in the *PMBOK® Guide* chapter, is a legitimate engineering function (equivalent to design, production, and test engineering) carried out by uniquely trained technical specialists. Its technical focus is system/equipment evaluation, not overall corporate management change. The topic belongs, as such, exactly where the *PMBOK® Guide* designates, but clearly identified as QA management.

I served as an RCA QA manager when, in 1980, the so-called quality revolution exploded onto America's management stage. Terms such as total quality management (TQM) transfixed people's minds on quality when they should have focused instead on the primary topic, i.e., management. Management is the noun in that title, while quality is merely the modifying adjective. This unfortunate confusion about a word associated with both a specialized engineering function and an overall management theory produced bizarre results, such as QA managers being assigned to direct new corporate TQM programs about which they knew nothing. Executives might just as well have had their finance, human resource, design engineering, or production directors assume the task. Relatively few people, including executives, understood this difference, causing numerous management-transforming enterprises to fail.

My primary quality management references include Shuster's Laws (see Appendix 1), and the pincer envelopment strategy, introduced in Chapter 2. These devices accrue from two decades of management-transforming consulting, implementing, teaching, and writing experience and owe much to giants on whose shoulders I stood, including (but not limited to): W. Edwards Deming, Joseph Juran, Kauro Ishikawa, Phillip Crosby, Genichi Taguchi, Arman Feigenbaum, Tom Peters, Anthony Downs, David Easton, Plato, professional peers, and thousands of deserving but unsung individual client employees.

## MANAGEMENT SIBLINGS

Quality management and project management resemble siblings—brother and sister. They are different and immediately distinguishable, yet genetically bonded. They share and represent:

- common management philosophies—e.g., customer focus, organic community, enabling environment
- teaming and process principles (although their performance periods differ—one never ending, the other duration centered)
- radical departures from hierarchical, command/obedience organizational structures.

Both quality management and project management practitioners must, therefore, face the traumatic burdens of overcoming resistance to corporate cultural change identified in the last two chapters. But, they do it from different and distinct perspectives. Quality management, defined in Chapter 1 at the philosophy level of analysis (recall the three pincer strategy levels of analysis discussed in Chapter 2), is "a never-ending journey toward an ever-rising and receding horizon of something better," while project management is "the act of creating something beautiful." Note quality management's teleological focus, approaching some unimaginably glorious, moving but unattainable, end. Contrast that with project management's aesthetic target: beauty that delights the senses and inspires awe. Their definitions also vary at the theory and technology levels of analysis.

Rephrasing *PMBOK® Guide* definitions, project management (at the theory level) is the act of directing a temporary endeavor undertaken to create a unique product or service. Project management at the technology level is the application of theory-based knowledge, skills, and tools and techniques to meet or exceed project stakeholder needs and expectations while balancing competing task and human demands.

I define quality management (at the theory level) as the act of inspiring and committing everyone to visibly and actively participate in the development, nurturing, and sustaining of a working culture that pursues the ethic of total internal and external customer satisfaction through dedication to continuous process, performance, and delivery improvement. This definition celebrates both human individuality and the bonding of distinct personalities into an enhanced community of great purpose and worth that serves a larger and meaningful enterprise with distinction, satisfaction, and joy.

I define quality management at the technology level, much like project management, as the application of theory-based knowledge, skill, and tools and techniques to internalize and actualize management transformation principles and practices.

These definitions illuminate fundamental similarities and differences driving both disciplines from their highest philosophical purposes, through their strategic theories, and down to the most concrete tactical practices they employ to satisfy those principles. They provide a framework within which to consider their compatibilities and incompatibilities.

## QUALITY/PROJECT MANAGEMENT INCOMPATIBILITIES

Quality/project management practitioners, like human brothers and sisters, sometimes fail to appreciate each other, thereby robbing themselves of possibilities lost in their separation. One especially unfortunate and self-inflicted incompatibility, I believe, is a shared myopia concerning common available theory-implementing technologies, i.e., a sense that the number of such tools and techniques for applying disciplinary philosophies and theories are limited and restricted. Presentations, for example, highlighting the seven [or more] tools of quality management, or the [x] tools of project management, exemplify that perception. I realize, of course, the value of specifying particular tools and techniques for defined situations, as I do in Chapter 6. Many such assertions probably fit that interpretation. But, not all! I have heard, over years of experience, far too many quality/project management professionals expound a deeply held belief that some narrowly defined set of separate methods, practices, applications, and tools and techniques surround and limit their disciplines. They look exclusively inward, failing to appreciate what others have to offer. And, they sometimes seem to arbitrarily select disciplinary tools without apparent theory-driven rhyme or reason.

What blinds people in both disciplines to ignore imaginative alternatives offered by the other, and by what theoretical model do they select one technique over another? I realize, for instance that the *PMBOK*® *Guide* is merely a guide, placing a system of order on an enormous body of knowledge, and cannot possibly offer detailed explanations of every element. And I commend its authors on their clear consistent process design, along which the specialized bodies of knowledge integrate and flow. Returning to *PMBOK*® *Guide* Chapter 8, however, I sometimes wonder why the authors happened to select a fishbone cause-and-effect diagram, a general control chart, and a Pareto diagram from the enormous universe of equally effective and trusted tools, a short list of which includes:

- why/because (causation), how/by (solutions) and if/then (consequences) logic tree analyses
- force field diagrams
- affinity diagrams
- nominal group technique
- quality function deployment
- reverse brainstorming and rotational ideation
- Delphi technique
- checklists
- personal, direct, and symbolic analogy.

I ask quality management practitioners the same questions. Seldom, if ever, do I see them delve into the rich sea of techniques offered by project management professionals (many of which appear in the *PMBOK® Guide*), including but not limited to:

- functional, matrix, and projectized organization analysis
- work breakdown structures (block diagrams and lists)
- Gantt and networking diagramming
- responsibility assignment matrix tables
- life cycles analysis
- earned value analysis
- scope analysis
- budget and estimating techniques
- risk quantification.

What good are process and teaming theories if we, as professionals, trap them in confining application prison cells? What do we gain in theoretical advances if we fail to follow creative conception with innovative implementation? Would physics deny engineering? We will have failed our primary quality management/project management mandates if, in a changing world, our future management technologies do not keep pace with vision and theory.

Quality and project managers share much in common and should strive to seek each other's counsel. Nowhere do they join more intimately than in their perspectives on process and teaming. Turning to those topics, we shall now probe their quality/project management compatibilities, and examine how we might improve them—process first, then teaming.

## QUALITY MANAGEMENT/PROJECT MANAGEMENT PROCESS COMPATIBILITIES

Processes were defined in Chapter 1 as conversion devices; i.e., A becomes B through a process. A process is, therefore, a becoming, and human organic processes involve complex blendings of supportive or impeding personal and social ideas, attitudes, habits, agendas, relationships, situations, and cultural influences.

## Recalling Control Systems Energy-Sustenance Input Effects

Standard control systems input-process-output-feedback models were also shown in Chapter 1 to exclude the crucial effects of supporting energy (sustenance) as an input without which systems can operate. I asked you to read Appendix II at that time for a full explanation (based on political scientist David Easton's remarkable analysis) of this principle. Please read it now if you skipped it previously, because the following discussion of the *PMBOK® Guide*'s approach to process depends upon that analysis. Appendix Figure AII-3, displaying the full control systems model, shows that the process input combines mixtures of demand information and sustenance, i.e., energy (human attitudes and behaviors), either supporting or impeding process operation.

A process (as defined in the *PMBOK® Guide*) is "a series of actions bringing about a result," a viewpoint quite compatible with the ideas of conversion and becoming. The Guide presents each of nine generally recognized project management knowledge areas (integration, scope, time, cost, quality, human resources, communications, risk, and procurement) as self-contained (and sequentially linked) input-process-output-feedback systems. Project life-cycles proceed through five process phases (intiating, planning, executing, controlling, and closing), into which the nine knowledge areas are distributed. Figure 4.1 (created by Aspen Group consultants Dennis Lane and David Maynard) shows, for example, that scope definition occurs in the planning phase, scope verification in the executing phase, and scope change control in the controlling phase. Lane and Maynard also condensed the overall *PMBOK® Guide* process flow onto one page (see Figure 4.2).

The *PMBOK® Guide*, therefore, compresses project management essentials into easily understandable cross-referenced sequences of life-cycle processes and knowledge areas, which fits quite well with quality management process perspectives and operations. They both, however, would profit from inclusion of energy-sustenance principles in the process model, especially project and quality management leaders responsible for ensuring enabling environments, open relationships, participant bonding, and effective teaming.

**Figure 4.1**
Process/Knowledge Areas *PMBOK*® Matrix

| Knowledge Areas | Initiating | Planning | Executing | Controlling | Closing |
|---|---|---|---|---|---|
| | | | **Process Areas** | | |
| 4.0 Project Integration | | 4.1 Project Plan Development | 4.2 Project Plan Execution | 4.3 Overall Change Control | |
| 5.0 Scope | 5.1 Initiating | 5.2 Scope Planning<br>5.3 Scope Definition | 5.4 Scope Verification | 5.5 Scope Change Control | |
| 6.0 Time | | 6.1 Activity Definition<br>6.2 Activity Sequencing<br>6.3 Activity Duration Estimating<br>6.4 Schedule Development | | 6.5 Schedule Change Control | |
| 7.0 Cost | | 7.1 Resource Planning<br>7.2 Cost Estimating<br>7.3 Cost Budgeting | | 7.4 Cost Control | |
| 8.0 Quality | | 8.1 Quality Planning | 8.2 Quality Assurance | 8.3 Quality Control | |
| 9.0 Human Resources | | 9.1 Organizational Planning<br>9.2 Staff Acquisition | 9.3 Team Development | | |
| 10.0 Communications | | 10.1 Communications Planning | 10.2 Information Distribution | 10.3 Performance Reporting | 10.4 Administrative Closure |
| 11.0 Risk | | 11.1 Risk Identification<br>11.2 Risk Quantification<br>11.3 Risk Response | | 11.4 Risk Response Control | |
| 12.0 Procurement | | 12.1 Procurement Planning<br>12.2 Solicitation Planning | 12.3 Solicitation<br>12.4 Source Selection<br>12.5 Contract Administration | | 12.6 Contract Closeout |

**Figure 4.2**
Process Area and *PMBOK*® Flow

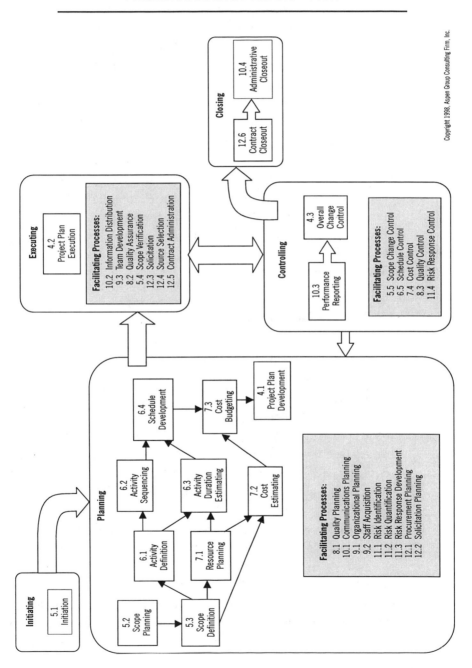

The appearance of what some people call virtual teams, or virtual projects (people separated by long distances working together), offers great opportunities for creating and using new technologies. Most virtual-teaming participants (as I, of course, view it) seldom, if ever, meet each other in a single location. They communicate electronically or through the mail. The Delphi (Greek Delphic Oracle) consensus-building technique is one example of numerous tools proven useful in this environment, because it summons ideas through the mail and adapts well to videoconferencing. (See Julius E. Eitington, *The Winning Trainer*, Chapter 11, for a clear explanation of Delphi and other techniques.) Global corporations, projects, and opportunities demand such enhanced process and multicultural communication skills, and quality management/project management practitioners have only themselves to blame if they choose not to technically expand. We can choose to avoid issues, but we cannot elude consequences (S/L #17, Appendix I).

## The Recursive Nature of Process

John Adams, past PMI president and chair, and Miguel Caldentey, in an article in David Cleland's *Field Guide to Project Management*, challenge the *PMBOK® Guide*'s view of process as simplistically suggesting that project life-cycle phases occur in neatly stitched, uninterrupted, beginning-to-end sequences. They argue that "real world" project life-cycle activities are recursive; i.e., events in later phases feed back and influence those in earlier phases, thereby requiring people to continuously revisit, update, and adapt what came before against what comes later. More directly, project life-cycle events skip back and forth rather than move steadily forward. The authors, of course, offer a corrective model. Caldentey is a systems analyst, and the authors' model, like the control systems model in Appendix II, reflects the recursive nature of projects.

Without judging the *PMBOK® Guide*, I suggest that quality/project management practitioners would benefit from pondering the recursive nature of project processes, keeping it in mind when considering the character of all processes. I do not doubt for a moment that the *PMBOK® Guide*'s authors understand the recursive element of real-world projects. Life's conversions and becomings seldom if ever flow unidirectionally. Modern physicists even question the arrow of time's uninterrupted unidirectional flow. Writing is certainly recursive. Progress through PIC teaming steps, stages, and phases, flows (as you will see when you conduct it) back and forth. Lessons of experience aside, periodic reminders of this principle would help quality/project management practitioners realistically envision the resources, time, and environments defining the constraints and opportunities characterizing their respective enterprises.

## QUALITY/PROJECT MANAGEMENT TEAMING COMPATIBILITIES

Time now to examine the contrasting words, team and teaming, and perhaps loosen my prohibition on using the former term. Everything discussed here applies equally to project management and quality management environments. Both disciplines seek organic communities, enabling environments, and innovation/consensus relationships. They are, in this context, totally compatible.

Phrases such as project team, teamwork, team goals, team this, and team that are permanently embedded in our minds and vocabulary, and I do not oppose that reality. I simply ask that when you hear or use them, please recall political strategist Anthony Downs' crucial admonition that "groups do not act ... people do" (S/L #4, Appendix I)! Groups (whether project management or quality management derived) influence and modify individual behavior, but only living breathing individuals can act.

Imagine, for example, that you are instructing a class of fifteen adult students on financial management. You and they comprise a group—a team, if your heart so desires. Your group character is defined by 1) certain roles (you, teacher; they, students), 2) rules (you define agenda; they participate) and 3) expectations (you require their serious attention; they trust that you know what you are doing). Picture their surprise if you walked into your class and began by playing a guitar and singing two or three top 40 songs—

oops on expectations. Your school classroom (group) roles, rules, and expectations do not include such individual instructor behavior.

Now, imagine that after class dismissal all of you adjourn to the local pub for an hour of froth, friendship, and karaoke. You are the same people, but you now comprise an entirely different group with substantially different roles, rules, and expectations. You now, being always the one to surprise others, tell your students (or are they students at this moment?) to open their texts and review Chapter 12. Picture their surprise again.

Your behaviors are not, themselves, bizarre. Singing, guitar playing, and lesson reviewing are perfectly sensible and even entertaining activities. Context, alone, makes them bizarre. Had you reviewed in class and entertained in the karaoke bar, all would have been judged proper and appropriate.

The primary lesson of this story is that teams are groups, holistic patterns of abstract concepts defining roles, rules, and expectations concerning members' individual behaviors and collective relationships. Concepts and holistic patterns are invisible; so are relationships. Only individuals are visible, and the holistic patterns defining their group associations only become quasivisible by observing and interpreting repeated individual member actions. Teams, in other words, become quasivisible through teaming.

Why, I am often asked by new clients, do I place such stress on this seemingly trivial distinction? My constant answer is that the distinction is not trivial. As we saw in Chapters 2 and 3, individual employees typically swim in the collective brew of one of their corporate organization chart's boxes. Blended with peers and isolated from other boxes, their individuality sinks into the oblivion of group think. I exaggerate the point only to make it clear and familiar. Visible consequences seldom appear in static command/obedience hierarchies. Nowhere, however, does the condition become more evident and defining than when project or transforming teaming efforts are initiated. Such radical changes awaken all of the resistance to change devils and cultural taboos discussed earlier—watch out!

# DIVERGENT AND CONVERGENT THINKING

Effective teaming activities involve recursive iterations of individual creative thinking and collective decision-consensus building. Creative thinking (sometimes called divergent thinking) is, by nature, chaotic and unpredictable. Consensus building involves more analytic and ordered convergent thinking.

Imagination, intuition, and leaps of insight drive divergent thinking. Picture an upside-down funnel with a question such as "What could happen if ... " resting on the inside bottom point. The funnel expands (diverges) upward, its opening ever enlarging to swallow a potential infinity of possible responses. Divergent thinking is constraint free, random, chaotic, and turbulent—always seeking surprises and delving into the to-date incomprehensible universe of things we don't know we don't know. Great as-yet unimagined truths that radically alter our lives (relativity, quantum theory, DNA, Beethoven's Ninth Symphony, classical and Keynesian economics) periodically drop into our hands from divergent exercises. Important and equally beneficial gems await those practicing divergent thinking in teaming environments.

Convergent (consensus building) thinking involves more analytical, rational, and calculational methods. Consensus builders seek collective agreement on one or more answers to broad questions. Imagine, for instance, a collection of variables pertaining to some question pouring into the funnel opening. Convergent thinkers sift through the data according to some model (mathematical or other), retaining only useful variables as they drop down through the ever-narrowing space (converge) on the funnel point containing the answer(s). Convergent thinking is constrained to logic, and the model driving analysis is ordered, structured, and serene, always avoiding surprises and seeking a certain end; i.e., the thing we know we don't know.

Of the many pleasures that teaming affords, I find its continuous striving to blend chaos and order (complementarity, as discussed in Chapter 3) the most fascinating, and I designed the PIC with that in mind. Various divergent thinking (brainstorming, NGT, and psychic irrelevancy) and convergent thinking (CDAM, multivoting, NGT, and discrete summation) devices were selected to acutualize these principles.

You must, therefore, internalize chaos/order complementarity before engaging the PIC model in Chapter 5. Management theorist and consultant Margaret Wheatley, in her book, *Leadership and the New Science: Learning about Organization from an Orderly Universe*, eloquently explains how physical and natural science chaos/order principles apply to organizations and management. The following paragraphs summarize her message and provide insights I want you to retain, as you delve into teaming mechanics. It is, as always, easy to lose the forest in the trees.

## ORDER AND CHAOS: PARTNER IN THE NEW MANAGEMENT

John Dewey, in *The Quest for Certainty* (1929), said, "Every great advance in science has issued from a new audacity of imagination." Prepare yourself for Wheatley's audacious advance by imagining a flock of geese or a school of fish swarming, bee-like, in an ordered but shifting pattern, flitting now in one direction, jerking then in another, but always holding to their cloud-like pattern. The motion of any one creature in the swarm is random, chaotic, and unpredictable, as is the direction that the swarm might take at any instant. Although changing shape, the ordered pattern into which the individual beings cling retains its mysterious cohesion, or, what Wheatley defines from chaos theory, strange attraction (analogous to Adam Smith's economic *Invisible Hand*). Some instinctive force or inclination commands their close-ordered association. The new science tells us, says Wheatley, that order and chaos exist together in nature, as complimentary, rather them competing, aspects of reality.

Order emerges from random unpredictable chaos. Such a vision runs counter to our intuitive picture of the totally ordered, predictable, and certain universe proclaimed by the seventeenth century science of Sir Isaac Newton. To understand Wheatley's management principles, however, we must willingly surrender our perceptions of reality, based on everyday commonsense experiences, and enter the quantum land of Oz. For instance, tiny to us is a grain of sand or a flea; yet to quantum physicists, those infants are as large as the sun compared to subatomic particles. In our world, we experience a second as an instant in time, but physicists divide that seeming wink into ten billion parts, durations totally meaningless to us. More strangely, in the quantum Oz, when we simply look at a particle, it changes; that idea defies all human experience. When we look at a house or a sheet of paper, it does not change. Nonetheless, these paradoxes (and more) define the new science, and Wheatley states that the tools of good management reflect universal scientific principles governing nature at every level of existence, from the very large (macrolevel) to the very small (microlevel). She too is perplexed by these alien concepts but uses her admitted confusion as a window to enlightenment. Even the physicists are boggled by their discoveries. For example, Wheatley quotes the great quantum theorist Niels Bohr in her book: "Anyone who is not shocked by quantum theory has not understood it." Her message is, nonetheless, that microworld chaos and macroworld order comprise a total reality governed by their symbiosis.

Wheatly suggests that discoveries in different disciplines tend to parallel each other and that, over the last 350 years, physics, as the most rigorous science, has shaped our methods of reasoning. Frederick Taylor's clock-like mechanical hierarchical management theory reflected, for instance, Newton's classical model of the universe. She argues, therefore, that the new quantum-inspired, open, participative, information-exchanging, facilitative, relationship-focused management theories are valid permanent fixtures on our organizational horizon. They are not mere fads.

If Wheatley's paradigm could be expressed in one sentence, it would probably be the following: Appropriate organizational order cannot be directed; it must be allowed to emerge from the random creativity of its personnel. She suggests that "companies highlight a principle that is fundamental to all biological self-organizing systems," that of self-reference; i.e., they respond to environmental disturbances signaling a need for change by adapting to survive, maintaining their unique integrity, and self-renewing. Easton's control-systems theory rests on the same assumption, i.e., that political systems survive by responding and adapting to environmental signals (1965). One key to this adaptive behavior is recognizing that organizational cohesion (order) depends upon maintaining an internal environment allowing the random exchange of information between freely associated individual personnel (chaos). Macrosystems do not, therefore, "change randomly; in any direction. They always are consistent with what has gone on before, i.e., with the history and identity of the system." As Erich Jantsch notes about nature and organizations, "the more freedom in self-organization, the more order."

Eighteenth century economic free-enterprise capitalism and Jeffersonian democracy are founded on those same principles; i.e., free (chaotic) exchange of both goods and ideas create stable (orderly) societies.

Self-reference, open relationships, and information exchange are the necessary and sufficient elements of healthy organizational leadership, reflecting universal principles established in nature and governed by symbiosis between microlevel chaos and macrolevel order.

Consider again the geese, who, with feathers bound, cannot fly, but, with wings freely spread, may obey nature's dictate to soar free over unchartered waters toward unimagined horizons.

## THE NEXT STEP

Enter now the world of PIC. Chapter 5 presents the strategic model (see Table 2.2, Cell 2B in the pincer strategy components classification scheme). Chapter 6 guides us through the implementing tactics (see Table 2.2, Cell 2C), designed to actualize teaming philosophy and theory.

Remember that every recommended strategic and tactical PIC rule, phase, and step rests on higher order philosophical and theoretical assumptions (valid or invalid). Judge them, as you will, on that basis—but not before doing them. Once you have internalized the process, you can modify, add, subtract, and do whatever you want to alter and adapt those devices. Chapter 6 offers what I believe are effective and minimally sufficient tools and techniques to make teaming work. Recall my claim that while teaming philosophy remains invariant, its strategies and tactics offer virtually infinite alternatives. There are many effective teaming approaches in the quality/project management universe. PIC is one of them.

*5*

# Teaming Philosophy and Theory: The Process for Innovation and Consensus Model

The constitution was framed upon the theory that peoples of the several states must sink or swim together, and that in the long run prosperity and salvation are in union and not division.

Benjamin Cardozo

All for one, and one for all

Alexander Dumas

## FOUNDATION AND PHILOSOPHY

Teaming potentially begins when two or more people decide to join in some discussion or enterprise. Note, however, the cautionary word, potentially. Collective efforts must meet stringent teaming standards before being admitted into that select category. These standards derive from the overarching philosophies of quality management and project management, discussed in Chapters 1–4.

The spirit of teaming was philosophically well defined by Shakespeare's King Henry VI, when admonishing his most trusted advisors to "join your hands, and with your hands your hearts, that dissonance not hinder governance." He showed (without using the word teaming itself) the formula for instilling that deep intellectual and moral bonding implanted within individuals living in organic communities. Here is that glorious, but too often rarest, commonwealth of souls simultaneously celebrating individual differences while cherishing collective unity.

Note also Henry's visionary goal: governing without dissonance. Therefore, people simply blending is not enough to establish teaming. Henry insists that they must join forces with that driving governance purpose always in mind.

Remember from Chapter 2 that preserving, nurturing, and sustaining an organic community is the central objective underlying all transforming managing efforts, regardless of specific issues and circumstances. Resolving distinct issues at the cost of undermining the organic community is a recipe for short-term satisfaction presaging ever-growing long-term difficulties. Here again we face the age-old dilemma of balancing immediate personal gratification and consumption with long-term preservation of those collectively held ecological resources allowing such periodic spending. Must tomorrow pay for today? And where is the balance between I and we?

Enter the teaming world without serious, prolonged, and revisited contemplation of these principles, and your transactions will eventually reduce to formulaic rituals of form without substance, despair without progress, and cynicism without change. I expect that many of you reading this admonition have already experienced such disappointments, but do not give up. Just remember (S/L #6, Appendix I) that you are not responsible for incoming obstacles, but you are responsible for how you choose to respond to them. Discovery rewards perseverance, not surrender.

# PERSPECTIVE

Remember the admonition stated earlier: Forget Teams! Think Teaming! At least for now! This deceptively simple semantic shift offers an entirely new way of looking at both quality management and project management and their universe of possibilities.

Teaming, as an act, can occur anytime that two or more people communicate with each other. They might be transacting as members of a formal group, committee, or team. Conversely, they might be simply enjoying snacks in the cafeteria, sitting around their work area, schmoozing at a picnic, talking on the telephone, or trading E-mails. The point is that the way they are communicating, not the character of their organization, determines whether or not they are teaming. Teaming, in other words, concerns what people are doing, rather than where they are or how they are grouped.

Two critical questions emerge from this viewpoint. First, how do we know when we are teaming and when we are not? Second, why does it matter? The answer to question one is that teaming theory tells us when we are teaming and when we are not teaming; this chapter provides that theory. It matters because teaming produces significant performance improvements supporting both personal and corporate objectives.

Everything that follows in this and the next chapter is an expansion of these questions and answers, including necessary teaming principles, practices, methods, and tools and techniques. Teaming within a formal group is addressed first, although most teaming takes place in informal conversations. Informal teaming is discussed in Chapter 7.

# THE TEAMING UNIVERSE

One of the most prevalent misconceptions about teaming is that it pertains almost exclusively to problem solving. This idea severely restricts the teaming universe and violates one of the central tenets of management transformation, i.e., that the real breakthroughs in performance come after severe, lingering, and chronic problems in an organization are eliminated, and totally new questions are asked about fundamentally new ways of doing things. A giant cultural hurdle is crossed when the idea of innovation is internalized in the minds, hearts, and habits of more and more people. Teaming, therefore, must be viewed through the lenses of innovation and consensus.

The universe of teaming issues is virtually unlimited. Some issues might concern correcting things that are wrong (problems). Others might involve preventing future problems. Still others might turn us toward doing better what we already do well, or doing what we have never done before. Think, therefore, of Process for Innovation and Consensus (PIC) teaming as a process for considering limitless kinds and quantities of issues.

## APPROACH

Countless books and essays have been written about effective meeting principles and group dynamics; numerous how-to guides about quality teams have also been published. I do not intend to reinvent those wheels. Instead, I shall borrow, twist, and adapt portions of existing ideas, salt them with a few original thoughts, and present them in PIC dress—to advance the frontiers of participative management. My immediate purpose is to suggest a common vocabulary through which we can jointly build the PIC model and understand its dynamics.

But, remember this! No amount of tinkering or gadgetry will ignite, open, and transform closed hierarchical organizations if people cling to the letter, but violate and deny the spirit, of what follows. Too many of us have committed this error only to watch their transforming efforts stall, fail, and flame out—leaving ashes of cynicism, ignominious defeat, lowered morale, and stunted productivity.

## THE PROCESS FOR INNOVATION AND CONSENSUS MODEL

I suggest that the investigation of any issue is conducted in the following three phases:
1. Diagnosis.
2. Prescription.
3. Action.

The issue is defined, and its underlying causes identified and prioritized, in the diagnosis phase. What should be done to resolve the causes of the issue is determined in the prescription phase. The action phase involves executing and evaluating the resolution(s). The PIC includes only Phases 1 and 2. Phase 3 is post-PIC. My experience suggests that those teaming partners best suited to conduct the first two phases are not necessarily those most appropriate to perform Phase 3. And, although many of the techniques used during the earlier phases can be used during the last phase, execution differs enough from analysis to warrant their separate consideration.

Each phase is conducted in two or more stages that are themselves divided into very specific tangible steps. The phase/stage relationships are illustrated in Table 5.1.

The Symptom Selection stage (see 1A in Table 5.1) is designed to define a broad issue in terms of one specific symptom selected from a ranking of suggested alternatives. Each issue can be defined (in whole or in part) in terms of some existing condition, effect, or symptom. A symptom is an observed, perceived, or imagined condition, or state of things or events, that is so broadly defined that no readily obvious solution, corrective action, or response appears. For instance, a stomachache is the symptom of a problem. It might be observed visually (swelling), by touch (heat), or by any of our five senses. It is either perceived or imagined by its victim. The symptom of an innovation-directed issue might originate, for example, in a shared perception that an existing customer service process, although satisfactory, could be significantly improved if customers' expectations and intentions were better understood, thereby increasing potential market share. During Stage 1A, that general feeling might be refined into a specific symptom statement, such as, "Our knowledge of customers' inclination to repurchase our product is uncertain."

We shall see, in Chapter 6, that the symptom statement must be phrased in terms that imply no direct, tangible resolution. This is due to the fact that human beings tend to jump to conclusions by assuming that they know the causes of a symptom immediately after becoming aware of the condition. Aside from the fact that this impatience might lead us to the wrong resolution, it prevents us from probing more deeply into causation and, thereby, opening our

---

### Table 5.1
### Issue Investigation Phases and Stages

---

| Process | Phase | Stage |
|---------|-------|-------|
| PIC | 1. Diagnosis | A. Symptom Selection |
| | | B. Cause(s) Identification/ Prioritization |
| | 2. Prescription | A. Resolution(s) Selection |
| | | B. Implementation Planning |
| Post-PIC | 3. Action | A. Execution |
| | | B. Evaluation |
| | | C. Adjustment |

---

minds to unimagined and innovative insights, alternatives, and opportunities. Both of the example symptoms stated earlier meet this no-implied-solution criterion. The symptom statement, "I have a stomachache," suggests no direct or unique tangible solution. Imagine, for instance, your reaction if the doctor unhesitatingly replied to your complaint with the proclamation, "I am scheduling you for immediate surgery." The very absurdity of the response makes the point. What you properly expect from the physician is an examination and diagnosis. You want her to determine the cause(s) of your affliction and treat (resolve) the cause(s), not the symptom.

The Cause(s) Identification/Prioritization stage (see lB in Table 5.1), therefore, begins with a speculative search for all the potential causes of the selected symptom. It ends with verified evidence about which few of the suggested potential causes contribute most to the symptom. At this point, both Stage lB and the Diagnosis phase (Phase 1) end. We know, at the time, the symptom, and we know its primary contributing causes.

The next obvious question is: "What should we do about it?" This prescriptive question leads us directly into Phase 2, Stage A, Resolution(s) Selection (see Table 5.1). During Stage 2A, potential solutions are defined, means to their accomplishment are considered, their potential consequences (positive and negative) are analyzed, and refinements are added to accommodate feasibility and consequences considerations.

Stage 2B, Implementation Planning, follows directly and logically from Stage 2A (see Table 5.1). Once the nature and implications of resolutions are understood, the next logical stage is to determine the mechanics, logistics, funding, scheduling, and measurement tools required to execute and evaluate the resolution(s). Hard data must be obtained to predict with some precision the expected cost/benefit outcomes of the projected resolutions. This involves translating resolution concepts into a concrete plan of action.

At this point, all that remains is to take action on the implementation plan. Phase 2 is complete, thereby terminating the PIC teaming effort with respect to the selected symptom. Phase 3, Action (see Table 5.1), may be conducted by the same team members, a totally new team, or any desired mix of people. The three stages included within the third phase are designed to initiate, conduct, complete, and assess the results of the implementation plan. The final stage is to adjust operations in accordance with the results of the total process and, perhaps, begin again with another symptom related to the same issue. By this time, everyone's perspective on the issue will be substantially different than it was when it all started. New horizons, earlier unknown, will open new windows of opportunity and suggest alternatives only now becoming evident. From this rising yeast, new heights of understanding are reached.

Figure 5.1 outlines PIC teaming phases and stages. Note that resolution(s) are targeted only to those few critical causes that have been verified as contributing to the bulk of the symptom. It makes little sense to expend energy and resources on trivial causes that contribute insignificantly to the symptom. The overall process is, then, very simple in design:

- Isolate a condition of interest.
- Define it as a symptom.
- Verify its critical causes.
- Specify reasonable, feasible resolutions.
- Define expected costs/benefits.
- Plan implementation of the resolutions.

## Figure 5.1
### Process for Innovation and Consensus Model

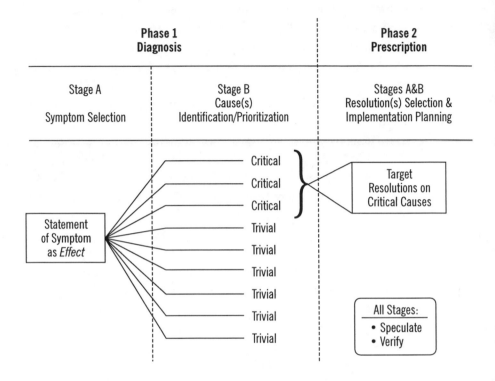

Remember that symptoms must be stated in terms that imply no direct tangible solution(s) to prevent the frequent human tendency to leap to wrong, unwarranted, or limited resolutions. Symptoms are to be viewed merely as the effect of one or more causes, which must be identified, ranked, and verified in terms of their degree of contribution to the effect. Solutions are targeted onto those few verified critical causes that, when treated, will resolve the symptom.

Figure 5.1 presents PIC in outline. But, before moving on to its tools and exercise (see Chapter 6), we must define the specific steps into which each of its stages is further subdivided. These steps define the tangible actions comprising the phases and stages. Table 5.2 illustrates this subdivision. Specific steps are identified with three-character alphanumeric codes; for example, Step 2B1 is Phase 2 (Prescription), Stage B (Implementation Planning), Step 1 (Scheduling/Resources Speculation). The purpose of dividing and subdividing the PIC is to prevent people from forgetting the forest during their trek through the trees. Teaming partners too often and too easily lose sight of the overall investigation process as they become entrenched in specific techniques and steps. It is a perfectly natural trap to fall into and worth the up-front expenditure of time and thought to be remembered. One of the teaming facilitator's most important tasks is to prevent such tunnel vision from occurring.

Steps are merely those specific activities that must be conducted in order to proceed through the PIC journey and accomplish its purpose. Table 5.2 should be reviewed periodically to keep a full perspective of the process. It can also be used to reorient those individuals who have temporarily lost their way.

## PROCESS FOR INNOVATION AND CONSENSUS PHASES, STAGES, AND STEPS ANALYSIS

Important insights are gained by examining the steps in some detail. Note, for instance, that many of the steps involve speculation, the act of intellectual inquiry without need or recourse to demonstration, proof, or verification. Speculation is the key to free flights of imagination, creative insight, new perspectives, originality, expanded vision, and altered horizons—i.e., the mechanics of innovation. It makes sense to speculate in every PIC stage.

Eventually, however, speculations must be ranked in terms of their usefulness in accomplishing our teaming purpose—that is, they must be demonstrated as operational, measurable, applicable, and real. This is the purpose of the several PIC verification steps. For instance, the physician might speculate that one potential cause of a stomachache is an ulcer; other speculative causes could be gas, appendicitis, food poisoning, or whatever. Eventually, however, we shall expect tests to be taken—that is, empirical measurements of temperature, pain, blood count, blood pressure, and other required vital signs verifying which, if any, of the speculated causes are the real causes.

**Table 5.2**

Process for Innovation and
Consensus Phases, Stages, and Steps

| Phase | Stage | Step |
|---|---|---|
| 1. Diagnosis | A. Symptom Selection | 1. Symptom Speculation |
| | | 2. Symptom Verification |
| | | 3. Symptom Specification |
| | B. Cause(s) Identification/ Prioritization | 1. Causes and Roots (C&R) Speculation |
| | | 2. C&R Verification |
| | | 3. C&R Prioritization |
| 2. Prescription | A. Resolution(s) Selection | 1. Solution(s) Speculation |
| | | 2. Consequences Speculation |
| | | 3. Solution(s) Refinement |
| | B. Implementation Planning | 1. Scheduling/Resources Speculation |
| | | 2. Feasibility Verification |
| | | 3. Action Item Speculation |
| | | 4. Presentation |

The PIC, therefore, is a logically connected sequence of steps alternating between speculation and verification, with a sprinkling of prioritizations, refinements, and presentations inserted as catalysts in key spots. Clearly, innovation is central and evident throughout the process.

Consensus is less evident in this outline. Basically, it occurs at the end of each step, because what participants must agree on is that the step they are conducting is complete and that it is time to move on to the next step. Consensus is implied in the very act of progressing through the steps.

"But," you might ask, "how do you know when one step is finished and that it is time to move on to the next step? What criteria does one use to come to such a conclusion?" The answer is that each step of each stage begins with a question that reflects PIC flow. Each step ends, therefore, when its initiating question has been satisfactorily answered—with 100 percent member consensus. The rule of progression states that "when one step ends (by consensus), then the next step's question is automatically asked." The PIC ends when Stage 2B4 ends—i.e., with consensus that its initiating question is satisfactorily answered.

Table 5.3 is an expanded version of Table 5.2. Each step's initiating question is inserted between the Stage and Step columns. Take time now to carefully study the table. Read each step-initiating question in order of occurrence, keeping in mind its phase/stage context. Everything that follows in Chapter 6 is predicated on this logic. PIC fundamentals are condensed in Table 5.3, and, like Table 5.2, it should be referenced as questions arise.

The only questions remaining before examining PIC technology are: "What exactly does 100 percent participant consensus mean?", and "How do we know it when we see it?" The answers reside in the wonderful world of *satisficing*.

## SATISFICING: ACHIEVING 100 PERCENT CONSENSUS

Talking about win-win environments and 100 percent agreement on collective decisions is one thing; achieving them is another. The three PIC voting techniques, fully explained in Chapter 6, do achieve them. You can exercise them any time you choose to do so. Simply follow the steps, and keep in mind the philosophical and theoretical spirit of the process, as well as the letter of the technique.

You will achieve what decision-makers call a satisficing consensus, thoroughly explained in Appendix IV. You should read it when you arrive at the discussion of voting in Chapter 6.

The term satisficing emerged from the famous 1958 (reissued in 1993) book, *Organizations*, by James March and Herbert Simon. Briefly, they contrast satisficing with optimizing intentions of voting participants. Optimizing-minded people demand receiving only their personally highest priority alternative in any collective agreement into which they enter. Majority voting works well for them, because they do accept the idea of winning and losing. Win-lose makes sense to them, while 100 percent agreement makes no

## Table 5.3
### Process for Innovation and Consensus
### Teaming Phases, Stages, and Steps Analysis

| Process | Phase | Stage | Initiating Question | Step |
|---|---|---|---|---|
| PIC | 1. Diagnosis | A. Symptom Selection | 1. What is the observed or imagined condition (the symptom)?<br>2. a. What empirical data are required to measure the speculated symptom?<br>b. Are required data available?<br>c. Do the data verify the speculated symptom, as stated?<br>3. Is the validated symptom stated as an *effect*? | 1. Symptom Speculation<br><br>2. Symptom Verification<br><br>3. Symptom Specification |
| | | B. Cause(s) Identification/ Prioritization | 1. What are the potential causes and roots (C&R) of the specified symptom (the effect)?<br>2. a. What empirical data are required to measure the relative contribution of each C&R to the specified symptom?<br>b. Are required data available?<br>c. Do the data verify each speculated C&R, as stated?<br>d. Can the verified C&Rs be ranked in terms of their relative contribution to the specified symptom?<br>3. Which C&Rs are *critical* and which are *trivial*, in terms of their ranked contributions to the specified symptom? | 1. C&R Speculation<br><br>2. C&R Verification<br><br><br><br>3. C&R Prioritization |

*continued on next page*

sense. They go along to get along, under accepted principles of majority rule with minority rights.

Satisficing-minded people purposefully seek 100 percent agreements. They perceive greater value in a true coming together of people mutually willing to accept less than their personally highest

## Table 5.3—*Continued*

| Process | Phase | Stage | Initiating Question | Step |
|---|---|---|---|---|
| PIC | 2. Prescription | A. Resolution(s) Selection | 1. a. What are the most preferred potential resolutions to be targeted against the critical C&Rs?<br>b. How can selected potential resolutions be accomplished? | 1. Resolutions Speculation |
| | | | 2. What are the potential positive and negative consequences of the most preferred potential resolutions? | 2. Consequences Speculation |
| | | | 3. How can each preferred resolution be refined or improved? | 3. Resolutions Refinement |
| | | B. Implementation Planning | 1. What are the predicted major milestones, who does it, who approves, and how is it funded? | 1. Scheduling/ Resources Speculation |
| | | | 2. What are the expected costs/ benefits, and are they feasible? | 2. Feasibility Verification |
| | | | 3. What specific action items are required to accomplish resolutions implementation? | 3. Action Item Speculation |
| | | | 4. How and to whom should these findings be presented? | 4. Presentation |
| | | **PIC Termination** | | |
| Post-PIC | 3. Action | A. Execution | 1. Are all required resources available and ready? | 1. Readiness Confirmation |
| | | | 2. Is the plan initiated and operating? | 2. Accomplishment/ Monitoring |
| | | B. Evaluation | 1. What are the results? | 1. Assessment |
| | | C. Adjustment | 1. Is change or revision necessary? | 1. Adjustment/ Confirmation |

priority alternatives in collective decisions than in each participant sticking exclusively to his highest preference choice. What they will not do is go along to get along; they demand that the agreement accommodate some minimal acceptable amount of their personal preferences. That provided, they all join in the decision (win-win). The three voting techniques described in Chapter 6 produce 100

**Figure 5.2**

Degree of Satisfaction

| | | Optimizing | Non-Optimizing |
|---|---|---|---|
| **Interests Satisfied** | **Individual** | 1<br><br>Self-Serving<br><br>Group Sacrificing | 3<br><br>Self-*Satisficing*<br><br>No Sacrificing |
| | **Collective** | 2<br><br>Group Serving<br><br>Self-Sacrificing | 4<br><br>Group *Satisficing*<br><br>No Sacrificing |

percent satisficing agreements. The PIC requires that participants go back several steps in their investigation if and when voting procedures fail to achieve total consensus. Participants, in some earlier PIC step leading up to the vote, failed—an exceptionally rare occurrence once participants internalize the techniques.

Read the PIC mechanics. Try them out with friends. Never lose sight of their intent and complementary spirits of individual dignity and collective unity. True consensus can be lost at any time, in any substep, by just one person digging in heels and optimizing. The only thing required to succeed is clearly stated and genuine willingness to make it work. Do not frustrate yourselves in its absence. Drop it! Come back again another day.

# 6

# Putting Principles into Practice

It is sweet to let the mind unbend on occasion.

Horace

Criticism comes easier than craftsmanship.

Zeuxis

Teaming is not easy; neither is it a panacea. Participants typically report a sense of mental exhaustion at the end of extended sessions. But, it is a sweet infirmity, accompanied by the exhilaration of victory, the elation of real accomplishment, and a confirmation of one's capacity to overcome and achieve. The secret to all this is almost too simple to believe—in principle. The tough part is making it work—in practice.

Technique is the secret to making the Process for Innovation and Consensus (PIC) work—that is, properly using the tools of the trade. The trade is the PIC. Techniques are the tools. Techniques are rigorously defined, logically related actions conducted to perform PIC steps. Hammers, screwdrivers, and saws, by analogy, are the tools of the carpentry trade, including, of course, appropriate rules for their use.

There is a tendency for PIC newcomers to confuse the process (PIC) with the techniques (tools). This is perfectly natural, but potentially frustrating. To be forewarned can help you to be fore-armed. A few words now can prevent confusion later. This chapter is devoted to defining and explaining techniques.

Some teaming participants who become confused between process and techniques compensate (usually unconsciously) by overritualizing technique performance. They tend to blindly and arbitrarily chant the rules, insisting that their peers march more to the letter of the law, rather than to its spirit. Remember that inno-vation and consensus are the desired outcomes of the process. Techniques are tools that are justified only to the extent that their use serves the accomplishment of appropriate process ends. Tech-niques are means to achieve ends. To raise the techniques, them-selves, to the status of ends is equivalent to the carpenter treating the hammer, rather than the house, as the desired end. There are few dilemmas that can disorient and unmotivate people more quickly than this particular situation.

To prevent such an occurrence, I offer a principle, often recited in words, but forgotten in application, and vital enough to be engraved as S/L #32 (Appendix I):

> Techniques serve the process ... the process does not serve techniques.

Dismay and frustration await those who forget this dictum. Sad (and unnecessary) histories, recording the demise of quality circles and other teaming efforts, abound with wreckage run aground on this concealed shoal. Consider, again by analogy, the frustrated car-penter who fails to finish constructing a house because her hammer breaks. Connecting various boards of lumber is crucial to the construction process, and there are many tools available for accomplishing that end.

> Ritual must not supplant meaning!

# FAILURE AND FEAR

A sure sign that team members are forgetting S/L #32 (Appendix I) is a growing aura of frustration insidiously encircling participants, ultimately manifesting itself in a collective failure to proceed effectively through PIC phases, stages, and steps. Alert people sense it first in body language, blank stares, and assumptions implied by individual comments. Eventually, the drift becomes quite explicit. A typical cry expressing such advanced gridlock is something like, "The process isn't working," or "See, it's failing."

Recall, however, that a process cannot fail! Techniques cannot fail! Only people can fail! Remember S/L #4 (Appendix I)? Processes are concepts. They do not biologically live and breathe and act. In this same sense, techniques are also ideas, expressed as precisely defined rules for action. But techniques cannot, themselves, do the acting. Only people can act! Obviously, then, only people can fail!

Teaming process techniques never fail. Individuals fail—sometimes singly, sometimes collectively, but always as individual people. Why is this distinction so important? There are three reasons:

1. If people can fail, then people can fix.

2. The keys to fixing are contained in the process and the techniques.

3. There is nothing wrong with failure; failure is worthwhile and valuable, often preventing disasters.

Let us examine these three reasons in reverse order. First, what is so wrong with failure? Should good ends be abandoned for risk of failed means? Does the ten-month-old infant learning to walk fail by falling on his ample bottom in the attempt? Of course not! People learn techniques by trying, failing, and trying again. Ultimate success in completing the process comes from trying the techniques. This operating principle is contained in S/L #29 (Appendix I):

Failure is fine; fear of failure is not!

W. Edwards Deming's eighth point (within his famous fourteen points of quality management) says, "Drive out fear." Sage advice! He did not say, "Drive out failure." Failure teaches! Fear destroys! Sophocles said it well: "To him who is in fear, everything rustles." Self-esteem and worthy enterprises drive out fear of failure or at least control its effects. This lesson is learned well in the doing.

Reminding teaming participants of these truths and guiding them to act in their accordance are crucial duties of facilitators. As in all things, prevention is better than the cure. Skilled facilitators read moods and stop dysfunctional behaviors before they start.

As for reversing failures, while you read through this (and the next) chapter and imagine yourself acting a member's role, hold fast to the doctrine expressed in S/L #30 (Appendix I):

The process will set you free!

This law's message is deceptively simple. When you are failing to conduct the PIC effectively, look to proven fundamentals for a remedy—that is, to the explicit rules of the process and its techniques. Your failure is in forgetting and/or abusing those guidelines. The remedy, therefore, is to remember and/or properly use them. Go back to them! It all comes with practice. Both PIC principles and techniques are user friendly. Practice soon approaches perfection. All that you have to do is be willing to:

- recognize failures
- admit them
- do something about them
- return to the process.

Given such willingness, remedies come with relative ease. Appropriate remedial action always works and for logical reasons. Consider for a moment that if only you and your peers can act, and only you and your peers can fail, then it follows that only you and your peers can succeed. It is in your hands. Granting my overly simplistic reasoning, this fact holds quite true within all operating contexts.

## TECHNIQUES MENU

Whenever I think I have an exhaustive menu of techniques, something new crops up. Sources are bottomless. A few of the included PIC tools are original; others come from literature, media, or someone else. Almost everyone will have heard of or used one or more of them, perhaps with variations of title or procedure. That is good. Avoid treating them as absolutes. Be creative. If you can substitute, add, or enhance the list, do so. I certainly expect to add to the list. However, do not make the mistake of being frivolous or sloppy with the use of any technique once it is selected. The rules of application are not arbitrary. They emerged with reason—wise or unwise but reason nonetheless. I shall endeavor to satisfactorily explain each rule for each technique. Do not violate the rules until you have exercised them enough to fully understand their intents, uses, and limits. Freedom of choice is no excuse for arbitrary license.

- Your teaming peers are also trying to comprehend the process and techniques, and a common language is crucial for effective communications and mutual understanding.
- The techniques are not designed to be fully independent. The rules for each are derived with the others in mind. They are mutually interdependent, i.e., organic. Consequently, when the rules of one technique are arbitrarily changed, its partner techniques are affected, thereby influencing process phases, stages, and steps in unpredictable ways.

Although nothing is sacred, everything deserves sufficient respect to be changed only with reasonable care, insight, and sensitivity to potential consequences. Table 6.1 outlines and numbers PIC techniques; review the entries to become familiar with the technique names and subelements before proceeding through the chapter.

## COGNITIVE AND AFFECTIVE TECHNIQUES

Innovation requires the unrestrained use of all our creative juices. Sometimes ideas arrive as conclusions tied to the end of a precise chain of reasoning, such as the final answer to a complex mathematical equation or a set of formally defined propositions. For instance, if I propose that:

---

## Table 6.1
### Process for Innovation and Consensus Techniques

---

1. Divergence/Convergence
   1.1 Divergence
       1.1.1 Nominal Group Technique (NGT)
       1.1.2 Brainstorming
             1.1.2.1 Random
             1.1.2.2 Structured
   1.2 Convergence
       1.2.1 Numbering
       1.2.2 Clarifying
       1.2.3 CDAM
             1.2.3.1 **Combining**
             1.2.3.2 **Deleting**
             1.2.3.3 **Adding**
             1.2.3.4 **Modifying**
       1.2.4 Lobbying
       1.2.5 Voting
             1.2.5.1 Multivoting
             1.2.5.2 NGT
             1.2.5.3 Discrete Summation

2. Stream Analysis

3. Cause/Effect Diagramming (Fishbone/Ishikawa)
   3.1 Factors Type
   3.2 Process Type
       3.2.1 Block
       3.2.2 Flow

4. Why-Because Pursuit

5. Process Internalization
   5.1 Informal Process Internalization
   5.2 Formal Process Internalization

6. Data/Information Accumulation
   6.1 Information and Data
   6.2 Pareto Presentation

7. How-By Pursuit

8. Force Field Analysis

9. Psychic Irrelevancy

---

- All boys have red hair, and
- Joe is a boy,

deductive logic tells us, therefore, that

- Joe has red hair.

This deduction is an example of a cognitive process, meaning thinking in the sense of formal reasoning. The conclusion is said to make sense because it appeals to logic. Knowledge gained through rules of formal reasoning is said to be derived logically.

Of course, someone will eventually remind us that all boys do not really have red hair. The term really appeals to our understanding of the world, as we perceive it through our five physical senses. Knowledge gained through our senses is said to be derived empirically.

At the risk of oversimplifying such rich disciplines as learning theory, psychology, logic, and any number of branches of metaphysics, I suggest that ideas derived either logically (through formal reasoning) or empirically (through one or more of our five senses) be classified within the general category of cognitive PIC techniques.

Some ideas seem to simply occur to us through some avenue we cannot describe—for example, intuition, inspiration, emotion, whimsy, faith, divine communication, extrasensory perception (senses other than our five empirical senses), and any number of other sources defying explicit description. I shall suggest that ideas derived from such sources be classified under the general category of affective PIC techniques.

Cognitive techniques appeal to the scientist in us; affective techniques illuminate our artistic qualities. Human beings are complex organisms, and bureaucracies are equally complex mixtures of human beings. It should hardly be surprising, therefore, to discover that creative thinking involves the use of both cognitive and affective faculties. Few creative enterprises are exclusively one or the other. Insight is an element of the scientific method, just as logic and perception are components of art. Nonetheless, the primary thrust of each included PIC technique is either cognitive or affective.

## TECHNIQUES DESCRIPTIONS

Table 6.2 is a matrix showing which of the techniques described in this chapter are used to conduct each of the PIC phases, stages, and steps. Treat the table as a guide. Elements of techniques can be used in process steps in ways limited only by the imagination of team members, but this table shows the primary PIC step focus for each technique.

Refer to Table 5.3 as you read the following technique descriptions to refresh your understanding of the PIC; refer to Table 6.1 to recall detailed sequencing of PIC techniques. For simplicity's sake, each technique is described in the following sections as if it is being conducted by a facilitator for individuals, organized into a

## Table 6.2
### Process for Innovation and Consensus
### Techniques and Applications

| | Process | | | | | |
|---|---|---|---|---|---|---|
| | 1<br>Diagnosis | | | | | |
| | 1A<br>Symptom Selection | | | 1B<br>Causes ID/Prioritization | | |
| **Techniques** | 1A1<br>Symptom<br>Speculation | 1A2<br>Symptom<br>Verification | 1A3<br>Symptom<br>Specification | 1B1<br>C&R<br>Speculation | 1B2<br>C&R<br>Verification | 1B3<br>C&R<br>Prioritization |
| 1.1 Divergence | X | X | X | X | X | |
| 1.2 Convergence | X | | X | X | | |
| 2 Stream Analysis | X | | X | | | |
| 3 C/E Diagramming | | | | X | | |
| 4 Why-Because Pursuit | | | | X | | |
| 5 Process Internalization | | | | X | | X |
| 6 Data/Info Accumulation | | X | | | X | X |
| 7 How-By Pursuit | | | | | | |
| 8 Forcefield Diagramming | | | | | | |
| 9 Psychic Irrelevancy | X | | | X | | |

*Continued on next page*

formal teaming group, who are learning the process and techniques for the first time.

## 1. Divergence/Convergence

Divergence/convergence (D/C) is the most pervasive technique used during the PIC. It appears, in whole or in part, during every PIC step. It is also used in conjunction with some of the other techniques.

## Table 6.2—Continued

| Techniques | Process | | | | | | |
|---|---|---|---|---|---|---|---|
| | 2<br>Prescriptions | | | | | | |
| | 2A<br>Resolution(s) Selections | | | 2B<br>Implementation Planning | | | |
| | 2A1<br>Resolutions Speculation | 2A2<br>Consequences Speculation | 2A3<br>Resolutions Refinement | 2B1<br>Scheduling Resources Speculation | 2B2<br>Feasibility Verification | 2B3<br>Action Item Speculation | 2B4<br>Presentation |
| 1.1 Divergence | X | X | X | X | X | X | |
| 1.2 Convergence | X | X | X | | | | |
| 2 Stream Analysis | | | | | | | |
| 3 C/E Diagramming | | | | | | | |
| 4 Why-Because Pursuit | | | | | | | |
| 5 Process Internalization | | | | | | | |
| 6 Data/Info Accumulation | | | | X | X | | X |
| 7 How-By Pursuit | X | | | | | | |
| 8 Forcefield Diagramming | | X | | | | | |
| 9 Psychic Irrelevancy | X | | | X | | | |

Divergence exercises cognitive and affective faculties almost equally, the balance depending on the character of the issue under consideration. Convergence is primarily cognitive.

Divergence is the act of generating as many ideas as possible with respect to some stated area of interest. For instance, assume that a department head has been receiving complaints from personnel about the use of office computers; complaints vary across a wide spectrum. The manager convenes ten people in the conference room, those who have complained and those who know most about computer capabilities. Their charge is to diagnose and resolve whatever problems exist with respect to office automation. They are, in effect, entering the PIC as a formal group at Step 1A1, Symptom Speculation (see Table 5.3). Other people might be given a specific symptom statement and asked to determine its causes. For instance, the given statement might be, "Computer terminals are not available when needed." In this case, they would be entering the PIC at Step 1B1, C&R Speculation. Both formal teaming groups will perform D/C within the PIC. The second group's participants will also use additional techniques specified in Table 6.2 for Step 1B1.

Convergence is the act of prioritizing or ranking ideas generated during divergence. The purpose is to identify the one or few explicit statement(s), from out of the total generated, that most appropriately specify, by general consensus, the desired issue(s). For instance, the second group's members want to identify the few most significant causes for computer unavailability, while the first group's participants desire to isolate the one most crucial office computer problem from out of the pack, to attack first.

### 1.1 Divergence

#### 1.1.1 NOMINAL GROUP TECHNIQUE

*Features*

Nominal group technique (NGT) is a private divergence technique. Brainstorming is public. I personally find NGT most satisfying as a thinking stimulator. It lets people go into their own relaxing mental corner for a few moments of quiet contemplation. It also provides anonymity for people who would prefer that the source of their ideas remain confidential, at least temporarily, for any number of private reasons.

*Procedures*

**Note**: This divergent NGT procedure is described as if it is being conducted excluding combinations with any other technique, such as cause/effect diagramming or why-because pursuit.

- Hang flipchart sheet on the wall (prior to beginning of the session).
- Provide enough to accommodate five or six ideas per sheet.
- Distribute two or three three-by-five-inch cards to members.
  - ◆ Distribute two cards, if nine or more people.
  - ◆ Distribute three cards, if eight or fewer people.
- Instruct members to write one, and only one, idea on each card.

- Allow no talking.
- Cautions
  - *Print* neatly.
  - Use either pen or dark pencil.
  - Be brief, no essays; suggest ten words or less as a general guideline.
  - Set a time limit (five to ten minutes), but do not push someone for the difference of a few moments (good time for a working break).
  - Ask everyone to retain cards until everyone has completed the task.
- Collect and shuffle cards (for anonymity).
- Ask for volunteers to write entries on flipchart sheets hung on wall, one person per sheet.
  - Give volunteers the same dark-color marker, for example, black, brown, blue, violet. (Save bright colors for later convergence markings.)
  - Rules
    - Allow no talking.
    - Allow no more than six ideas per sheet, evenly spaced, with about six to eight inches between entries.
    - Do not number ideas.
    - Establish a six-inch left margin, and draw a bullet on that margin at the beginning of each entry.
    - Allow *absolutely no editing*. Write each entry *exactly* as written on card, including spelling and/or syntax errors.
    - *Be neat.* Remember that people must be able to read the entries from their seats.
    - Volunteers return cards and markers to facilitator or specified central area when sheet is completed, then return to seat.
    - Individuals at table should read entries as they are being written on sheets.
      - Search for surprising ideas.
      - Try to think of additional ideas that are inspired by what you are reading.

## Figure 6.1
### Typical Flipchart Sheet: Divergent NGT

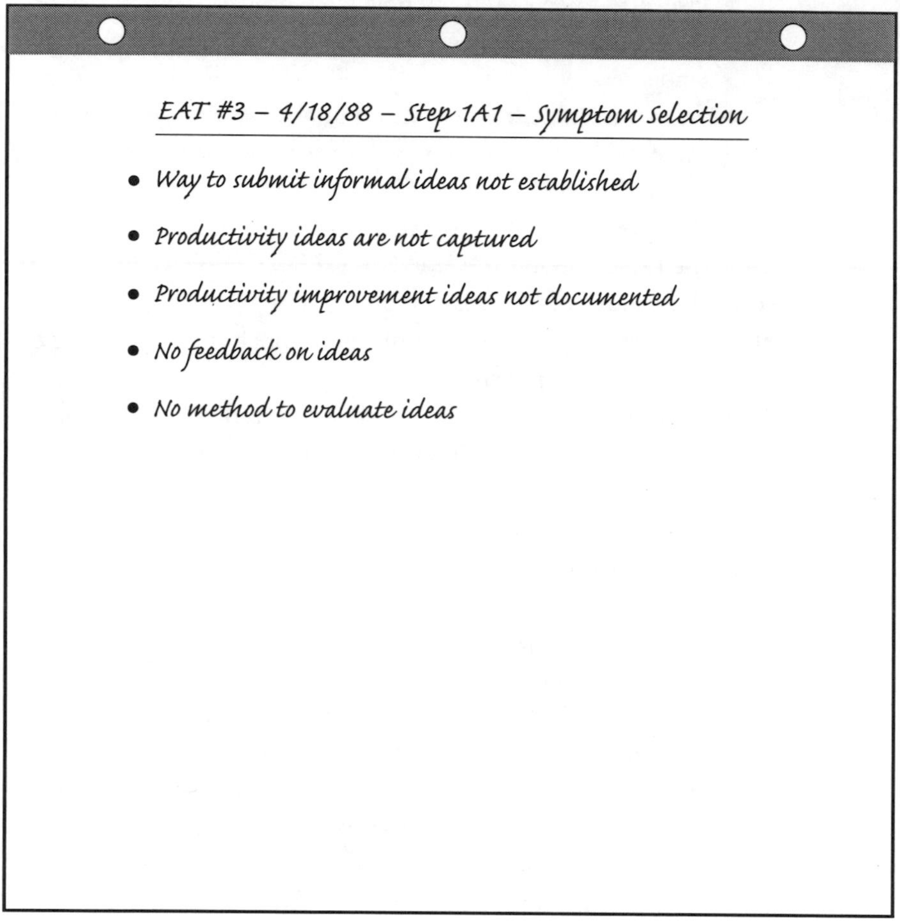

---

*EAT #3 – 4/18/88 – Step 1A1 – Symptom Selection*

- *Way to submit informal ideas not established*
- *Productivity ideas are not captured*
- *Productivity improvement ideas not documented*
- *No feedback on ideas*
- *No method to evaluate ideas*

---

- Write any newly inspired ideas on a sheet of paper for later entry.
- Await directions to begin new technique.

*Typical Flip Chart Sheet: Divergent Nominal Group Technique*
The most striking aspect of NGT divergence to the newcomer is the speed with which twenty to thirty ideas are generated and

## Figure 6.2
### Typical Flipchart Sheet: Brainstorming Added

*EAT #3 – 4/18/88 – Step 1A1 – Symptom Selection*

- *Way to submit informal ideas not established*
- *Low morale inhibits suggestions*
- *Lack of coordination for new ideas*
- *Productivity ideas are not captured*
- *Company fails to share ideas*
- *Average age of employees is 28 years*
- *Productivity improvement ideas not documented*
- *No incentives to share ideas*
- *No feedback on ideas*
- *Managers do not accept new ideas*
- *No method to evaluate ideas*

recorded, for all to see, within the space of ten or fifteen minutes. I always ask initiates what their reaction would have been if I had given each of them ten or fifteen minutes to come up with twenty to thirty original ideas on the subject of concern. They recognize immediately the low probability of successfully achieving that target.

### 1.1.2 BRAINSTORMING

Brainstorming's great virtue is that it allows (in fact, demands) individuals to generate a continuous chain of new ideas on insights gained by building on what peers have to say. It is a symbiotic activity. Properly conducted, brainstorming establishes a rhythm of linked-statements generation that captures participants' imaginations in a flowing tide of new ideas. It is not a solitary endeavor. Each individual must listen carefully to what is being said and grab insights inspired by the chain of ideas circling the room. In this sense, brainstorming is very much an affective technique.

Random brainstorming is conducted by allowing everyone to state an idea as soon as it occurs to her. Each person simply shouts it out. The scribe writes the idea on flipchart sheets as fast as possible, being careful to record it accurately (exactly as stated by the author). The process is disorderly but not chaotic. It works best when flashes of insight are being sought—that is, when affective faculties are called on, such as in technique 9, Psychic Irrelevancy.

Structured brainstorming is conducted in an orderly sequence; each person offers one idea per turn. Turns move from individual to individual in a continuous, unbroken flow around the room. The process is as much cognitive as it is affective. Each individual carefully considers the flow of ideas and develops new entries for contribution during subsequent turns. I tend to favor this form during most of the PIC steps, but this is a personal inclination. Members set their own rules regarding when to use either form of brainstorming.

Regardless of the form used, do not fool yourself into thinking that groups of people are brainstorming simply by offering isolated individual ideas within a collective setting. If they are ignoring each other's contributions, then (by my standards) they are not brainstorming; they are simply recording isolated individual thoughts. It is the holistic character of the process that makes it so very powerful: individuals listening carefully to each other and joining their intellects into a symbiotic network of ideas accelerated to new heights by the energy of collective reinforcements. E pluribus unum! Many as one!

**Note:** It is vital that statements be recorded exactly as expressed by their authors. Neither scribes, peers, nor facilitators may paraphrase or suggest that the author change, explain, or justify the statement wording or syntax. The idea belongs to the offerer and to no one else. Violation of this critical rule (in either letter or spirit) ensures loss of consensus.

### Procedures

*1.1.2.1 Random Brainstorming.*

- Individuals call out ideas as they occur to them.
- Facilitator or scribe writes ideas on flipchart sheets.
  - Add entries on wall-hung sheets if continuing from NGT divergence or if the brainstorming is being conducted as part of another technique employing specialized diagramming—for example, fishbone diagramming or how-by pursuit.
  - Enter ideas at the top of a new sheet if beginning divergence with brainstorming, and no other technique's specialized diagramming is being used.
  - Rules
    - ➤ Observe simple rules of courtesy to prevent chaos; *ideas traffic* can become congested.
    - ➤ Individuals listen carefully to flow of ideas, and let new thoughts develop from them.
    - ➤ Individuals read ideas as they are written on the sheets. (Visual cues strike us differently than audio cues, and we can increase our insights by using both perceptual faculties.)
    - ➤ Allow no additional talking or comments about entries.
    - ➤ Make clear that all ideas are acceptable; no idea is absurd.
  - End process when no one has an idea to offer.
    - ➤ Do not stop, even if only one person is continuing.
    - ➤ Do not make that person self-conscious about holding up events.
    - ➤ Remember that the last ideas could be the best ideas.
    - ➤ Remember that those last few ideas could rekindle a whole new set of ideas in other people's minds.

> ➤ Early completion is not the object of the exercise; full expression of ideas is the object.

*1.1.2.2 Structured Brainstorming.*

■ Note that random brainstorming rules hold, except as noted below.

◆ Allow no talking, except during turn.

◆ Allow no killer phrases or body language to intimidate individuals.

◆ Rotate turns either clockwise or counterclockwise.

◆ Allow one idea per turn.

◆ Do *not* stop flow of process.

◆ Must say "pass" if:

> ➤ Nothing to contribute during turn.
>
> • Ensures individual is participating.
> • Stimulates listening and thinking.
> • Is important for peers to know person is listening.
> • Is a courtesy to next person in line.
>
> ➤ Not sure how to state idea.
>
> • Compose idea on sheet of paper for next turn.
> • Do *not* ask peers to help with phrasing.
>   ❖ Interrupts flow.
>   ❖ Disturbs individual thoughts.
>   ❖ Loses ideas.

■ Try to hold any questions about the brainstorming process itself until it is completed.

◆ Interrupts thinking.

◆ Ideas are lost.

■ Process ends when everyone passes.

◆ Circle room twice for passes.

◆ Encourage person with last few ideas.

> ➤ One final statement could stimulate whole new round.
> ➤ Squeeze out every last idea.

The session formally ends when one participant so moves, and there are no objections. Remember that there is no seconding or "the ayes have it" in PIC Teaming. Majorities count for nothing; there must be full consensus on any motion. Therefore, the proper response to the motion is for the facilitator or selected participant to state, "We have a motion to close brainstorming. Are there any objections?" If there are no objections, then the activity ends. But if just one person objects, then the activity continues.

This rule is not arbitrary. Remember that consensus is lost if one person is intimidated or forced to go along with the group. That person has been denied choice, the one thing that cannot be tolerated in PIC teaming. If consensus is lost during any step of the PIC, the price will be eventual lost creativity and consensus. The seeds of failure can lay dormant through several steps and even stages— the longer the worse. Its consequences multiply because later decisions are based on earlier false consensus. The results can be demoralizing. If the truth is suppressed until the end, people will surely ask questions that will eventually uncover the latent divisions among participants. The results can be personally and organizationally devastating. Take my word for it; you do not want to learn this lesson the hard way. Do not violate this hard and fast rule:

Never take away a person's choice. (S/L #31, Appendix I)

### 1.2 Convergence

#### Features

Convergence includes ranking. The idea is to select (by consensus) the few (or one) best ideas (idea) from out of the population of total ideas generated during divergence. The technique is best introduced by looking at its component steps backward (refer to Table 6.1, items 1.2.1 to 1.2.5). The last step in convergence is to vote (item 1.2.5). But this is not the familiar kind of one-vote-majority-wins balloting that most of us have experienced; we are looking for satisficing consensus. Consensus voting requires many elimination ballots, similar to what is done during the Miss America Pageant. The winner is not selected when all the contestants appear on the stage for the first time. Numerous rounds of voting take place to eliminate individuals, leaving an ever-smaller population of candidates eligible for the next round of voting. Early ballots focus on eliminations; later, ballots focus on ranking finalists. The three voting techniques described in Table 6.1 are designed for just this kind of multiple balloting.

Yet before members vote, it is only fair to give each of them the opportunity to influence their peers' votes—that is, to convince others to vote for certain ideas listed on the sheets. Therefore, before voting, everyone gets this opportunity during the lobbying part of convergence.

But why lobby and vote for ideas until their language has been simplified and clarified? Remember that the entries on the sheet were the product of individual thoughts generated as they occurred. They might not be worded as clearly as possible and might not accurately convey the authors' true meanings. Therefore, they must be clarified sufficiently for members to know for what they are voting. Several of the diverged entries might say the same thing in different words. Why should members have to vote for the same idea more than one time? To prevent such redundant behavior, members are given the opportunity to combine like ideas before voting. They also get a chance to add, delete, and/or modify listed entries. This phase of the convergence technique is called combine, delete, add, and modify (CDAM). Prior to these actions, the entries are sequentially numbered and clarified (if necessary), but only by their authors.

### Procedures

#### 1.2.1 NUMBERING
- Number entries (1 to N) sequentially.
- Refer to entries by number throughout convergence.

#### 1.2.2 CLARIFYING
- Ask the author of each entry to give a short explanation of the essential meaning of the statement.
- Ask members if further clarification is required.
- Rules
  - Statement belongs to the author until clarifying is completed.
  - No discussions; the intent is to ensure that everyone understands the author's meaning and intent.
  - It is not necessary for members to agree with the statement.
  - The author can change the wording, as desired, to further clarify his own statement.

## Figure 6.3
### Typical Flipchart Sheet: Convergence Numbering

---

*EAT #3 – 4/18/88 – Step 1A1 – Symptom Selection*

1 Way to submit informal ideas not established

2 Low morale inhibits suggestions

3 Lack of coordination for new ideas

4 Productivity ideas are not captured

5 Company fails to share ideas

6 Average age of employees is 28 years

7 Productivity improvement ideas not documented

8 No incentives to share ideas

9 No feedback on ideas

10 Managers do not accept new ideas

11 No method to evaluate ideas

◆ Every statement should be reviewed, or have individuals ask for specific clarifications if number of entries is very large.
◆ Clarification can be reopened at any time during the subsequent convergence phases, but it should be completed as much as possible at this time.

**Figure 6.4**
Typical Flipchart Sheet: Convergence Clarification

---

*EAT #3 – 4/18/88 – Step 1A1 – Symptom Selection*

1  *Way to submit informal ideas not established*

2  *Low morale inhibits suggestions*

3  *Lack of coordination for new ideas*

4  *Productivity ideas are not captured*

5  *Company fails to share ideas*

6  *Average age of employees is 28 years*

7  *Productivity improvement ideas not documented*

8  *No incentives to share ideas*

9  *No feedback on ideas*  — positive or negative

10  *Managers do not accept new ideas*

11  *No method to evaluate ideas*  — documented

---

### 1.2.3 COMBINE, DELETE, ADD, AND MODIFY

*1.2.3.1 Combining.*

- Purpose is to simplify voting.
- Select any *two* statements that seem to say the same thing.
  - ◆ Decide which of them would make the better lead statement.
  - ◆ Refer to the statements by their respective numbers.

## Figure 6.5
### Typical Flipchart Sheet: Convergence Combining

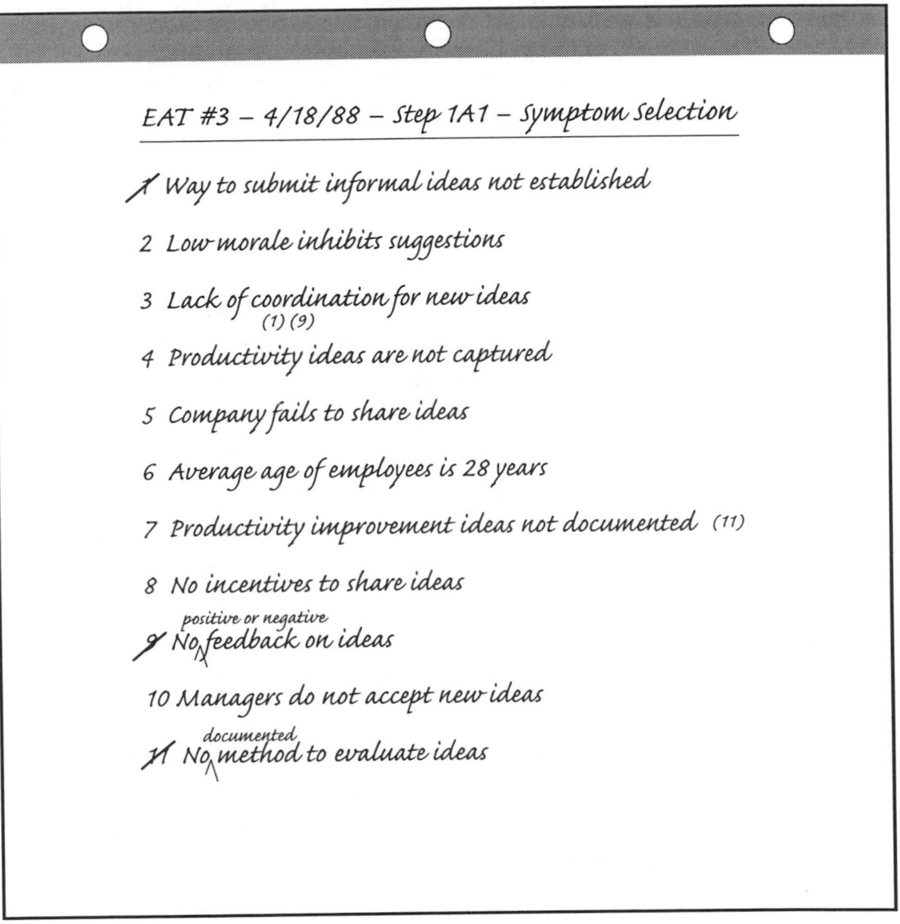

---

*EAT #3 – 4/18/88 – Step 1A1 – Symptom Selection*

~~1~~ *Way to submit informal ideas not established*

2 *Low-morale inhibits suggestions*

3 *Lack of coordination for new ideas*
 *(1) (9)*

4 *Productivity ideas are not captured*

5 *Company fails to share ideas*

6 *Average age of employees is 28 years*

7 *Productivity improvement ideas not documented (11)*

8 *No incentives to share ideas*

 *positive or negative*
~~9~~ *No feedback on ideas*

10 *Managers do not accept new ideas*

 *documented*
~~11~~ *No method to evaluate ideas*

---

◆ Recommend that the two seemingly similar statements be combined; i.e., "I recommend that number 11 be combined with number 7." The second number 7 is the *lead* statement.

■ If no objections, then the scribe writes the combination on the flipchart sheets, as shown in Figure 6.3 (combining number 11 with number 7).

- ◆ Cross out the identifying number of the statement being moved (number 11).
- ◆ Write that number under the text of the lead statement (number 7) at the left edge of the text in parentheses.
- ■ Rules
  - ◆ Combine any number of statements as one statement, but only one combination can be recommended at a time.
  - ◆ Allow recommendations to be made randomly.
  - ◆ Cancel the combination if one person objects to any recommendation.
  - ◆ Objecting person simply says, "Objection."
  - ◆ Allow no discussion concerning objection.
    - ➤ Objection simply means that the objector believes that the two statements are distinct and different enough to warrant separate votes.
    - ➤ Objecting is *not* a negative act, and the facilitator must remind participants of this fact.
    - ➤ Objections to combinations are accepted without discussion, because individual choice is the most important factor to preserve, and no person should be forced to implicitly vote for any statement simply because it is combined with some other statement that he wishes to choose.
    - ➤ When in doubt about a recommended combination, I suggest an objection, because the convenience of simplified voting is not as important as preserving individual choice during voting.

  *1.2.3.2 Deleting.*
- ■ Delete statements that appear to be irrelevant to the topic.
- ■ Do not delete statements in lieu of combining them under similar statements.
  - ◆ It is important during voting to see how many times the same idea has been suggested.
  - ◆ Different versions of the same idea add nuances that are important, if a statement (and its combined partners) is chosen for further consideration.

## Figure 6.6
### Typical Flipchart Sheet: Convergence Deleting

---

*EAT #3 – 4/18/88 – Step 1A1 – Symptom Selection*

~~1~~ Way to submit informal ideas not established

2 Low morale inhibits suggestions

3 Lack of coordination for new ideas
   *(1) (9)*

4 Productivity ideas are not captured

5 Company fails to share ideas

~~6 Average age of employees is 28 years~~

7 Productivity improvement ideas not documented *(11)*

8 No incentives to share ideas

~~9~~ No ⌄feedback on ideas
   *positive or negative*

10 Managers do not accept new ideas

~~11~~ No ⌄method to evaluate ideas
   *documented*

---

- Rules
  - A deletion can be suggested by anyone.
  - One objection stops the deletion; no explanation is required.
  - Best guideline for deletion is consensus that the statement is totally irrelevant to the topic (number 6).

## Figure 6.7
### Typical Flip Chart Sheet: Convergence Adding

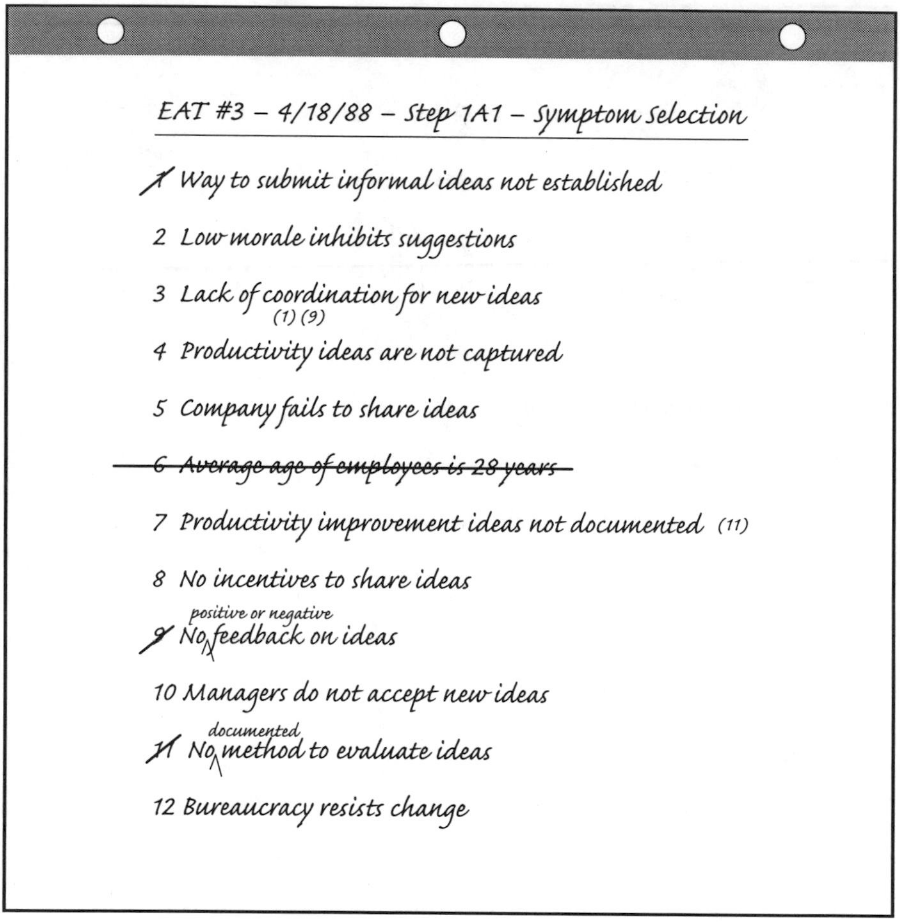

---

*EAT #3 – 4/18/88 – Step 1A1 – Symptom Selection*

~~1~~ Way to submit informal ideas not established

2 Low morale inhibits suggestions

3 Lack of coordination for new ideas
  (1) (9)

4 Productivity ideas are not captured

5 Company fails to share ideas

~~6 Average age of employees is 28 years~~

7 Productivity improvement ideas not documented  (11)

8 No incentives to share ideas

  positive or negative
~~9~~ No feedback on ideas

10 Managers do not accept new ideas

  documented
~~11~~ No method to evaluate ideas

12 Bureaucracy resists change

---

*1.2.3.3 Adding.*
- Adding is conducted similarly to random brainstorming (see number 12).
- Rules
  - Anyone can add a statement.
  - Number additions sequentially with existing statements.
  - No one can object to an addition.

## Figure 6.8
## Typical Flipchart Sheet: Convergence Modifying

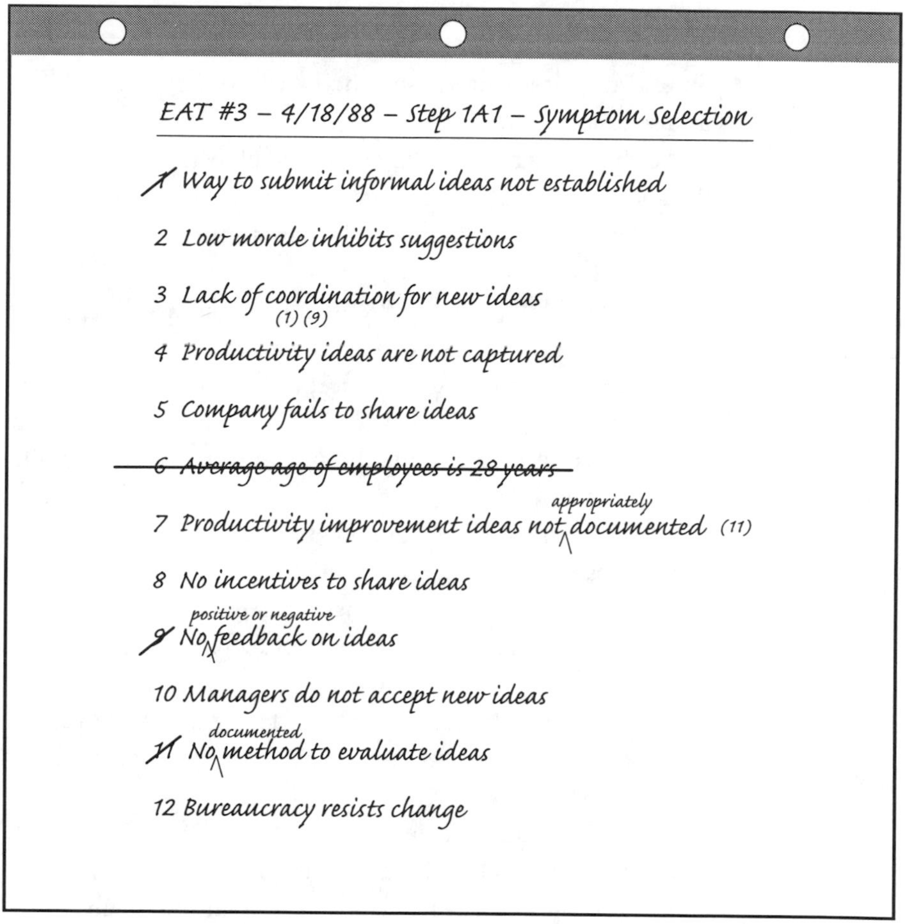

*EAT #3 – 4/18/88 – Step 1A1 – Symptom Selection*

~~1~~ Way to submit informal ideas not established

2 Low morale inhibits suggestions

3 Lack of coordination for new ideas
    *(1) (9)*

4 Productivity ideas are not captured

5 Company fails to share ideas

~~6 Average age of employees is 28 years~~

    *appropriately*
7 Productivity improvement ideas not documented  *(11)*

8 No incentives to share ideas

    *positive or negative*
~~9~~ No feedback on ideas

10 Managers do not accept new ideas

    *documented*
~~11~~ No method to evaluate ideas

12 Bureaucracy resists change

---

◆ Clarify all additions.
◆ Additions are eligible for combining, deleting, and modifying, along with all other entries.
◆ Adding is a good way to combine statements that seem to defy combining, but require only a generic statement that can accommodate all of them.

*1.2.3.4 Modifying.*

- Anyone can suggest a change in the wording of a statement, since all statements are collectively owned after clarification (see number 7).
- Rules
  - ◆ State the desired change succinctly, without explanations or discussion.
  - ◆ Make the change in wording if no one objects.
  - ◆ If someone objects, the change must be discussed; the objection does not automatically carry in this case.
  - ◆ Rules for Discussion
    - ➤ Do *not* debate your disagreement over the wording, as this causes meetings to break down.
    - • Concentrate on what you *agree*; for instance, the original statement was originally accepted by everyone.
    - • Start discussion by asking the suggestor to briefly explain the reason for the suggested modification.
    - • Objectors must listen carefully to and seriously consider the reasons for the modification.
    - • If there is more than one objector, get consensus between the suggestor and the first objector before going on to the other objections.
    - • The objector, after seriously considering the suggestor's reasons for the change, gives a short explanation for the objection.
    - • *Remember* that the object is to find a common ground, not to stick stubbornly to *my* interpretation.
    - • If no consensus is reached after explanations, each person should again concentrate on the areas of agreement, and determine the usually very minor spot of disagreement.
    - • Each person should ask herself the following questions: "What could the other person say that would turn me to accept his interpretation?", or "How could the wording be changed to accommodate both of our meanings?" *Listen! Empathize! Seek accommodation without sacrificing your intent!*

- If no accommodation is found, one person should simply add a new statement, and both statements can stand.
- Seek advice from other team members; they usually can find the appropriate words to satisfy both persons because they are more objective, being separate from the debate.
- *Repeat*, seek a working consensus that satisfies, that each individual can accept, and that enjoys general acceptance.

■ At the end of CDAM, circle the numbers only of those statements remaining as candidates for voting.

### 1.2.4 LOBBYING

■ Before voting, each individual has a chance to explain her preferences.

■ The object is to suggest reasons for peers to vote for your preferences.

■ Rules

♦ Must lobby for a statement—with positive tone.

♦ Must never lobby against a statement with negative tone; this immediately puts someone on the defensive.

♦ Suggest a random lobby—that is, a person simply calls out, "I want to lobby for number X because. ... " (Keep it brief.)

♦ Lobby for as many items as you wish, but only one per turn.

♦ Lobbies supporting previous lobbies are perfectly reasonable and permitted.

♦ If lobbies are confusing, ask for reclarification of the entry in question by the original author.

♦ Do not argue, debate, or discuss; just listen and make your own choices.

### 1.2.5 VOTING

Remember that we seek consensus, not majority winners and minority losers. We desire a 100 percent satisficing consensus on which of the alternative statements are the best statements, with respect to the issue under consideration. Therefore, each person must have a chance to vote at least once for every statement—that is, there must be multi (many) voting ballots. Succeeding ballots are arranged for elimination voting, very much like the Miss America Contest, where in the first round fifty-plus women appear on the stage. The winner is not selected by one ballot representing one vote per judge, as stated earlier. Instead, a series of elimination ballots are taken to winnow the population down to semifinalists and finalists, who are then ranked to determine the runners up and final winner.

Considering that in any given PIC step, the initial population of statements can grow to over two hundred-plus alternatives, the value of all the preceding convergence techniques becomes obvious. The intense and repeated deliberations conducted between numbering and voting allow people to develop ever-more sophisticated understandings and opinions about the relative worth of statements. After a few excursions through the entire D/C exercise, individuals become expert at the process, and conduct it with mutual trust, empathy, and ease. It is very user friendly.

Of the three included voting techniques, only multivoting is usable for balloting on twenty-five or more alternatives. Convergent NGT works best with twenty-five or fewer alternatives, and discrete summation loses favor with more than ten remaining choices. Multivoting works regardless of the number of alternatives, from two to hundreds. The ranking of finalists typically occurs when twenty-five or fewer alternatives remain, and different individuals usually favor one of the three techniques at this time. But it is seldom difficult to gain consensus on one. In fact, individuals usually enjoy trying all three techniques during votes conducted in subsequent PIC steps.

Sometimes the mechanics of one technique do not produce a real sense of satisfying satisficing consensus among members. The numbers on the sheets indicate ranking, but the spirit of agreement is clearly missing. A change of technique often changes that unhappy result. If this does not work, then participants must go back to some previous convergence step—for example, clarifying, CDAM, or lobbying—and work their way back to voting for finalists. As always, the answer to a roadblock in the activity is to let the process set you free (S/L #30, Appendix I).

The probabilities are that voting will begin with a few dozen to hundreds or more statements remaining as available choices after CDAM and lobbying. Multivoting eliminates alternatives having little or no chance to become finalists. The process is the same regardless of whether the particular PIC step being conducted requires choosing just one item, such as Symptom Specification (PIC Step 1A3), or more than one item, such as Causes and Roots Speculation (PIC Step 1B1). In the latter case, the number of causes that will finally be chosen need not be predetermined. The mechanics of the voting techniques will draw that final number out as a reflection of the consensus in the room. Voting, then, is a discovery exercise. The underlying consensus in the room is discovered through the mechanics of the voting techniques.

*1.2.5.1 Multivoting.*

### Features

Multivoting is a public form of convergent voting. Members vote for available remaining statements by raising their hands as the statement numbers are called. After all the votes are called, counted, and recorded, a decision is made, through consensus, regarding which statements should be eliminated for the next round of voting. This seems straightforward enough, but the real power of multivoting is found in a few vital rules that make it a true reflection of organic consensus rather than simply a summation of individual choices.

The first vital rule regulates the number of alternatives for which individuals can vote during each round of voting. Basically, this restriction can be summarized as:

- Round 1: rule of all
- Round 2: rule of halves.

During the first round of voting, each individual can vote once for every candidate statement. Therefore, if the initial number of candidates is fifty-two, then each member can vote for as few as zero, all fifty-two, or some number in between. This guarantees that no member will ever lack an opportunity to express a choice for each and every candidate. Remember that in consensus building expression of individual choice is the glue that cements unity. Therefore, at the conclusion of the first round, those statements that received zero or only a few votes can truly be viewed as lacking general favor. During the first round of voting, choices are free; no one is required to give up a vote for one statement as a price to pay for choosing an alternative.

During the second and subsequent rounds of voting (however many are required), voting is preceded by a consensus decision about which alternatives should be eliminated as candidates in that particular exercise. Understand that the term *elimination* does not mean destroy or remove. In the PIC, nothing is ever lost! Even items deleted during CDAM are not obliterated; they are simply removed from contention at that time. One learns very quickly that in the PIC ideas have a way of rising, phoenix-like, from irrelevance in one step to pertinence in some subsequent step. However, once the elimination process for the second voting round is completed, the number of remaining candidates is counted, and the rule of halves is involved. Simply put, each member can vote for a maximum of one-half of the remaining candidates. If the number of remaining alternatives is thirty-four, then each person can vote for as few as zero, as many as seventeen (one half of thirty-four), or some number in between. If there is an odd number of remaining alternatives, then the number of votes is to be one-half of either the next-higher or next-lower even number. I prefer the next-lower even number, because one must prioritize that much more carefully and think that much more critically with one less available choice. But this is my personal preference; group consensus determines the issue.

In fact, the rule of halves itself is a matter of consensus. It could just as easily be a rule of three-quarters or a rule of two-fifths. I recommend the rule of halves because of hard experience. Mechanically, it seems to fit well with inherent senses of fairness and individual efforts to evaluate priorities. But its real value is in what it prevents, and that is the waste of time and good energy that people begin to sense over an issue of relatively trivial moment. It becomes very obvious very quickly that the rule should provide enough candidate statements to allow fruitful choice, and should simultaneously restrict candidates to a population small enough to stimulate careful individual evaluation, prioritization, and ranking.

If ever a golden mean for cooperative behavior existed, the rule of halves in this situation must surely be it.

The mechanics of voting in the second and subsequent rounds is the same as for round one. Hands are raised for each candidate, and votes are counted and recorded. How many rounds of voting are required? There is no set number. Each episode of multivoting is unique in this regard, but the principle underlying the determination the of number of voting rounds is expressed in the second vital rule that makes multivoting a true reflection of consensus.

The second vital rule establishes the subtle shift in individual mindsets that occurs as each episode of multivoting progresses from start to finish. The two mindsets should be:

- initial rounds: eliminate nonfinalists
- late rounds: rank/prioritize finalists.

Regardless of whether a particular episode of multivoting is aimed toward one or a few end choices, the initial rounds express a quality of getting rid of alternatives. But, as these elimination rounds progress, certain statements begin to visibly exhibit a character of staying power, which implies their near certainty as finalists. When this occurs depends on the number of initial candidates: what PIC phase/stage/step is being conducted, the character of the issue under consideration, results of previous verification steps, and many other variables. My experience indicates that semifinalists begin to appear when about fifteen to twenty-five candidates remain, and the finalists emerge with about five to ten surviving alternatives. The facilitator should be cognizant of this shift, and point out its virtues as questions arise about voting procedures.

Throughout the multivoting episode, questions such as, "Can I ask for further clarification on number X?", "Can I recommend more combinations?", or "Can I modify number X?" can arise. The answer should, with few exceptions, be "yes." But, as always, it is up to team consensus. Be prepared, however, to bear later costs for early impatience. Consider the third vital rule, making multivoting a true reflection of consensus. I call it the role of recapitulation:

> Allow reopenings of previous convergence techniques between individual rounds of multivoting, but not during them.

It should be obvious at this point that the entire convergence process, from numbering of statements through voting, is a critical thinking and learning exercise. As people probe into the subject and ideas fly around the room, a synthesis of understanding occurs in every mind, and sophistication of insight opens doors to perspectives that earlier were unobtainable. Therefore, the mood in the room should be conducive—even eager—to welcome a new arrangement of candidates that might remove a roadblock to prioritizing finalists and resolving individual uncertainties.

The one limit (stated above) I suggest is that recapitulation be allowed only between rounds of voting and not during a round. Constant interruptions of voting cloud thinking and tend to create growing impatience and irritation—for obvious reasons. But, as always, such a limit is a matter of group consensus. Better to learn the hard way and agree than to suffer imposed constraints.

■ Multivoting ends at one of two junctures. First, it may end when the final single choice or multiple choices have been selected. Second, it may end at or near the finalist stage, and there is a consensus to end voting by using convergent NGT or discrete summation. Convergent NGT works best with twelve to twenty-five remaining candidates. Discrete summation is most suited for three to ten alternatives. I know of no general rule for deciding which technique to choose during the end game; let consensus decide. However, I can suggest that the best way out of the impasse that sometimes occurs, when the mechanical voting technique employed fails to satisfy the underlying sense of consensus, is to shift techniques. If that fails, then somewhere in the convergent process, before voting, consensus was missed. The team must go back and retrieve it. In fact, consensus might really have been lost during some early step, stage, or phase of the PIC itself. Whatever the case, backtracking and consensus retrieval are the only answers.

### Procedures

■ Facilitator/leader/scribe draws a blank voting grid with a felt pen on flipchart sheet(s) prior to voting period (as shown in Figure 6.9).

## Figure 6.9
### Typical Blank Flipchart Sheet:
### Convergence Multivoting

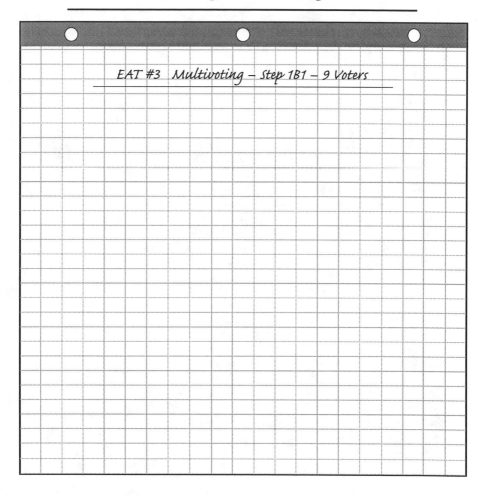

*EAT #3   Multivoting – Step 1B1 – 9 Voters*

- ◆ Make grid space density about eighteen columns by twenty-five rows.
- ◆ Label the top of the sheet, for later identification, with the following data:
  - ➤ Team name or number.
  - ➤ PIC step, for example, 1B1.

125

## Figure 6.10
### Typical Flipchart Sheet:
### Convergence Multivoting

EAT #3  Multivoting – Step 1B1 – 9 Voters

| Left column | | | | | | Right column | | | | | |
|---|---|---|---|---|---|---|---|---|---|---|---|
| 2 | 1 | | | | | 41 | ⑧ ⑧ ⑦ ⑥ | (# ③) | | | |
| 3 | ④ 2 | | | | | 42 | ⑨ ⑧ ⑧ ⑧ | (# ②) | | | |
| 4 | ⑨ ⑧ ⑧ ⑨ | (# ①) | | | | 46 | ⑦ ⑥ ⑤ ③ | (# 6 tie) | | | |
| 5 | ⑤ ⑥ ④ 2 | | | | | 47 | ⑤ 1 | | | | |
| 7 | 1 | | | | | 48 | ② 2 | | | | |
| 8 | 0 | | | | | 50 | 1 | | | | |
| 10 | 2 | | | | | 55 | ⑤ 3 | | | | |
| 12 | 2 | | | | | 58 | ③ 4 4 1 | | | | |
| 13 | 2 | | | | | 59 | ③ 0 | | | | |
| 14 | ③ 3 | | | | | 60 | ④ 2 | | | | |
| 15 | ④ 3 | | | | | 61 | 2 | | | | |
| 18 | ③ 1 2 | | | | | 66 | ⑧ ⑥ ④ 1 | | | | |
| 23 | ⑤ 5 1 1 | | | | | 67 | 0 | | | | |
| 25 | ⑦ 5 5 4 | (# ⑤) | | | | 68 | 1 | | | | |
| 26 | ⑧ 8 7 5 | (# ④) | | | | 69 | 2 | | | | |
| 27 | ⑤ 3 | | | | | 70 | ④ 2 | | | | |
| 28 | ③ 2 | | | | | 71 | ③ 1 | | | | |
| 29 | ③ 1 | | | | | 72 | ② 3 | | | | |
| 30 | 2 | | | | | 73 | 2 | | | | |
| 32 | 2 | | | | | 74 | 1 | | | | |
| 35 | 1 | | | | | 75 | 8 5 1 2 | | | | |
| 36 | 0 | | | | | 80 | ⑤ ⑤ ④ ③ | (# 6 tie) | | | |
| 37 | ⑤ ⑤ 2 | | | | | 84 | ⑥ ④ 2 | | | | |
| 38 | ④ 2 | | | | | | | | | | |
| 40 | ③ 0 | | | | | | | | | | |

➤ Title, for example, Multivote.
➤ Name of any other special technique during which the convergence is being conducted (for example, Cause and Effect Diagram, or Why-Because Pursuit 1.
➤ Total number of people voting.

- Facilitator/leader/scribe enters into the grid the numbers of the candidate statements remaining after CDAM and lobbying. They are the statements for which identifying numbers were circled at the end of CDAM.
  - ◆ Enter the numbers in numerical sequence beginning in column 1, row 1 (1,1).
  - ◆ Continue entering candidate numbers down the first column to the last row—that is, space 1, 25.
  - ◆ Enter the next numbers in column 10, beginning with space 10, 1, and proceeding to 10, 25.
    - ➤ Leave enough columns for eight rounds of voting—that is, one column per round per candidate.
    - ➤ Use a second flipchart grid sheet if more than fifty candidates exist.
- Each individual takes a clean sheet of paper and sequentially lists the candidate statement numbers in columns.
- Individuals take five to ten minutes to determine for which candidate statements they intend to vote during the first round of voting.
  - ◆ Facilitator/leader ensures that everyone understands the rule of all for the first round of voting.
    - ➤ Since, under the rule, choices are free, you (as a voter) should feel free to vote for any candidate, even if you feel that it is low on your priority list as a finalist in subsequent voting rounds.
    - ➤ Do not vote for those candidates that you reject.
  - ◆ Individuals circle the identifying numbers of those, and only those, candidates for which they intend to vote in round 1.
  - ◆ Allow additional time for personal consideration. *Do not rush people.* True consensus is the goal, not a savings of five to ten minutes.
  - ◆ Allow no talking.
- If the facilitator is scribing, then she can call out the candidate numbers, count the raised hands for each candidate, and enter the voting totals for each candidate.
  - ◆ Since the facilitator does not participate, this function is relatively easy to perform.

- ◆ If no facilitator is present, then participants must appoint a caller/counter and a scribe.
  - ➤ Since they are participants, they must pay very careful attention to their split responsibilities, or they will make mistakes.
  - ➤ Other team members should help them as much as possible.
- ■ When everyone is prepared to vote, the facilitator gives the following instructions.
  - ◆ When a number is called, those voting for it must raise one hand high, and keep it there until the total count is called.
    - ➤ Do not raise hands halfway.
    - ➤ Do not drop hands early.
    - ➤ Be careful about moving arms in such a way as to cause the facilitator to count such movements as votes—for example, scratching head, leaning back with arms behind head.
  - ◆ Allow no talking.
- ■ Facilitator begins round by calling out the first candidate number.
  - ◆ Counts raised hands.
  - ◆ Enters the sum total in column 2, space 2,1.
  - ◆ Continues the process until votes are entered for each candidate, at which point the voting round ends.
- ■ Facilitator asks, "Are there any recommendations for dropping (eliminating) candidates for the next round of voting?"
  - ◆ Instructs members that they should consider, in their own minds, the minimum number of received votes that should qualify candidates for survival into the next round of voting.
  - ◆ Members should also consider the importance of statements that might be dropped if any given numerical threshold for rejection is defined. Pure numbers of votes received are not the sole criterion.
  - ◆ Such considerations vary, as the voting rounds progress.
- ■ Explains that the appropriate language for recommending candidate elimination is: "I recommend that, for the next round of voting, all candidates receiving a vote of X (for example, three or less) be dropped."

- ◆ If no one objects, then the list of available voting candidate statements is reduced by eliminating those that receive a count of X votes or less.
  - ➤ Someone might object by stating, "I object and recommend dropping those receiving X – 1 votes or less (for example, two votes or less), instead of the originally recommended three votes or less."
    - • If this is the only objection raised, then members are obliged to accept the lower number (two votes or less), because the objector would lose choices if the higher reject value were accepted.
  - ➤ It is perfectly reasonable for the team to accept dropping all candidates with X votes or less, while exempting one (or a few) about which a member feels strongly. For example, "I recommend dropping candidates with two or less votes with the exceptions of numbers 48 and 72" (which both have two votes).
  - ➤ The principle is to eliminate as many as possible without any member losing a sense of choice—that is, never sacrifice consensus.
- ◆ Once elimination is decided, the facilitator draws a single line through the dropped candidate numbers (and their first-round count) on the matrix sheet.
  - ➤ Asks someone to cross out equivalent numbers on the wall-hung text flipchart sheets.
  - ➤ Calls out numbers being crossed out to ensure that there are no errors, and that everyone knows which numbers to cross out on their personal count sheets.
- ◆ Round two of voting begins with the facilitator telling members to review candidates, and choose a maximum of half of them for the second round of voting.
  - ➤ Count total remaining; declare one-half number.
  - ➤ Give sufficient time for members to think privately on choices (obviously depends on number remaining).
  - ➤ Remind members not to exceed maximum number of allowed votes.

➤ Round two votes are called, counted, and recorded, using same procedures as in the first round.
  • Vote count is entered in the third column of the matrix sheet (next empty column to the right of the round one column).
◆ Procedure continues through elimination rounds, as defined earlier.
  ➤ Ends under one of the following conditions.
    • Final choice (or choices) are completed.
      ❖ Occurs when members decide that they are satisficed with final surviving candidate(s).
    • Surviving candidates are few enough to finish voting, using either convergent NGT or discrete summation, and members decide to use one of these techniques.

*1.2.5.2 Nominal Group Technique.*

### Features

Convergent nominal group technique (NGT) is a private technique for ranking or prioritizing statement candidate finalists. I have found that it works best when approximately twenty-five candidate statements remain to be considered. Members seem to be able to juggle that many ideas with relative ease, but NGT becomes visibly more difficult when the number of candidates gets larger.

The results of voting are not significantly changed by the choice of technique to be used during the finalist rounds. I have tested this proposition numerous times and feel quite confident with the results. Considering that the same people are looking at the same candidates under the same conditions, there is little reason to expect a difference in finalist selections.

The most positive remarks that I hear about convergent NGT are that it gives participants a quiet time to think and allows them to cast private ballots. However, as I mentioned earlier, people often agree to switch techniques during successive D/C episodes just for the sake of variety. Regardless of the technique used, during the finalist rounds of voting, each individual is privately prioritizing or ranking surviving candidates in his own mind. The different techniques are, in effect, merely different ways of summing and expressing these singular private decisions.

The decisions remain quite constant, regardless of the technique chosen to express them. The NGT process is mechanically easy. Each member is given a number of three-by-five-inch cards and asked to format them to record two distinct numbers. With approximately twenty-five remaining candidates, I usually distribute five cards per person. If there are twelve or fewer remaining candidates, I distribute four cards per person. Members are asked to select five (assuming five cards were distributed) candidate statement finalists from the survivors. They are then asked to write the statement number of each of the five finalists on the cards, one number per card, in a designated format area.

Using what has sometimes been called an overly ritualistic (but I believe necessary) ceremony, each member is then asked to rank his five finalists with respect to each other. The most favored of the five finalists selected by each individual is given a weight score of 5 on the card (in another designated format area) bearing that candidate's statement number (the 5 score signifying the most favored finalist for that individual). From the four remaining cards, individuals are asked to select the least-favored candidate, and give it a score of 1 in the appropriate formatted area. This most-favored, least-favored sequence is repeated (with scores of 4 and 2), and the last remaining card is given the median score of 3.

This most-least device reflects the fact that it is easier to choose extremes than it is to choose between median preferences. With this technique, the median choices are identified by default; it works with any number of choices and cards.

When voting is completed, the cards are collected and sorted, first by individual statement numbers and then by weights for each statement. The necessity for the ritualistic procedure required during voting becomes obvious at this juncture. If card formats vary and numbers are illegible, inconsistent, or unintelligible, the entire ranking process is jeopardized. Once the cards are mixed, it just about always proves impossible for individuals to recognize their own cards or to reconstruct their exact thought processes. Clarity and precision are vital.

The weights for each statement receiving them are written underneath the appropriate statement text on the flipcharts. The top finalist is the one receiving the highest cumulative weight. If two or more statements score the same weight, then the tie is broken by counting the total number of cards (reflecting the total number of individuals who chose that candidate as a finalist) submitted for each of the candidates. A tie is declared between any two (or more) statements receiving both equal weights and equal numbers of votes.

I have found convergent NGT very helpful when the mechanics of multivoting, carried down to final selections, fails to reflect a true sense of consensus in the room. In fact, any one of the three finalist techniques described here makes a fine consensus assurance device, when one of the other two leaves an atmosphere of dissatisfaction hovering in the air.

### Procedures

- Facilitator distributes cards (five, for example) to members.
  - ◆ Gives following instructions.
    - ➤ Lay cards in pattern (see Figure 6.11A).
    - ➤ Make no marks or entries on cards until instructed. *Please observe this restriction* (explain reason).
    - ➤ Format each card with # symbol in center and large circle in bottom-right corner. Use dark pencil or pen, and be neat (Figure 6.11B).
    - ➤ Each member should consider the remaining semifinalist candidates, and select five finalists. (Provide ample time.)
    - ➤ Enter one finalist statement number on each card, next to the # symbol, neatly and clearly (Figure 6.11C).
    - ➤ Do not—repeat—do not proceed further, and please do not move ahead of pace.
- Individual members follow the instructions, and stop after each of their five cards contains the formats and the numbers of their chosen statement finalists.
- Facilitator gives following instructions.
  - ◆ Weight (1 to 5) finalists with respect to each other. A weight of 5 is to be given to the most preferred finalist, and a weight of 1 is to be given to the least preferred finalist;

## Figure 6.11
### Convergent NGT Voting Procedure

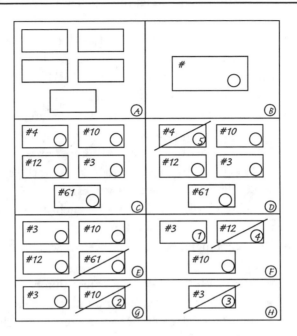

intermediate weights are to be distributed in descending order of preference.

◆ Repeat, do not enter weights now—follow the pace.
◆ First, select most preferred finalist, enter a weight score of 5 in the bottom-right circle, turn the card over, and stop (Figure 6.11D).
◆ Second, there are now four finalist cards. Select the least preferred of the four finalists, enter a weight score of 1 in the bottom-right circle, turn the card over, and stop (Figure 6.11E).
◆ Third, there are now three finalist cards. Select the most preferred of the three finalists, enter a weight score of 4 in the bottom-right circle, turn the card over, and stop (Figure 6.11F).

◆ Fourth, there are now two finalist cards. Select the least preferred of the two finalists, enter a weight score of 2 in the bottom-right circle, turn the card over, and stop (Figure 6.11G).

◆ Fifth, there is now one finalist card. Enter a weight score of 3 in the bottom-right circle, collect all five cards, and pass them to the facilitator (Figure 6.11H).

■ Declare a five to ten minute coffee break, and ask two members to assist with the card-sorting procedure.

◆ Sort cards by statement number, and lay the piles on the table in sequential statement-number order.

◆ Sort each pile by weight values, 5's on top, 1's on bottom, in descending order of weight values.

■ The facilitator writes the scores for each statement underneath the text on the wall-hung flipchart sheets.

◆ One team member reads the weight scores aloud for each pile of cards.

➤ Begin with the lowest statement number.

➤ Recite the weight scores individually, beginning with 5's and continuing in descending order of weights through 1's—that is, "Statement number 17: 5, 5, 4, 4, 4, 3, 2, and 2."

➤ The facilitator writes the weights under the text for statement number 17, exactly as recited.

➤ Total the number of cards for statement number 17—that is, 8.

➤ Add the sum total of the weights:
$5 + 5 + 4 + 4 + 4 + 3 + 2 + 2 = 29$.

➤ Write the two totals (number of scores/total weight) under the statement text on the far-right side of the flipchart sheet—that is, 8/29.

➤ Read the scores for statement 17 as follows: "Statement 17 received 8 votes for a total weight of 29—that is, 8 for 29."

➤ Repeat the process for every pile of sorted cards.

■ Seek the statement on the flipchart sheets with the highest total weight score, and declare that as the consensus preference.

- Repeat the process for the second, third, and so on highest weight score.
- Rank statements with equal weight scores, according to the number of votes received.
- Declare statements with both scores equal as *tied* in rank.
- Note that the number of statements receiving high finalist scores does not necessarily equal five (because five cards were distributed to each member).
- Total number of high-scoring finalists depends on distribution of individual member choices during the card-writing process.
- Note aloud that rather large score differences separate the cluster of big winners from the median and small winners. This top-scoring cluster is usually the group on which to concentrate as the team moves on to the next PIC step and the next set of techniques.

*1.2.5.3 Discrete Summation.*

### Features

I coined the title discrete summation for this convergent technique; however, the device itself is hardly original. I have seen it described in a number of documents, always with some variation of form or structure. My experience indicates that, like convergent NGT, psychological barriers reduce the usefulness of discrete summation as the number of statements to be ranked grows beyond a certain number. I suggest that it is best employed with no more than ten to twelve statements. For simplicity's sake, I shall explain it under the assumption that there are six finalist statements to rank. The principle is as easily learned with this number as it would be with ten to twelve statements.

The term discrete refers to choices between two distinct, separate, clearly distinguishable alternatives. This is exactly the task given to each individual during the first part of the process. Each person privately ranks each alternative against each of the other alternatives in a kind of round-robin contest. Therefore, each comparison pits one candidate finalist against one other candidate finalist—for example, 1 versus 2, 1 versus 3 ... 2 versus 3, 2 versus

## Figure 6.12
### Typical Flipchart Sheet: Convergence NGT

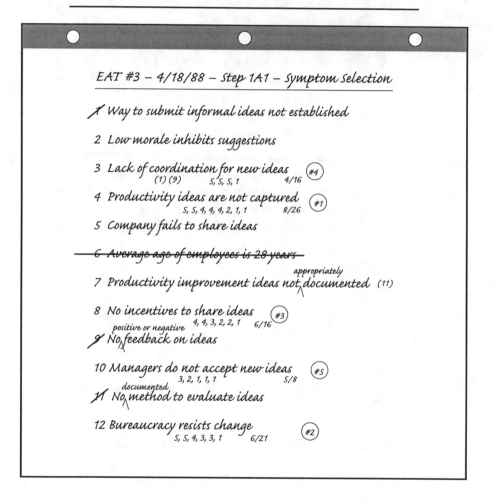

*EAT #3 – 4/18/88 – Step 1A1 – Symptom Selection*

1̶ Way to submit informal ideas not established

2 Low morale inhibits suggestions

3 Lack of coordination for new ideas  (#4)
   (1) (9)   5, 5, 5, 1   4/16

4 Productivity ideas are not captured  (#1)
   5, 5, 4, 4, 4, 2, 1, 1   8/26

5 Company fails to share ideas

6̶ ̶A̶v̶e̶r̶a̶g̶e̶ ̶a̶g̶e̶ ̶o̶f̶ ̶e̶m̶p̶l̶o̶y̶e̶e̶s̶ ̶i̶s̶ ̶2̶8̶ ̶y̶e̶a̶r̶s̶

   *appropriately*
7 Productivity improvement ideas not documented  (11)

8 No incentives to share ideas  (#3)
   *positive or negative*  4, 4, 3, 2, 2, 1  6/16
9̶ No feedback on ideas

10 Managers do not accept new ideas  (#5)
   3, 2, 1, 1, 1   5/8
   *documented*
1̶1̶ No method to evaluate ideas

12 Bureaucracy resists change  (#2)
   5, 5, 4, 3, 3, 1   6/21

4 ... 3 versus 4, 3 versus 5 ... 4 versus 5, 4 versus 6, 5 versus 6. Each specific contest is between one of two distinct alternatives, and the choice of one alternative is taken at the cost of the other. Mechanically, the winning choice is simply circled, in each binary contest, on a specially prepared form.

The second individual task is to add (sum) the number of times each of the finalist candidates (six in the example) wins a discrete contest. This is easily done on the special form by simply counting the number of times each candidate's number is circled. With six alternatives, there are a total of fifteen discrete round-robin contests. With five alternatives, there would be ten contests, and, with seven alternatives, there would be twenty-one contests. Therefore, a parity check of the total number of votes made by each person against the total number of available choices can be easily made.

When all have completed their private voting, the forms are collected, and the total votes for each of the six finalists are tallied (summed) on the special team form. A parity check is also available on this second form. If, for instance, five voters (as assumed in the example) are involved, then the total number of available team votes would be seventy-five: (fifteen votes per person) × (five people).

Each person can also check the logic of his discrete choices. Logical inconsistencies can occur in the process. For instance, a person could choose candidate X over candidate Y and candidate Y over candidate Z but, at the same time, choose candidate Z over candidate X. Such inconsistencies become relatively easy to discover, as the device becomes more familiar with repetition. As a final ranking tool, discrete summation is probably best constructed to illuminate such inconsistent thinking. Regardless, it is simply one more mechanical tool to help individuals calculate and present their principal ideas and conclusions.

No doubt, other techniques are available to conduct convergence voting, and I encourage everyone to seek them, and use them to their best effect. Just be careful to examine the strengths, weaknesses, and limits of each device, and be sure that it is employed for the right reasons with respect to the particular PIC phase/stage/step under investigation. Refer to Julius Eitington's, *The Winning Trainer*, Chapter 11, for effective variations.

### Procedures
- Facilitator distributes discrete summation individual voting forms, one per member, and explains the voting process.
  - Enter statement numbers of finalists to be ranked.

# Figure 6.13
## Discrete Summation: Individual Voting Form

| | Vote Summation Table | | | | | | | | | |
|---|---|---|---|---|---|---|---|---|---|---|
| Discrete Voting Matrix | Finalist Numbers | | | | | | | | | |
| | 3 | 4 | 10 | 12 | 61 | 109 | | | | |

Discrete Voting Matrix rows: 10, 9, 8, 7, 6

| Row | 3 | 4 | 10 | 12 | 61 | 109 |
|---|---|---|---|---|---|---|
| 5 | 3 | 1 | | 1 | | |
| 4 | | 4 | | | | |
| 3 | | | 2 | 1 | | |
| 2 | | | | 2 | | |
| 1 | | | | | 1 | |
| Totals | 3 | 5 | 2 | 4 | 1 | |
| Rank | 3 | 1 | 4 | 2 | 5 | |

Parity Total: 15 / 15

➤ Assume that the six finalist statements used in this example are 3, 4, 10, 12, 61, and 109.

➤ Order the numbers, low to high.

➤ Enter the numbers in the heading squares of the vote summation table section of the individual voting form (see Figure 6.13).

➤ Enter the number 15 in the bottom-right segment of the parity total square (fifteen discrete votes with six candidates).

> Note that the Discrete Voting Matrix section of the form is constructed of ten numbered discrete comparison levels, each level divided into two rows and a number of column squares.

> Each of the six finalist statement numbers can be individually contested five times—that is, once for each of its five competitors.

> Find level 5 in the matrix, and enter the candidate numbers, as shown in Figure 6.13.

◆ Conduct individual discrete voting.

> Begin at level 5.

> Decide your preference for number 3 versus 4.

> Circle the winning number.

> Repeat the process for the remaining four comparisons in level 5.

> Repeat the process in levels 4 through 1.

> If you are totally indifferent about the two alternatives in any discrete contest—that is, your preference for one is exactly equal to your preference for the other—then circle neither of them.

◆ Sum the votes for each candidate finalist.

> Add the number of circles around each number in level 5.

> Enter totals in the appropriate columns of the summation table (see Figure 6.13).

> Repeat the process for the remaining levels.

> Add the entries for each candidate in the appropriate columns of the summation table.

> Enter totals at the bottom of the summation table.

◆ Conduct the parity check.

> Note that the parity number (the maximum number of available votes with six alternatives) is 15.

> Add the total number of votes cast, and enter it in the upper-left segment of the Parity Total square.

> Ensure that the total is less than or equal to the parity number. (Indifference votes reduce the total.)

> If the total votes cast number more than the parity total, review the entries on the form, and correct the error(s).

## Figure 6.14
## Discrete Summation: Participant Voting Form

| Team Member | Finalist Candidates | | | | | | | | | | Parity |
|---|---|---|---|---|---|---|---|---|---|---|---|
| | 2 | 3 | 4 | 7 | 8 | 10 | 12 | 34 | 61 | 109 | |
| 1 | | 3 | 5 | | | 2 | 4 | | 1 | | 15 |
| 2 | | 1 | 4 | | | 3 | 4 | 1 | | | 13 |
| 3 | | 2 | 5 | 1 | 1 | 1 | 3 | | 2 | | 15 |
| 4 | | 3 | 5 | | | 2 | 4 | | | 1 | 15 |
| 5 | 1 | 2 | 4 | | | 1 | 5 | | 1 | | 14 |
| | | | | | | | | | | | |
| | | | | | | | | | | | |
| | | | | | | | | | | | |
| | | | | | | | | | | | |
| | | | | | | | | | | | |
| | | | | | | | | | | | |
| Totals | 1 | 11 | 23 | 1 | 1 | 9 | 20 | 1 | 4 | 1 | 72 / 75 |
| Final Ranking | 6 | 3 | 1 | 6 | 6 | 4 | 2 | 6 | 5 | 6 | |

- The facilitator collects the forms.
- Participants select two members to enter individual voting totals on Discrete Summation: Team Voting Form, as shown in Figure 6.14 (assuming five team members in this example).
  - Enter parity check totals, as required, for individuals and for team.
    - Enter the number 75 in the bottom-right segment of the parity total square (15 votes/person x 15 people).

➤ Ensure that the sum of individual parity totals is less than or equal to 75.

➤ If the total votes cast number more than 75, review all forms, and correct the error(s).

➤ Enter final ranking numbers in the bottom row of the form.
  • The finalist with the highest vote total is ranked 1; that with the lowest total vote is ranked lowest.

### Convergence/Divergence Summary

Many pages have been devoted to explaining detailed D/C mechanics. A newcomer to the PIC might infer that any device requiring so many pages of explanation must be complex, difficult to learn, intricate, and user unfriendly. However, the opposite is true. During my typical teaming orientation workshops, people who have never heard of such processes exercise D/C with sufficient skill to use it the next day in their own organizations. One complaint that I hear from people attending some quality improvement seminars and schools is that instructions for conducting suggested processes are not provided in sufficient detail to actually exercise. Well, D/C, as explained here, is one of those exact tools for bringing management transformation principles to sparkling life. Of course, you can best learn the technique by participating in an orientation workshop. Failing that, you can construct the event with the blueprint provided here. If you start participative decision-making, motivation enhancement, morale boosting, personnel enabling, and communication improvement with nothing more than a D/C experiment, you will come away with a solid feeling of accomplishment and a renewed faith that you can beat back the devils plaguing your corporate halls.

If you try D/C without a trained facilitator, you will stumble. But just remember S/L #29 (Appendix 1) about failure and fear of failure; it is all part of learning. By all means, I recommend that you hire a trained facilitator; it will be one of the best investments that you have ever made. But if that is impossible, distribute some copies of this book, read and discuss D/C (within the context of the previous chapters), and give it a try. Properly executed, the D/C experiment will be so successful, liberating, and uplifting that the motivation for probing deeper into management-transforming practices will be firmly established in enough individuals to rethink a few priorities.

## 2. Stream Analysis

### *Features*

Remember that PIC Stage lA, Symptom Selection, is a three-step process for speculating about a symptom of interest, verifying the speculations, and finally specifying an exact symptom statement. Stage lA, then, is the anchor for any fully extended PIC investigation, because it is the reference point against which causes and resolutions for a symptom are compared and evaluated. It is meaningless to seek causes and resolutions for a symptom until the symptom itself is clearly identified.

Stream analysis is a technique for logically defining symptom statements by separating them from other kinds of expressed statements—for example, cause, resolution, or impact. It is therefore used during PIC steps lAl and 1A3, both before and after symptom verification.

Remember that symptom statements must be expressed in broad descriptive terms suggesting no specific causes or solutions—for example, "I have a stomachache" as opposed to "My ulcer is giving me a stomachache." The most important early decision to be made in any issue-resolving situation is to determine the condition of interest that the symptom statement is to express. For instance, is the ulcer the condition of interest, or is it the stomachache? Or is it perhaps the impact of it all, for example, that I cannot go to work with the pain? Clearly, a logical reference point must be established against which the symptom can be expressed, its causes identified, and potential impacts or results estimated. Like motion, all such standards are relative. For instance, how fast is a jetliner flying? Is its speed to be measured with respect to the velocity of the air streaking across its wings (airspeed), or is it to be fixed with respect to a stake driven into the ground (ground speed)?

How should we measure the length of a room—by inches, meters, centimeters, cubits, miles, parsecs, or feet? And what is a foot? How do we know that any given strip of imprinted wood (ruler) represents a true foot? What if two different rulers are different in length by a factor of one-sixteenth of an inch? Which of the two sticks represents the true foot? Are they both off the mark? What is the standard? The answer is that the standard is conventional; that is, it is not ingrained in an absolute law of nature. Conventional standards are contrived by human beings, defined for convenience, and accepted by consensus. In the case of conventional rulers, they can be calibrated for accuracy by comparing them to a standard rod that is probably encased in a temperature-controlled atmosphere somewhere in the tombs of the Bureau of Standards. That rod, by consensus, represents the standard foot; therefore, the term accuracy is meaningless when applied to rulers until the standard foot is defined. So it is also in stating the speed of an aircraft; it must wait upon the standard of evaluation (airspeed or ground speed).

Think of symptom definition as equivalent to driving a standard reference stake into the ground, against which all related elements can be gauged. It is equivalent to driving that stake into the ground as a reference against which to measure the ground speed of the jetliner.

Stream analysis suggests the flow of cause and effect; for example, the ulcer causes the stomachache (effect), which itself causes absence from work (impact), as illustrated in Figure 6.15(a). If we wish to investigate this stream of events, our first step is to focus on the element that best expresses the condition giving rise to our interest. If we decide that absence from work is our proper focus, then we must express it in terms that do not suggest specific causes—that is, as a symptom. An example symptom might be as follows: "Average weekly absence rate is 22 percent of employee population." This is now our symptom, stated as an effect. Clearly, stomachaches are only one of many potential causes for this effect; reduced productivity is one potential impact of absence.

However, if we decide to focus on the stomachache, then the symptom (effect) might be stated as: "Employees are reporting

## Figure 6.15
## Stream Analysis Cause/Effect Relationships

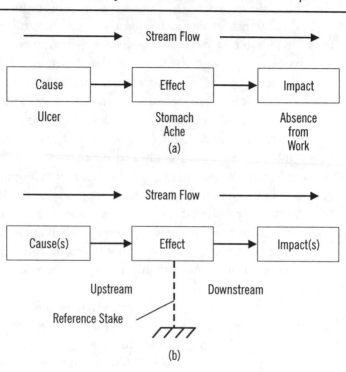

increasing incidences of stomachaches." Absence then becomes an intermediate impact, with productivity losses representing an even further end impact.

Maybe an increasing incidence of ulcers is the focus of interest. The ulcers are then treated as the symptom (effect), with potential causes including stress, drinking, and so on. One intermediate impact could be stomachaches, with further ramifications of absence and lowered productivity.

The point of all this is that the most critical mental threshold to cross in selecting a symptom statement is to establish the location in the flowing stream of cause and effect where the reference stake is to be driven and against which all other elements are to be evaluated. Figure 6.15(b) illustrates this concept. The symptom (effect) is defined as that element in the cause/effect stream determined to be the staked reference point against which all other elements are defined. Clearly, with respect to the direction of cause/effect flow, all causes are upstream of the symptom, and all impacts are downstream of the symptom.

Frankly, I have found the stream-analysis concept to be the most abstract in my current arsenal of techniques. It is the one that newcomers to PIC find the most tricky to use, but it is essential. An issue must be defined before it can be resolved. The key to comfort rests in understanding that the approximate condition (issue) of interest must be clarified before stake driving is considered. All sorts of daily pressures constrain us from taking the time to think through such basic questions. The initial question to ask is: "What is the condition in the working environment that caught our attention in the first place?" This condition (or issue of interest) becomes the effect—that is, the location of the stake. The next step is to state that effect as a symptom. Cause and impact statements are relatively easy to isolate once these basics are determined.

### Procedures

- Obtain a general working consensus regarding the general issue of interest.
  - ◆ Does not have to be exact.
- Identify those statements written on the flipchart sheets that are:
  - ◆ *Symptoms* or statements that:
    - ➤ Directly express the issue of interest (effect).
    - ➤ Do not imply a direct, tangible solution.
    - ➤ Do not imply a cause.
  - ◆ *Causes* or statements that:
    - ➤ Create or account for the symptom.
    - ➤ Imply resolutions.
    - ➤ Are located upstream of the symptom.
  - ◆ *Impacts* or statements that:
    - ➤ Result from (or are caused by) the symptom.
    - ➤ Imply consequences of the symptom.
    - ➤ Are located downstream of the symptom.
  - ◆ *Resolutions* or statements that:
    - ➤ Suggest recommendations for action.

## Figure 6.16
### Typical Flipchart Sheet: Stream Analysis Notations

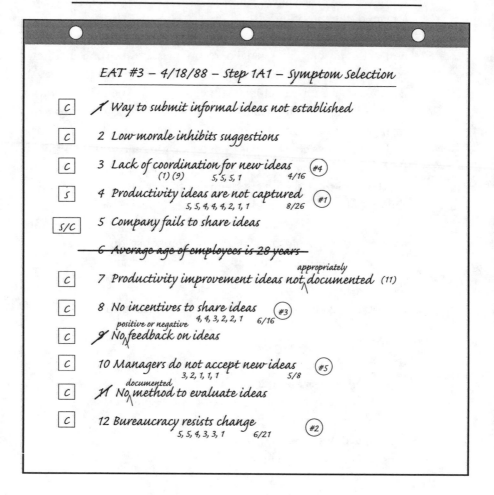

> Imply some improvement in the symptom.
◆ *Facts* or statements that:
> Verify symptoms, causes, impacts, and resolutions.
> Are stated in precise numbers, for example:
• "The average loaded labor rate is $24.59/hour."
• "Eighty percent of respondents declared that they do not share their ideas with other people."

- Label statements near the left margin, as follows (see Figure 6.16):
  - ◆ Symptoms: S
  - ◆ Causes: C
  - ◆ Impacts: I
  - ◆ Resolutions: R
  - ◆ Facts: F
- If a statement appears to fit into more than one category, label it accordingly (see statement 5, Figure 6.16).
  - ◆ Statement 4 in Figure 6.16 is the only entry unambiguously labeled S.
- Actual case history is as follows (see Figure 6.16).
  - ◆ Team convened to consider general condition of interest: "Employees often develop better ways to do their own jobs, but no one else ever seems to hear about them."
  - ◆ There was a total of thirty-two statements generated during Step lAl, twelve of which appear in Figure 6.16.
    - ➤ Stream analysis identified three statements as symptoms, labeled S.
    - ➤ Four statements were identified as facts, labeled F.
    - ➤ The remainder were identified as causes, labeled C.
  - ◆ Final converged Step lAl statement became: "Company fails to capture individuals' productivity improvement ideas."
  - ◆ Verification (Step 1A2) and further refinement (Step 1A3) confirmed statement with no changes.

### 3. Cause/Effect Diagramming (Fishbone/Ishikawa)

#### 3.1 Factors Types

*Features*

Dr. Kauro Ishikawa, in *Guide to Quality Control* (1976), developed the "fishbone" diagram to logically identify, sort, and categorize all the potential causes for a specified effect (symptom). He defines high quality as "nondispersion of quality characteristics" (1976, Table 2.1). He wondered why, at the output of a manufacturing process, individual items of the same product differed in some quality characteristic. For example, why do the diameters (quality characteristic) of ball bearings differ (dispersion) as they come off the assembly line? Or why does the roundness (quality characteristic) differ (dispersion) between individual bearings? He wanted to isolate all the potential factors (causes) that might account for such dispersions. Factors might include temperature variations and pressure changes in machines or actions taken by employees. They might also include features of raw materials or elements of the total manufacturing process, itself.

Ishikawa was interested in ensuring clarity of thinking and focused concentration during the causation discovery process. He was also interested in simplicity of display and ease of comprehension. As Figure 6.17(a) illustrates, the familiar outline of a fish, including the internal skeletal structure, enjoys all these virtues. It also conveys a sense of flow and direction. One's eye naturally moves left to right across the page, tail to head, toward some implied end or destination. These virtues are retained in the abstracted illustration of the fishbone (see Figure 6.17(b)). The tendency to look to the right culminates in the head block.

- The chosen symptom (effect) is written in the block. Each rib bone becomes the main trunk of a general category of potential causes. Ishikawa refers to a symptom as a quality characteristic and to causes as factors. Therefore, using the ball-bearing example, the symptom might be stated as follows: "Ball bearing diameters vary from the specified length by +/– 15 percent" (see Figure 6.18). Teaming participants are free to determine the appropriate causation categories for any given diagram. An example is shown in Figure 6.18, where four categories (ribs) are defined: Press Machine, Environment, Process, and Employees—one rib per category.

Divergence is used to generate as many statements of causation as possible. It is vital that team members focus on the symptom at all times. The fishbone format facilitates this, since the eye is easily drawn to the symptom statement written in the head box. During a typical divergent brainstorming session, one person suggested that Temperature Variations (in Figure 6.18) be entered under the Press Machine category. This started people thinking, and, sometime later in the exercise, someone suggested that one cause for

## Figure 6.17
### Derivation of Ishikawa "Fishbone"
### Cause and Effect Diagram

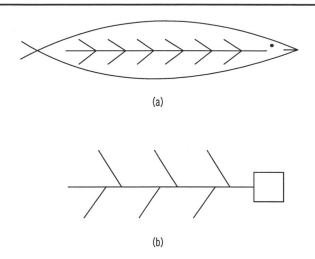

(a)

(b)

the temperature variations could be Poor Temperature Monitoring, leading to the subsequent suggestion that an underlying cause could be Insufficient Metering.

The number of fishbone entries is limited only by participants' knowledge, expertise, imagination, and patience. Of course, the sheet can get very crowded very quickly. I always tape a two-by-two collection of four flipchart sheets together when constructing a factors Ishikawa diagram, Attention to spacing and clarity of printing also helps. Additional sheets can always be added. Another way to approach the crowding is to tie all entries directly to the main rib of each category. The gain in neatness and crowding is offset, however, by a loss of the logical linkages between general causes and their root subcauses. These linkages can subsequently be defined by using the why-because pursuit technique, described later in this chapter.

One of the most pervasive myths surviving to this day is that this technique is useful only for manufacturing issues. Perhaps it is related to Ishikawa's original manufacturing focus of interest.

## Figure 6.18
## Sample "Factors" Type Fishbone Diagram

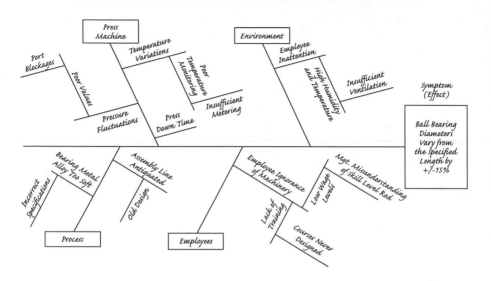

Forget it! Purge this imagined limitation from your mind! If the exercise is to link causes to effects, then this technique works— regardless of issue.

One interesting twist on the factors-type diagram is the 4Ms' categorized version. It can become very bothersome to try to identify major factor categories up-front or to keep adding them during the divergence process. The way around this is to define four categories that cover all factors common to all production processes, manufacturing, and service. These universal factors of production are defined in basic management and economics courses and should be familiar to students: land, labor, capital, and management/ entrepreneurship.

The 4Ms' equivalents are material, manpower, machinery, and methods; all causes pertaining to the symptom will fit within one or more of these four categories. A 4Ms factors-type fishbone diagram therefore requires only four ribs, thereby simplifying and universalizing the format. Individual causes are entered into a category according to the suggesting person's best guess. They are

**Table 6.3**
Definitions of Cause/Effect Diagram
4Ms' Categories

| Category | Source or Cause |
|---|---|
| Manpower | *Individual* behavior and attitudes |
| Methods | The *way* things are done—for example, rules, procedures, resource allocations, specifications, standards, instructions, organization, management |
| Machinery | What people *work with*—for example, facilities, resources |
| Material | What people *work on*—for example, raw materials and information received to be further processed, inputs |

rearranged by category only at the end of D/C (as described earlier), when all entries have been thoroughly thought out and ranked in importance. Table 6.3 defines the 4Ms in terms of the sources of causes that contribute to a specified symptom (effect).

During the initial divergence exercise, it is most important to get potential causal statements onto the sheets. Therefore, the suggestor's initial guess is good enough, and the scribe should enter the statement wherever the member chooses. Remember that divergent exercises such as brainstorming and NGT are not to be interrupted for any reason, including categorizing. To get used to the 4Ms' terminology, consider under which category some of the ball-bearing statements in Figure 6.18 might best be entered.

For instance, any entry that can be traced to inherent faults in the capital equipment, such as the press machine, would be entered under machinery, that is, capital equipment. Possible candidates are "press downtime" and "poor valves." Causes traceable to inherent flaws in the raw materials would be entered under materials—for example, "bearing metal alloy too soft." Entries such as "low wage levels," "lack of training," and "courses never designed" are rooted in management decisions, and would be properly entered under methods. A possible manpower candidate is "employee inattention."

Sometimes the true category is not so obvious at first. For instance, "press downtime" could ultimately be traced more to poor maintenance and inspection than to an inherent flaw in the press machine itself. Or it might be traced to both factors, thereby justifying its entry under machinery, methods, and manpower, suggesting inherent machine failure, poor maintenance decisions, and worker apathy and inattention. Such meanings become more obvious as the divergence/convergence process develops.

The object, of course, is to diverge as many as possible causes, and then converge down to the one or few causes deemed most critical. The chances are very good that the highest-ranked causes will be verified during the next PIC Step (1B2). Once the few finalists are chosen, participants can develop a consensus about categorizing each of them. If all the finalists concentrate in one of the 4M categories, that says a lot about the character of possible resolutions. If, for instance, they all collect under methods, then resolutions will be aimed at management, policies and procedures, decision-making, and organizational matters. A totally different perspective would develop if the causes collect under machinery; this would suggest taking a very careful look at inherent flaws in facilities and capital equipment. If the critical causes spread throughout the 4Ms, then potential resolutions would have to cover a much broader range of actions.

The finalist causes derived in our investigation of the capturing and sharing of productivity ideas provide an illustration of how they can congregate in one or two 4M categories. Over eighty statements were generated on the fishbone diagram during divergence; they were reduced to the few critical causes shown in Figure 6.19. Note that the critical causes are almost evenly divided between Methods (organization) and Manpower (individual attitudes/behavior). Two entries [numbers (17) and (78)] are included in both categories, indicating a belief that both organization and attitudes are at the heart of these causes.

## Figure 6.19
### Convergent Fishbone Diagram

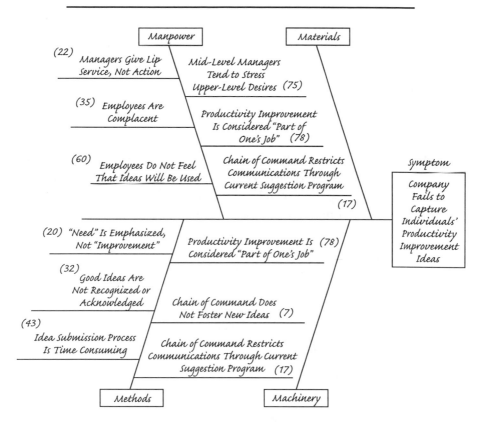

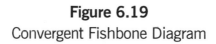

Some of these critical causes are stated in such broad terms that they do not suggest tangible and precise resolutions. The why-because pursuit, described later in this chapter, is a technique used to probe the root causes of broadly stated surface causes. The ultimate object is to isolate precisely stated critical root causes of the symptom. Once they are verified and ranked according to degree of contribution to the symptom, participants are well on their way to forming resolution ideas in their minds.

### Procedures
■ Tape four flipchart sheets together in a two-by-two pattern, and hang them horizontally on the wall.

- Draw the fishbone design on the sheet.
  - ◆ Write the symptom statement in the head box.
  - ◆ Write *Symptom* above the box.
- Conduct divergence exercise.
  - ◆ Ask members to state two things when offering an entry.
    - ➤ The 4M category into which the statement is to be included.
    - ➤ The statement itself.
- Conduct convergence exercise.
  - ◆ During CDAM, do not be concerned with the fact that combining statements will sometimes require moving them across categories. Go ahead and move them; their initial placement is merely suggestive.
  - ◆ After finalists have been voted upon, sketch a small version of the fishbone diagram in the corner of the large sheet, and enter just the numbers of the finalists into the categories that team members select (by consensus).
  - ◆ Take a few moments to consider the distribution pattern and its implications for potential resolutions—for example, the implications if all the finalists are concentrated in one or two categories, or if they are spread evenly throughout all of them.

### 3.2 Process Type

*Features*

Another type of Ishikawa cause/effect diagram is the process type. It is very useful when investigating the potential causes of a symptom occurring in an operation when the individual sequential steps in the process are clearly defined. Imagine, for instance, the step-by-step procedures for publishing a technical bulletin. Figure 6.20 illustrates an example of a very broadly defined publishing process. Assume that the symptom being investigated is: "The average actual processing time, from step 1 through step 7, is 2.5 times longer than the allocated time." What are the potential causes? The diagram allows members to focus on potential causes occurring in each of the specific steps. Figure 6.21 is a simplified reproduction of Figure 6.20. The lines extending from each process-step box are equivalent to

## Figure 6.20
## Example Publication Process Diagram

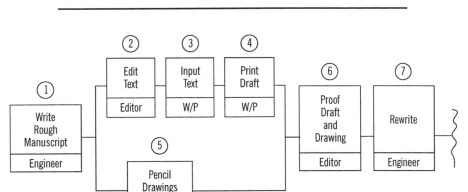

the rib lines of the 4Ms' fishbone diagram. Again, I recommend that the full-process diagram be drawn on four (or more) taped flipchart sheets, including full labeling of each step. During divergence, members state the box number and the cause; the scribe writes the cause statement on the appropriate rib, as illustrated in Figure 6.21.

The standard convergence technique is conducted (numbering through voting), and the critical causes are isolated similarly to the factors-type operation. Process-type fishbone diagrams can be as general or as detailed as people desire. I have facilitated investigations that stretch a process across the entire length of a thirty-foot wall. Standard flowcharting symbols, including decision (yes/no) diamonds, can be used to break down a process to its minutest details. Every flow diagram box is labeled with a number, an action identification, and responsible job categories. One of the most surprising discoveries that participants make, as they develop detailed process-flow diagrams, is the complexity and richness of the steps that have to be completed in order to accomplish what was thought to be a rather simple operation. The number of required feedback loops is also surprising. My experience shows that this particular technique is enlightening and very fruitful; it takes time and patience but results in very clear and tangible causes.

## Figure 6.21
### Example Process Fishbone Diagram

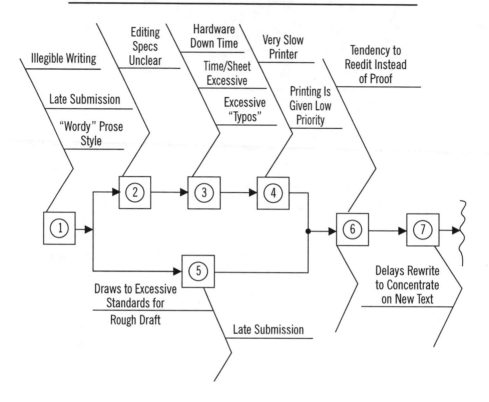

*Procedures*

■ Tape a number of flipchart sheets together, and hang them horizontally on the wall.

■ Conduct members through flowchart development to level of desired complexity.

■ Redraw final chart, distributing boxes at distances most conducive to extending fishbone ribs.

  ◆ If possible, format diagram to stagger adjacent ribs above and below the line of flow.

■ Conduct members through a typical divergence/convergence exercise.

## 4. Why-Because Pursuit

### *Features*

Why-because pursuits are extensions of the Ishikawa concept. I personally find it most useful as a device for extracting the deep root causes of individual fishbone finalists. The technique could be used directly against the symptom statement, and I do not doubt that some people use it just that way. But I suggest otherwise. The reason is that the Ishikawa technique is entirely open and freewheeling in its rules for divergence. Any entry is acceptable for inclusion in any category. The object is to generate as many causal possibilities as imagination and knowledge allow.

Why-because is more restrictive; the term pursuit is an apt descriptor of the technique. Designed in the form of a logic tree, the technique requires that entries bear a logical linkage to one or more previous entries. The object is to pursue the logical origin of a more broadly stated cause down to its fundamental roots. This is why I prefer to use the fishbone technique first. It allows totally open consideration of possible symptom causes, whereas why-because plunges one's mind into the depths of a single cause's genesis.

Figure 6.22 illustrates why-because pursuit logic. The initial causal statement is written in the box. During a divergent brainstorming exercise, the first suggestor states the cause, and then asks, "Why?" She then answers, "Because ... ," followed by the actual answer. The scribe writes the answer on the first available branch—for example, branch A. The scribe does not write "Because ... " for each statement; it is implied for every statement. However, I do recommend that the prefix statements, "Why?" and "Because," be audibly uttered, at least until people become very familiar with the pace and flow of the logical requirements for linking each statement to its predecessor.

The logic flows in the following manner (see Figure 6.22).

- D causes the original boxed statement.
- E, F, and H cause D.
- K and L cause E.

The most logical way to read the cause/effect relationship, however, is to stay on one horizontal path at a time, as follows:

## Figure 6.22
### Why-Because Pursuit Logic and Format

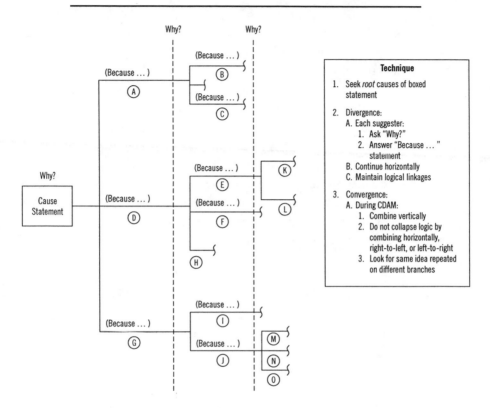

- K causes E.
- E causes D.
- D causes original cause.

To give this pattern more substance, consider the ball-bearing fishbone diagram illustrated in Figure 6.18. Note the cause listed under the Employees category: Employee Ignorance of Machinery. There are two root branches attached. Note how, in Figure 6.23, these root causes can be extended farther and farther, down into their deepest origins. Follow one line of reasoning:

- Employee Ignorance of Machinery. Why?
    - ◆ Because—of Lack of Training. Why?

- ◆ Because—it was Never Considered Necessary. Why?
- ◆ Because—we Never Did It Before. Why?
- ◆ Because—Managers Did Not Want Training. Why?
- ◆ Because—it is Time Consuming. Why?
- ◆ Because …

Numbers are not added to the diagram until divergence is completed. Remember that item numbering is the first step in convergence. A few more main branches of reasoning can be added to the diagram. However, I caution everyone to beware of too many main branches. The object is to think horizontally—that is, to get at the roots of the few main streams of causation. If more than four or five main lines of reasoning develop (vertically), then there is reason to suspect that members are freethinking the same universe of causes stated on the fishbone diagram; that is, they might be merely recreating the fishbone in a different format. Some of the statements will certainly appear on both diagrams, but the rationale for including them in the why-because pursuit should be logical linkage. This process of linking statements logically is sometimes called entailment.

The why-because pursuits are often cited as the favorite technique by PIC newcomers. The reason is that it leads to conclusions that are totally nonobvious at the start and yet are so logically valid. It is not at all uncommon for one to two hundred statements to be entered during divergence.

The rules of convergence are few, but vital:

- ■ Number top-to-bottom, left-to-right (see Figure 6.23).
- ■ During CDAM, combine vertically, not horizontally. Some people fall into the trap of collapsing horizontal lines of reasoning—for example, combining 16 under 11, then 16/11 under 6, then 16/11/6 under 2. This not only defeats the purpose of the technique, but it violates the rule of combining, which says: "Do not combine statements because one is the cause of the other." Statements should be combined only if they so closely restate each other that to vote for one would be tantamount to voting for the other. It simplifies voting by removing the need for redundant votes. Try to combine similar

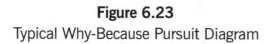

## Figure 6.23
### Typical Why-Because Pursuit Diagram

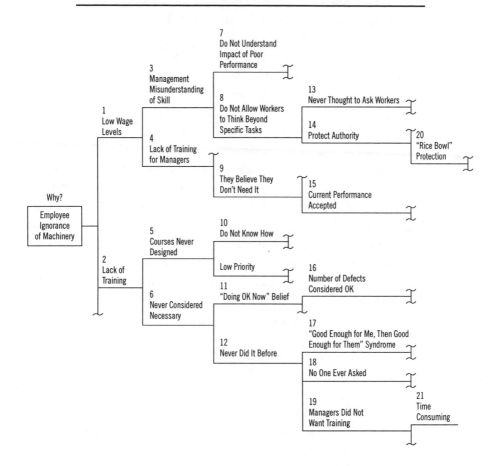

statements that appear in different branches; one possible combination in Figure 6.23 would be 16 under 15, or 15 under 16.

■ When combining two entries, all attached statements do not move with the subordinate statement. For instance, if item 12 is combined under another statement, items 17 to 21 do not move with it. Why-because, like its partner techniques, is merely a device to stimulate creative thinking and consensus. Once a causal statement is written in any logical path, it stands alone on its own merit and can be isolated or moved, as its criticality requires. The statements attached to it are helpful in generating more entries and become very useful as analytical tools for reasoning through solutions in PIC steps 2A1 to 2A3. Statement independence is a keystone of this technique.

Participants decide exactly how many why-because pursuits to conduct for any given assignment. I recommend that the universe be restricted to the number of fishbone diagram finalists, and there is no reason to assume that all the finalists must be put through the why-because pursuit. The critical determinant is the shared sense of having isolated the fundamental root causes of the symptom. If that can be done with several fishbone finalists and one or two why-because pursuits (one each for one of the fishbone finalists), then that is sufficient. My experience indicates that conducting two why-because pursuits sharpen everyone's insights so clearly, regarding the root causes of the symptoms, that people seldom see a need to go further. But I have always seen the need for at least one why-because pursuit.

### Procedures

- Tape sheets (two-by-two sheets minimum) and hang horizontally on wall.
- Draw box at left center and write in the fishbone finalist being analyzed.
- Write *Why?* above the box.
- Extend a short horizontal line to the right from the box, and then extend a vertical line, as shown in Figure 6.23.
- Conduct divergence using structured brainstorming.
  - ◆ Ask each member to state two things during a turn.
    - ➤ On which branch the statement is to be attached.
    - ➤ The statement itself.
    - ➤ A typical entry (see Figure 6.23) would be stated: "Off of 'Lack of Training for Managers,' Why? Because ... 'they believe they don't need it.'"
  - ◆ Add sheets as required.

- ◆ To best anticipate crowding, add first main branch at top, second at bottom, third in middle, and so on.
- ■ Conduct convergence as usual to isolate critical root-cause finalists.

## 5. Process Internalization

### *Features*

This technique is original, at least as presently constructed. Over the years, I have noted a recurring theme centering on the notion that the way things are supposed to be done and the way that they are done are often quite different. This insight is certainly no great shock; everyone seems to understand it, and almost everyone has experienced it. However, I began to ask what the signs might be when supposed and actual do approach each other and start to coincide; I turned again to the concept of process.

Assuming that, at the technology level of analysis, a process is any set of sequentially arranged actions for arriving at a desired end, I asked myself why one process becomes actualized while others are abandoned. The answer, when it came (intuitively), was almost too obvious to be useful; i.e., a process becomes actual (the way things really are done) when it becomes internalized within an organization. A process is internalized within an organization if and only if it is ingrained in the culture of the people doing the work (see Chapter 2). I reiterate my concentration on the individual as the origin and source of everything that happens in any organization.

### *Formal and Informal Processes*

We usually learn the strict and unforgiving rules of group norms and peer pressure in early school grades; those who are most dense usually suffer hard lessons as preteens and teenagers. We learn that, regardless of the rules, certain things are done, and other things are not done. One early personal and enlightening experience with this truth in a professional setting occurred at the beginning of my last assignment in the United States (U.S.) Air Force. I had spent almost three years at Keesler Air Force Base, Mississippi, teaching electronics and radar systems to future maintenance technicians and officers. Everything was taught by the book—for example: how to use a technical manual, how to troubleshoot a circuit, how to read a schematic, how to fill out maintenance reports, how to conduct preventive maintenance, and how to conduct test procedures. It was all formalized and neatly packaged, and I had spent three years of hard study learning and teaching the entire package. Hence, I enjoyed a twenty-three hundred-mile, first-class train ride to Yaak Air Force Station, Montana, confident and secure in my knowledge of it all, and certain of my value to the lucky people about to receive my technical knowledge and services.

It is amazing how quickly we learn when survival is at stake. The Riviera-like strip of Gulf Coast, from Mobile, Alabama, to New Orleans, Louisiana, in the U.S., bears little resemblance to a tiny military radar station perched atop a five thousand-foot mountain peak rising a minimum of sixty miles from even the most remote village, buried in ten-foot drifts of snow and embraced by chilling –60-degree breezes. Mountain lion, bear, and other assorted wildlife were also a bit of a change. Sum it all up with the words remote and isolated. My attitudes changed as quickly as the geography, technically as well as behaviorally, in this setting. For instance, there was never a dispute between maintaining and troubleshooting the equipment by the book or by some informal but universally understood process. There simply was no book. During the ten months of my tour, I do not remember ever touching a technical manual, let alone referencing one to use a procedure. Troubleshooting was some arcane ritual practiced by long-timers— that is, fifteen- to twenty-year NCOs, whose mysterious ways could have as easily been learned at the feet of a Far Eastern guru as in the gleaming classrooms of Keesler's Allee Hall. Ten years with the equipment taught them odd ways, and each sergeant's ways left when he did, only to be replaced by the equally shrouded expertise of his remaining disciples. I never did get the hang of it, but I was great at handing them tools.

I learned quickly about the difference between informal and formal processes, although I had not yet formed the concept in my mind. Informal processes are the stuff of culture; formal processes are the children of organizational policies and procedures. Organizations are bloodless; culture is imbedded in human marrow and sinew. In conflicts between the two, there is no contest. Marrow and sinew overwhelm roles and rules. One of the great advantages of both quality and project management over traditional management is their recognition of this crucial truth.

My thoughts on the application of this concept to management transformation began to crystallize years ago, as I heard this recurring theme in informal teaming discussions. It occurred most often during causation analysis. Statements such as, "It'll never happen," "Yes, we have procedures, but they never seem to work," "The procedures are not clear," "I never saw the procedures, but everybody says they exist," and so on became commonplace. This is when the dichotomy between informal process internalization and formal process internalization jelled in my mind, and I realized the potential power these concepts had for clarifying causation and therefore solution analyses. Process internalization statements typically arise during PIC causation and solution stages, as opposed to statements generated during symptom-finding steps.

Figure 6.24 identifies both formal and informal process internalization. A short period of consideration will show that 1) a process can be informally internalized without being formally internalized, 2) it can be both formally and informally internalized, but 3) it cannot be formally internalized without first being informally internalized. Very simply, if it meets all four formal internalization criteria, then it must (by definition) satisfy the informal internalization criterion.

Can a process be neither formally nor informally internalized? Frankly, I think not. Somehow, whatever an actualized process is, it gets performed. It might not get done properly, its results might always be unsatisfactory, and no one in the office might be capable of expressing how it is attempted. But unless there is absolutely zero action taken with respect to the process, it is by definition attempted, and the way it is attempted is the tangible indicator of the informal internalization.

# Figure 6.24
## Process Internalization

---

### Informal
A process is informally internalized within an organization if it is ingrained into the daily working habits of the people doing the work.

### Formal
The process is *formally* internalized if it is:

- **Documented**: Recorded on one or more tangible media (for example, print, film, tape, online).
- **Accessible**: Media within reasonably easy reach of intended users in the daily conduct of their work.
- **Communicated**: Critical process knowledge is transferred from the media into intended users' minds, such that they understand it as intended.
- **Used**: Process is employed by intended users with intended results.

### *5.1 Informal Process Internalization*

The definition of informal process internalization in Figure 6.24 should be self-explanatory, especially in light of the discussion in the last few pages. Habits need no justification. In fact, the surest way to scare the wits out of people is to challenge comfortable niches—even those that often irritate us (see Chapter 3). If you want to test this proposition, announce to people that you have decided to physically rearrange the office in the near future, and that you are currently deciding who will be placed where and with what facilities. Be prepared for every known sign of human stress; you will probably discover some new strains of which no one has ever dreamed. Remember that habits are hard to change, but not because new habits are hard to learn; it is rather because old habits are hard to unlearn. This is why some management transformation gurus say that it takes years for traditional organizations to rise when impregnated with quality yeast. The bulk of the time is spent unlearning.

I often hear that quality management principles are common-sense and obvious. Why then are they so scarce and so difficult to acquire? The answer is that we hold to our habits like hapless souls who cling tenaciously to a twentieth-floor balcony railing as the last protection from falling into a fearful 250-foot abyss. Lectures on how we might have avoided falling off the balcony in the first place are not really high on our list of priorities as our fingers slowly slip around the cold metal.

Habits, then, are the mortar binding informal processes together.

### 5.2 Formal Process Internalization

When informal processes are cited as causes of problem symptoms, the reasons always seem to center around four criteria that repeatedly emerged as I thought and rethought about the phenomenon. After several iterations, these four criteria are currently worded as shown in Figure 6.24. When team members focus on processes and procedures as the culprits underlying a symptom, I suggest that they try to isolate which of the four criteria best describes the character of the cause. The technique is easy to apply; the trick is to focus on the four criteria in order—that is, documented first and used last.

A process is formally documented if it is tangibly recorded, as stated in Figure 6.24. The issue is not so much the correctness of the documentation as its existence. Clues to its correctness and completeness are gleaned from answers to questions about the next three criteria.

Accessible documents are easily obtained. How many times have you heard, "I'm not sure who has it," "Yeah, it's somewhere," "We can send for it—maybe get it in eight weeks," "It's on disk, but we can't get one," or some such other disclaimer?

Communicated has a very special meaning in this technique; it gets to the heart of understanding. Documented processes are meaningless if they are either not understood or are insufficiently understood—as intended by the creators of the document. Information is communicated, in this context, therefore, if (and only if) it is fully transferred from accessible documents into the minds of intended users.

Sometimes people do not use what is properly communicated to them. A documented, accessible, and communicated process is used if (and only if) it is employed as intended by appropriate people.

A process is formally internalized if (and only if) it fully conforms to all four criteria. If it does not so conform, then the root cause can be accurately isolated by identifying which of the four criteria is first violated. Therefore, I recommend that this process is best introduced during the clarifying portion of cause/effect (fishbone) convergence. All the ideas have been entered on the fishbone diagram, and members are in the correct frame of mind to reconsider what they really meant when suggesting each idea during divergence. Their minds are focused in exactly the right direction to learn and use this concept.

### Procedures
- Read and discuss the meaning of the terms, *process* and *informal internalization*.
- Read and discuss the four criteria for formal internalization, in the following order.
  1. Documented.
  2. Accessible.
  3. Communicated.
  4. Used.
- Facilitator uses examples of fishbone entries to explain possible meanings, for example: "No standardized process for moving outgoing correspondence through the department."
  - First ask a question (answer yes or no): "Is a standardized process documented?"
  - If the answer is yes, then ask a second question (answer yes or no): "Is the documented standardized process accessible?"
  - If the answer is yes, then ask a third question (answer yes or no): "Is the documented and accessible standardized process communicated?"
  - If the answer is yes, then ask a fourth question (answer yes or no): "Is the documented, accessible, and communicated standardized process used?"

◆ If the answer is yes, then there is a standardized process, and the causal statement can be doubted.

◆ If the answer to any one of the questions, asked in the appropriate order, is no, then the causal statement is rein-forced (assuming later verification), with its root being identified as residing in that criterion for which the answer *no* was stated.

Further refinements of root causes can be accomplished by joining this technique to the causal statements diverged during the why-because pursuit and to solution statements diverged during the resolution stage.

## 6. Data/Information Accumulation

PIC Steps 1A2, 1B2, 1B3, 2B1, and 2B2 involve verification—that is, the accumulation and/or analysis of data for the purpose of testing the validity of speculations. Divergence/convergence steps are speculative, and their outcomes must be verified empirically. However, this book is not about specific techniques for conducting empirical research, developing questionnaires, sampling populations, and performing sta-tistical analysis. Joseph Juran's books discuss some of these topics, and pertinent general literature is easily found in any academic library.

There are, however, a few related ideas about empirical analysis worth discussing at this point. They include hints about how to ini-tiate the search for data, how to display it, how to use it to priori-tize and rank conclusions, and how to recognize the difference between information and data.

### 6.1 Information and Data

Information is substantive knowledge conveying meaningful insights about some topic of interest. Data (datum is the singular term) are specific isolated bits of empirically observed phenomena (sometimes numerical) that verify the truth, falsity, or degree of truth and falsity of information. For instance, suppose that a super-visor is told by a number of employees that the single computer ter-minal in the office is always busy, and that they never seem to be able to use it when required. The information to be obtained is something like, "Is the computer terminal sufficiently available to employees?" Examples of pertinent data include:

- number of employees
- number of employees who legitimately use the terminal
- number of terminals
- density of use during each hour of a typical workday
- specific hours of use by each employee over a period of one month
- specific hours of use by task over a period of one month.

Examples of nonpertinent data might include:

- height of Mt. Everest
- color of employees' hair
- local news broadcast time
- number of yearly personnel evaluations completed.

Suppose that an employee investigating the terminal availability issue walks into the supervisor's office one morning with the following statement: "Boss, I've got an answer." "Good," comes the hopeful reply, "let's hear it." Flashing a wide proud grin, the worker chirps "Two!" After a substantial pause, the supervisor, eyebrows pinched, leans forward and slowly asks, "Two—two what?"

"Just two," comes the reply.

Needless to say, we are leaving our hapless boss with a substantial communication problem, as well as a probable headache. Obviously, the number two is meaningless unless we can associate it with some pertinent aspect of the topic. For instance, what if the employee comes into the office with the following statement: "Boss, I've discovered that we actually have two computer terminals instead of one." Now that is pertinent datum, but it is not information in this case. The substantive information concerns the degree of availability of the computer terminal—now possibly two terminals—to employees. The specific fact that there are two, instead of one, terminals (terminal) available is one element of the total data set that will convey the desired information.

Teaming participants must realize that the act of verifying symptom and causation speculations involves this ability to determine what constitutes pertinent data, how to present it once obtained, and how to collect and analyze it.

The process works something like this:

- Precisely state the desired information—for example, "Are computer terminals sufficiently available?"
- List pertinent data that will convey that information. I prefer to write factual statements as if the data are already known. For instance, instead of asking, "How many people are employed in the office?", I would write the statement "There are ... people employed in this office." Another example would be: The average minutes of terminal usage, by hour, are:

HOURS AVERAGE MINUTES
0800–0900 _____
0900–1000 _____
and so on until closing time.

All that one has to do is collect the data, and fill in the blanks. The best way to display data is in any format that will lead most quickly and most obviously to the desired information. For instance, the final presentation of hourly use might best be a bar graph or trend line. It also might include users' names to enrich insights and convey more information.

The trick is to present the facts most succinctly and comprehensively to allow the audience (the supervisor) to visualize the information by viewing the data, and keep it simple. Do not decorate charts and graphs with gargoyles and fancy trim, like some late nineteenth-century government building. Decoration hides meaning; free it!

### 6.2 Pareto Presentation

Most of us are familiar with histograms, pie charts, bar graphs, line graphs, scatter plots, tables, and equations. They are generally accepted formats for displaying information. The one data-display format that might be less widely known is Pareto diagramming.

Vilfredo Pareto was a nineteenth-century economist who developed a number of principles that retain wide popularity. Quality and project management specialists have locked onto one such idea that was expanded by Juran just after World War II; the concept is generally known as the 80/20 Principle. Pareto, looking at mid-nineteenth-century Italy, found that 80 percent of the nation's wealth was in the hands of 20 percent of the population. Unequal income distribution is certainly no surprise to most of us, but we encounter the same general ratio operating in other instances. Have you managers, for example, ever noticed that about 80 percent of your personnel problems are caused by 20 percent (or fewer) of your personnel? And how many of us have joined some organization only to find that very few of the members perform the bulk of the work?

Juran discovered that the 80/20 principle also applies to symptom-causation relationships. Essentially, he suggested that 20 percent of all the causes contributing to a given symptom account for about 80 percent of the total causation. We have already discovered that fishbone and why-because techniques uncover large numbers of potential causes for a symptom; through convergence, we reduce these potential causes to a dozen or fewer. But even these dozen do not contribute equally to the symptom. The purpose of PIC causation/verification (Step 1B2) is to empirically determine the relative degree of contribution of each speculated final cause to the symptom. The Pareto principle suggests—and my experience tends to agree—that even out of the few finalists, anywhere from two to four of them contribute the bulk of causation. Therefore, these very few causes are the ones to resolve, because they effectively address the symptom. Such relationships are very amenable to pie chart and Pareto diagramming. Such presentations do not analyze data; they display analysis results.

Figure 6.25 illustrates a basic Pareto display in the form of a skewed histogram and a table. Assume that it illustrates the degree of contribution of the verified causes for the ball-bearing diameter dispersion shown in the fishbone diagram (Figure 6.18) and why-because pursuit (Figure 6.23). Assume also that the proportions of causal contribution are as follows:

- Critical Causes:

| | |
|---|---|
| Press Downtime | 30% |
| Temperature Variations | 20% |
| Low Priority for Employee Training | 15% |
| Belief That Current Performance Is Acceptable | 15% |
| Trivial Causes (all others) | 20% |

The histogram bars in Figure 6.25 are arranged left to right, in descending order of percent of contribution to the symptom. Therefore, Press Downtime, verified as contributing 30 percent of total causation, is the first column on the left. The last column represents the combined causal contribution of all the many trivial causes, too many to individually enumerate and display. The cumulative trend line plots the sum of the causal impacts represented by the columns under its slope. For instance, Press Downtime and Temperature Variations account for a combined total of 50 percent of the symptom causes. The slope of the cumulative trend line, therefore, plots an end point of 50 percent at the indicated coordinate. The Pareto histogram clearly illustrates that the four cited causes together account for 80 percent of the dispersion in the ball-bearing quality characteristic at the end of the production process. The many other causes account for only 20 percent of the dispersion. The tabular format, also illustrated in Figure 6.25, is quite succinct, but I have found it to be less popular as a display format in presentations. The choice is a matter of personal preference.

One very helpful variation on the histogram format becomes possible to use after further research uncovers the potential cost of resolving each of the symptom causes. For instance, one might assume that the best approach to resolving the ball-bearing symptom would be to eliminate or drastically reduce Press Downtime. This would effectively eliminate 30 percent of the symptom. The next cause to attack would then logically be Temperature Variation, thereby eliminating 20 percent of the symptom. But what about cost? Assume, for instance, that eliminating Press Downtime would be very expensive, but that eliminating Temperature Variation would be relatively very cheap. This could be (and should be) a critical consideration in determining how to resolve the issue.

Figure 6.26 respresents a revised version of the Pareto histogram. Column widths represent the estimated relative dollar costs of solving the ball-bearing dispersion by attacking each of the cited causes. Quite a different message is conveyed by this second histogram. The cost/benefit ratios suggest that attacking Temperature

## Figure 6.25
### Typical Pareto Histogram and Table

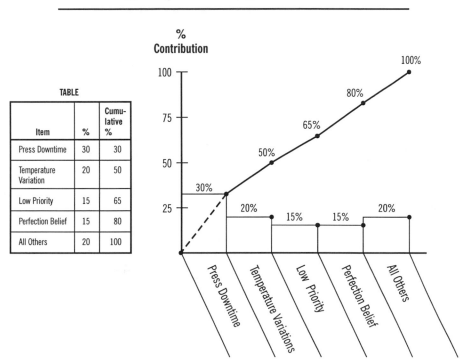

| | | Cumu-lative |
|---|---|---|
| **Item** | **%** | **%** |
| Press Downtime | 30 | 30 |
| Temperature Variation | 20 | 50 |
| Low Priority | 15 | 65 |
| Perfection Belief | 15 | 80 |
| All Others | 20 | 100 |

Variation and Performance Belief might be the most logical first steps. At relatively little cost, their resolution could account for removing 35 percent of the symptom causes—a not insignificant reduction in ball-bearing dispersion. The information gleaned by displaying the data in this format is impressive. The width of any column indicates its relative cost. The height shows its relative benefit, and the slope of the cumulative trend line located directly above that column indicates its combined relative cost/benefit impact on the symptom.

The initial causation-impact Pareto diagram, derived from causation data accumulated during Step 1B2, will not usually include resolution cost figures. Therefore, the diagram will look more like Figure 6.25 than Figure 6.26. Cost/benefit data are usually accumulated

## Figure 6.26
Cost/Benefit Pareto Histogram

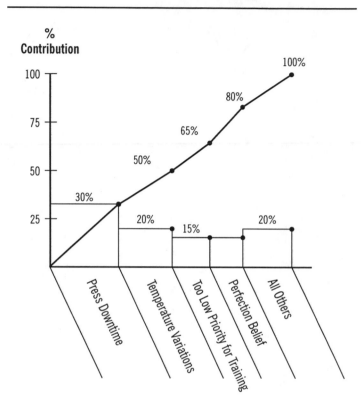

during the Resolution Implementation Stage (Step 2B1). Both diagrams are important. During causal analysis, resolution costs should not enter into one's thinking. The whole point of the PIC is to prevent such inhibitions from blocking people's thinking about the reality of situations. A real cause of a symptom is no less real simply because its resolution might be expensive. However, when costs of resolution do become appropriate considerations, it can be very valuable to compare cost-free and cost-encumbered Pareto diagrams. Such considerations become critical entries in force field analysis, described later in this chapter.

## Summary

Collecting, formatting, and analyzing data for the purpose of conveying meaningful information is often tedious and frustrating. But it is essential to any good investigation. Resist the temptation to avoid or reduce it. Nothing can be more frustrating than to complete an entire investigation only to find that the effort was unnecessary and the results ineffective. And there are few experiences more rewarding than presenting to an audience innovative performance improvements that shatter damaging myths of conventional wisdom with incontrovertible empirical evidence. Remember that the PIC phases and stages are divided into alternating steps of speculation and verification, each crucial to the effort and all combining to assure success.

## 7. How-By Pursuit

### Features

Structurally, the how-by pursuit is identical to the why-because pursuit; it is a logic tree. Ideas are entered onto branches according to the dictates of logical entailment. Divergence and convergence are also employed in the same manner for both techniques, but the similarities end at that point. Functionally, the how-by pursuit is designed to discover how broadly stated solutions and recommendations for action are to be accomplished.

Figure 6.27 shows the format of a typical how-by pursuit logic tree. The technique for diverging ideas is again similar in principle to the equivalent exercise in the why-because pursuit. The first suggestor reads the recommendation statement, which is a call to do something. Therefore, the member asks the question, "How?," meaning how is the recommended action to be done? After asking how, the member then says "By ... ," and makes a statement beginning with a verb.

Figure 6.28 abstracts one small corner of an immense how-by pursuit developed in the investigation of company employees not sharing the excellent ideas that most of them developed to make their own jobs easier and more productive. The causation and verification steps

175

## Figure 6.27
### How-By Pursuit Logic and Format

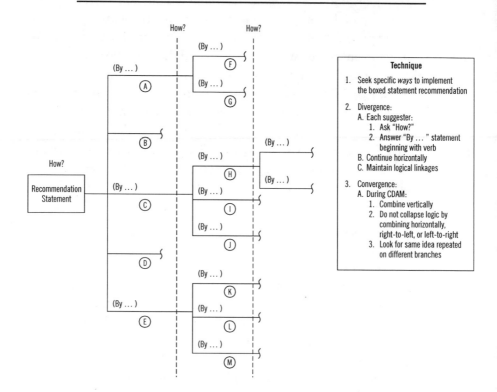

led participants to six overall solutions, one of which was: Develop a Productivity Improvement Idea (PII) Sharing Plan. The completed how-by pursuit diagram covered fourteen taped-together sheets and included over two hundred entries. The logic tree had twelve main branches, some of which spread out to as many as ten subtwigs.

The purpose of any how-by pursuit is to discover the critical steps required to implement abstract and generally stated recommendations. Along with cost/benefit analysis and consequence analysis, the exercise gets to the heart of recommendation feasibility. The timing of implementing actions and their relative sequencing is not a concern at this time. The object is merely to

## Figure 6.28
## Typical How-By Pursuit Diagram

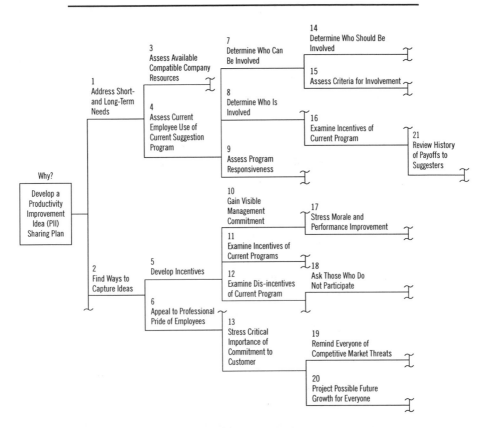

isolate and define the crucial steps required to conduct the recommendation; scheduling and sequencing can be done later. Once divergence is completed, team members converge down to the relatively few statements most critical for successfully implementing the boxed solution statement. Again, the rules of convergence are the same as applied in the why-because pursuit technique. Number entries top to bottom and right to left. Combine vertically, not horizontally—for example, numbers 9 and 11. With over two hundred entries spread over twelve main branches, clarification, combining, lobbying, and voting can take substantial time, but size, complexity, and time are usually measures of the complexity of the overall issue itself. The issue, by its very nature, takes care and patience. It would probably never have become such a monster if equally careful attention had been paid to it earlier. It is reality staring you in the face, so face it back. Do not fall victim to impatience and cries for taking shortcuts. It is at times such as these that commitment is truly tested. The PIC will work—if you work. If you don't, it won't!

### Procedures

- Tape a minimum of four flipchart sheets together (horizontally two by two), and tape them to the wall.
- Write the solution/recommendation statement at the left-center margin, and enclose it in a box.
- Write *How?* above the box.
- Draw the first vertical line of the logic tree.
- Conduct divergence.
  - ◆ Remember that each finalist can be treated as an independent statement, and that its selection does not impose the necessity of including attached statements as finalists.

Remember that CDAM combining in logic trees, such as why-because and how-by pursuits, should be done vertically (across parallel branches), not horizontally (serially along branches). Also remember that these techniques are designed to stimulate creative thinking that identifies critically important insights.

It is important to realize that every statement in a logic tree is independent. Therefore, when a statement is moved for combining, its adjacent, serially related branch statements do not move with it, and, when a statement is chosen as a finalist, all the statements in its serial branch are not selected with it.

However, the full line of statements within which a finalist is logically embedded provides very helpful hints regarding how to implement that idea. For instance, both the why-because and how-by finalist entries and their logical interdependencies would prove very helpful during consequence analysis (force field diagramming) and cost/benefit analysis. The particular example extracted here was crucial to the people who eventually wrote the PII sharing plan.

## 8. Force Field Analysis

### *Features*

Force field analysis is a technique for generating, displaying, and analyzing the consequences of a solution/recommendation. The how-by pursuit tells us how to do something; force field analysis tells us what will very likely happen because we did it. Typical force field diagrams divide suggested consequences of actions into two possible categories:

1. Driving forces.
2. Restraining forces.

Driving forces encourage (drive) us to implement the solution; that is, they are good, positive, or pro consequences. Restraining forces discourage (restrain) us from implementing the solution; that is, they are bad, negative, or con consequences. We have all heard of cures that are worse than the illness they are designed to eradicate; resolution feasibility is, in part, a function of consequences.

A separate force field diagram is developed for each recommended solution. Figure 6.29 is a force field diagram suggesting the possible consequences of implementing one of the six solutions recommended by the PII group participants. Statements are entered using typical divergence techniques. Members should be most careful to define all the possible restraining forces. Restraining forces can only be eliminated or minimized if they are admitted and clarified. You can be sure that the audience to whom the final conclusions are presented will probe such considerations, and it will confer substantial credibility to those who openly recognize and account for such considerations. Those who either cannot or will not admit, account for, and answer restraining forces are soon visualized as having done an incomplete job or as trying to hide consequences to sell an idea. Those who openly confront restraining forces and even suggest compensating factors gain immeasurable respect and attention. The bottom line is that real long-term resolutions require honest appraisal of restraining forces. Restraining forces often stimulate members to think of driving forces that mitigate or even eliminate their negative consequences. They also suggest ideas that can be added to a how-by pursuit to compensate for negative consequences. Restraining forces can often be turned into opportunities that were earlier unrecognized.

The solution for which the example in Figure 6.29 is drawn is Campaign PII with the Same Level of Effort and Enthusiasm as the Annual United Fund Drive. The numbers in the WT columns are merely rough indicators of the strength of each entry, in terms of impact of consequence—that is, how much the entry matters. I prefer the following very general estimates of impact:

- 1 = Small
- 2 = Medium
- 3 = Large.

These are ordinal (imprecise) indicators, and they cannot be added to some meaningful total. The number 1 is nothing more than a shorthand indicator for the word small. Its counterparts play the same role; therefore, you can no more add them than you can the words they represent. However, if most of the driving forces in a given force field diagram are 2's and 3's, and the restraining forces are 1's and 2's, then a sense develops that the overall consequences of a solution are reasonably good. They give one an overview of the relative impact of consequences and should be treated as no more than estimates. Some people use arrows pointing into the centerline to indicate weights. Three arrow lengths are used to indicate small through large impacts. Other people ignore weights entirely on the premise that they are so vague that they might be misleading. I prefer the system shown in Figure 6.29. After all, who are the participants going to mislead—themselves? Any device that helps convey and illustrate their sense of shared consensus is good, in my estimation. This is just one more small consideration for people to ponder. As a facilitator, I always go with expressed participant consensus on issues that do not impair the foundations of the PIC or its techniques.

Statements are entered onto the diagram through typical divergent exercises. Since the object of consequence analysis is to retain all entries, there is no need to converge down to the most critical few. I usually encourage members to perform convergence through CDAM, which ensures clarification and provides an opportunity to simplify the final draft by combining or modifying like entries.

# Figure 6.29
## Typical Force Field Diagram

---

**EAT #3 — 5/12/88 — Step 2A2 – Consequences Speculation**

---

**Solution #52:** Campaign PII with the Same Level of Effort and Enthusiasm as the Annual United Fund Drive

| WT | Driving Forces | Restraining Forces | WT |
|----|----------------|--------------------|----|
| 3 | Large # of ideas will be captured | Resistance to change | 1 |
| 3 | Professional importance will be recognized | More work for departments | 2 |
| 3 | Potential large $ savings | Cost to implement | 2 |
| 2 | Some people will feel more important in program | Management resistance to allocating required time | 2 |
| 3 | Potential morale improvement | Hard to sustain in long run | 3 |
| 2 | Increased awareness of process | Past history of similar programs not encouraging | 3 |
| 2 | Division visibility in corporate | Resources/people must be used to implement | 3 |
| 2 | Encourages participation | "Rice Bowl" syndrome discourages sharing ideas | 1 |
| 1 | Increases top level management awareness | | |
| 3 | Stimulates PII thinking | | |

1 = Small      2 = Medium      3 = Large

## Procedures

■ Draw the force field format on a single flipchart sheet.

◆ Enter the complete solution statement in the box at the top of the sheet.

➤ Include the number of the solution statement as recorded on the solutions sheets during PIC step 2A1.

- Derive the statements, using typical divergence techniques.
  - ◆ Ensure that members provide three bits of information for each entry.
    - ➤ The *vector* of the statement—that is, either driving force or restraining force.
    - ➤ The statement itself.
    - ➤ The estimated weight (impact) of the consequence statement.
- Clarify and simplify the entries, using typical convergence techniques through CDAM.
- Obtain a satisficing consensus regarding the weight of each entry.
  - ◆ A rough estimate is all that is required.
  - ◆ Begin by asking the statement author her reasons for suggesting the original weight estimate.
  - ◆ Do not belabor the issue.
  - ◆ Remember to concentrate on what is agreed, rather than what is disagreed, when consensus is lagging.
- Conduct a complete force field exercise for each solution finalist derived during step 2A1.
- Hang all completed force field diagrams on the wall, and cross-compare their consequences.
  - ◆ Take a fifteen-minute working break to allow each member to evaluate consequences.
    - ➤ Look for common driving and restraining forces.
    - ➤ Isolate specific consequences that might *kill* or *guarantee* one or more solutions.
    - ➤ Find driving forces in one solution that might eliminate or minimize restraining forces in another solution.
    - ➤ Seek and record additional entries to all diagrams.
    - ➤ Consider possible modifications to existing how-by pursuits suggested by the consequence analyses.
      - • Suggest additional implementing elements that might support driving forces and compensate for restraining forces.
  - ◆ Conduct a review of possible changes based on study.
    - ➤ Employ the rules of CDAM.

- Do *not* allow the review to degenerate into standard discussion/argument and debates between individuals.
- ◆ Obtain a consensus on the best-estimated mix of solution finalists, based on consequence analysis.
- ▪ Obtain a consensus on desirability of updating existing how-by pursuits, based on consequence analysis.

## 9. Psychic Irrelevancy

### Features

How many times have you found yourself so caught up in a situation that you could no longer think clearly about it? You needed some distance, some rest, and a new perspective. Then, having gained that distance, how many times did that new idea you craved just pop into your head when your thoughts were a million miles away—that is, when you were thinking about something entirely removed from the troublesome topic? Your flashing insight was no accident; it was (what I call) psychic irrelevancy at play.

This technique is, by no means, original. I have seen literally dozens of variations on the theme played out in different group (and individual) decision-making enterprises. I do believe that my title is original, however. I like titles to convey some sense of what is occurring during an activity. The term *psychic* emphasizes the employment of all our senses, imagination, and insight to create ideas at any and all levels of consciousness. It energizes all our potential cognitive and affective resources. The term *irrelevancy* pertains to the purposeful intent of seeking insights about one topic by allowing our psyches to drift off into contemplation about totally unrelated and seemingly irrelevant topics.

To illustrate the process, assume that participants are investigating ways to increase the capturing and sharing of ideas that will improve overall work performance. We are conducting Solution Speculation (step 2A1), and we are stuck. A number of solutions have been diverged, and we have even converged to some finalists. But we do not have a warm fuzzy feeling about our progress; that one really striking solution that we all seek is alluding us. We have reviewed our causes until we are blue in the face. We feel good about them; we are just dried out.

We could adjourn; sometimes that works. It certainly gives us distance, but that is simply passive adaptation to our stress. We want positive adaptation (see Appendix II). Let us act to regenerate ourselves, rather than quit and hope for the best. Someone suggests trying psychic irrelevancy. We agree. Psychic irrelevancy is a technique for drawing out of our consciousness ideas that are pertinent to one topic by seeking them in topics that are at first glance seemingly irrelevant.

The first step in the technique is to choose one or more of our senses to use as a vehicle to stimulate our consciousness. Should we, for instance, use our visual sense, or our auditory or nasal senses? Assume that team consensus says to use our visual sense by drawing pictures. Each person is asked to sketch a picture of something on a sheet of paper, and hand it in to the scribe, who hangs them side by side on the wall. Someone suggests which picture(s) to use in the exercise. Understand that there are no limits on this choice of pictures; one, a few, or all of them can be used. There are no restraints on the character of the pictures; they can be as simple or as complex as imagination and time allow. Figure 6.30 includes a sample of pictures; the circled picture is the one chosen for the exercise. Everyone immediately recognized it, and jokes began to fly around the room.

At first glance, Superman's crest is about as far removed from a creative solution about capturing and sharing productivity ideas as one could get. It is, so to speak, irrelevant. But maybe a second, third, or fourth glance offers commonalties between the topics. What we are really searching for are attributes, at the next higher level of abstraction, that are held in common by the act of sharing and the man of steel.

The technique is quite easy to practice. The scribe stands ready to write ideas on a flipchart sheet. Members look at the picture, and let their minds drift. Using random brainstorming rules, members call out whatever (one- or two-word maximum) ideas enter their heads, and the scribe records them as fast as possible. All sorts of ideas are forthcoming—some tangible and obvious, others less so.

Possible examples include: strong, alien, Clark Kent, Krypton, Lois, hero, flying, bulletproof, brilliant, virtuous, truth, justice, the American way, newspaperman, loyalty, bad guys, time travel, identity, secrets, make believe, comics, wonderful, lonely, different, homesick, inferior, winning, and on and on.

Suppose that ideas such as lonely, loyalty, and identity strike a chord somewhere in the corner of your mind. You begin to associate these attributes with certain individuals recognized around the company as kind of different, out of the in-crowd mainstream. You begin to see that one of the things that makes them different is their tendency to make lots of seemingly bizarre suggestions; that is, they have a reputation of always trying to rock the boat and poke their noses in where they do not belong. But they learned! Peer pressure quieted them, and now they remain alone and isolated. Suddenly you realize that they are not the only people who have learned to be quiet. You, yourself, have developed some very effective ways to better perform, and you find that it would give you a nice feeling to share them with others.

From that point on, it is only a matter of moments before you suggest a rather surprising solution involving a cultural change— that is, reteaching people to understand that new ideas are welcome and that some boats ought to be rocked. You now know that the odd balls are not so odd after all; indeed, they possess virtues that all of us would be proud to emulate. You will find yourself filling with new insights and in competition with your peers to get numerous newfound solutions recorded. Psychic irrelevancy is a kick-starter and a pump primer.

The exercise could just as easily have been initiated with recorded music, by smelling a flower, or by touching certain fabrics and surfaces. The sense-stimulating vehicle can be anything that our imaginations allow. As it is with the PIC itself, our only real limitations are self-imposed. As a facilitator, I inhibit the process only to the extent that the technique rules, once defined, are not violated. Within those rules, anything goes. Along with Wolcott Gibbs, I accept any action as valid, within the rules, as long as it is not immoral, illegal, or fattening.

### Procedures

- Stimulate a sense in one of the following ways.
  - ◆ Each member draws a picture on a sheet of paper.
    - ➤ Scribe hangs pictures on the wall.
    - ➤ Team decides which picture(s) to use.
    - ➤ Members look at picture(s) for a few moments.
  - ◆ Select music or some other locally convenient sound.
  - ◆ Members listen to music or sound for a few moments.
  - ◆ Pass a flower or some other locally convenient nasal stimulant around the room.
    - ➤ Members smell the stimulant for a few moments.
  - ◆ Pass some material around the room for people to touch.
    - ➤ Members touch the stimulant for a few moments.
  - ◆ Pass some food around the room for people to taste.
    - ➤ Members concentrate on the stimulant taste for a few moments.
    - ➤ Imagine, for instance, the taste of a sugar doughnut.
- After a few moments of real or imagined sensory stimulation, begin a random brainstorm, and record attribute ideas suggested by the stimulant on a flipchart sheet.
- When brainstorm is completed, look for attributes that encourage associations with the original topic of consideration.
  - ◆ Develop the associations, and record new ideas pertaining to the original topic on appropriate flipchart sheets.
  - ◆ Continue, according to the rules of divergence.

## CONCLUSIONS

The detailed techniques discussed in this chapter define PIC mechanics. In Chapter 5, the theory and logic of PIC phases, stages, and steps (conducted by using the techniques as tools) were defined.

We have journeyed from teaming philosophy, through theory, to technology. Specified technique rules, regulations, and procedures are justified back to those origins. None of them are arbitrary. You will successfully create an organic enabling, innovative, and con-sensus-building community with the PIC if, and only if, everyone involved remains consistently true to its moral spirit and procedural

## Figure 6.30
### Psychic Irrelevancy Sample Drawings

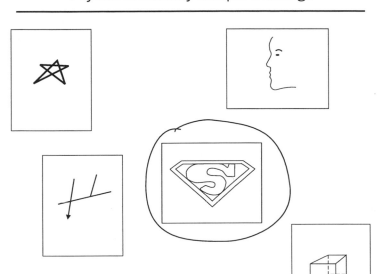

letter. Satisficing consensus, especially, is a fragile flower, destroyed before you know it without constant nurturing.

Just listen to any group of employees tell stories about how their organizations' teaming experiments (quality circles, quality improvement teams, and so on) withered and died. They either had no PIC-like processes and/or they arbitrarily imposed techniques like fishbone diagrams and Pareto diagrams into traditionally conducted meetings; without the slightest comprehension of philosophical or theoretical foundations. They locked themselves, in other words, into Figure 2.2, cell (2) (C), without considering cells (2) (A) or (2) (B).

Even worse, they paid no attention to the fact that complete quality/project management transformation requires both Cultural Change, Column (1), and Process Engineering development, Column (3), along with Teaming, Column (2). They were doomed from the start, and they did not know it. But now you know it. Others have succeeded; so can you.

Begin with the simple act of informal teaming with a few peers, as described in the next (and last) chapter. Most of us spend more time informally conversing with peers than we converse in formal meetings; therefore, most teaming is informal. Follow the few unadorned hints offered in those last pages, picking and choosing techniques appropriate to the topic of conversation. Have fun! Chill out! You will surprise yourselves and each other, as seemingly intractable concerns go away and as yet unimagined alternatives materialize.

# 7

# Informal Teaming:
# Romance Revisited

We took sweet counsel together.

Psalms 55:14

Against stupidity the very gods themselves contend in vain.

Schiller

There are horizons—frontiers to be expanded and pushed outward. Our shared ultimate end is to celebrate both human individuality and the bonding of distinct personalities into an enhanced community of great purpose and worth. That purpose is to serve a larger and meaningful enterprise with distinction, satisfaction and joy; e.g., in General Electric's phrase, "to bring good things to life." As Q admonished Star Trek's Captain Picard, "That is the exploration that awaits you. Not mapping stars and studying nebula, but charting the unknown possibilities of existence. See you 'out there!'"

My purpose remains to point your management vision "out there," and to provide sufficient principles and practices to launch you on your way. Lao-tzu said, "A journey of a thousand miles must begin with a single step." The Process for Innovation and Consensus (PIC) is our first step on the road leading toward the highest quality/project management aspirations. We know the character of organic communities, enabling environments, corporate cultural change, resistance to change, innovation, satisficing consensus, and effective teaming.

All that remains is to do it.

# DOING IT

Think like Lao-tzu! Start small! Small pleasant tastes stimulate appetite. Instead of dragging people into formal teams, chartered to find and resolve quality problems having little or nothing to do with their work, enable them to approach their own work more effectively. People reject interference, but grasp eagerly at help.

The first thing some employees say to me as a visiting consultant is, "Who are you to come in here from the outside and tell me (us) my (our) job?" After convincing them that I would never presume to do that, I ask them if everything is perfect. The answer is, of course, "No!" I then ask them if there are some relatively small but irritating matters (events, not people) that refuse to go away. I have never yet received a no answer to that question. Lastly, I ask if they would like to get rid of them. "Yes, yes," comes the reply. When I remark that we shall approach and treat the issues in somewhat strange ways, their interest perks. They never refuse to accept my process rules and catch on immediately to their nonthreatening qualities.

Note the following hints that you as a peer facilitator can use to interest a few coworkers:

- Focus on work deemed important by your peers.
- Gain their initial trust.
- Ask them if they would like to resolve work impediments.
- Ask them for several small irritants that can be addressed quickly.
- Have them choose one to start. If a dozen or more issues arise, exercise them through convergent nominal group technique to immediately experience satisficing consensus on a few most preferred issues.

- Ask them to let you, as facilitator, select a topic (from out of their most preferred) that 1) you see can be addressed in a few hours or less, 2) is under their primary control, and 3) requires exercise of only one relatively short PIC technique.
- Do not lecture or explain the process. Start them immediately on exercising individual issue-appropriate PIC techniques under your careful facilitation.
- Ensure that they eventually address several of the selected small issues, involving only interested participants.
- Once they feel confident enough to ask questions about the techniques, give them short interactive explanations, and suggest some readings.
- As issues involving internal suppliers and customers (often from other departments) arise, encourage them to become involved.
- Do not generate reports. Simply implement consensus actions under their control.

## PERSONAL EXAMPLES

A few personal examples will show how these hints work. A military engineering station division head asked me to help resolve a crucial issue demoralizing his eleven engineers and technicians. They regularly traveled back and forth between two test facilities almost two hundred miles apart. Both technical and personal problems, associated with traveling, plagued them for years. Equipment unavailability and breakdowns constantly occurred, and their families grew more and more upset over their continuous absences. They developed six less-than-satisfactory solutions, none of them earning anything close to consensus.

The division head asked me how long it would take to resolve this years-long albatross. I told him three hours. "Seriously," he laughed, "how long?" "Three hours, plus or minus thirty minutes," I said. It took three hours and thirty minutes.

We constructed force field diagrams on large flipchart sheets for each of the six existing solutions. Hanging them side by side on a wall, I facilitated them through a random brainstorming exercise that clearly illuminated competing positive and negative conse-quences of each solution. They discovered one entirely new short-term solution and, by mixing a few elements of them all, settled on one of the six as their long-term solution—all with 100 percent satisficing consensus. They expressed total disbelief over the result, wondering why they had allowed such shared suffering to go on for so long. They wanted to do more; they did, and they successfully implemented their two solutions.

The next example is even more astonishing. A friend and five of his colleagues working in the public works department of a huge industrial complex had used the PIC to generate seven solutions to a vexing problem. They found out that all seven recommendations violated both corporate and county regulations. Giving up on what now seemed illegal and useless solutions, my friend asked me to help. I told him to reconvene his group, bringing in one county and one corporate officer. Their task was to 1) examine the limits and specific applications of the relevant regulations, 2) rethink and reinterpret their still viable solutions keeping what they learned about the reg-ulations in mind, and 3) rebrainstorm their solution set. They gen-erated fourteen new solutions within fifteen minutes (each of them variations on the original set), converging them down to five final-ists with 100 percent consensus in ten more minutes. Two of the five also turned out to be illegal, but three of the new interpretations were quite legal. The entire exercise took about half an hour, culmi-nating in three perfectly workable solutions, drawn imaginatively from a basket of ideas they had nearly discarded.

Finally, another engineering friend did his teaming essentially alone; yes, he teamed with himself. He could not figure the cause of an intermittent failure in a missile fire-control system. He drew a why-because pursuit logic tree on a large sheet of paper and puzzled over it for several days, slowly but surely driving deeper and deeper into potential root causes. He stopped people in the hall, the lunch-room, the gym, and the parking lot for instant insights, and he got them. He even showed them to his wife and children, who knew nothing about the technology but could reason logically. They gave him some important entries. He finally converged (with the assis-tance of six peers) approximately 150 entries down to eight possible root causes (five of which had never occurred to him earlier). Careful circuit analysis and equipment troubleshooting verified two of the final roots as causes of the breakdown. The entire exercise consumed about four days of concentration and not only fixed that specific problem, but also suggested a design change guaranteeing that the problem would never occur again in any of the systems installed around the world.

## REITERATION

Think back! Imagine working in a totally fulfilling professional environment. Picture a genuinely transforming corporate culture driven by confident peers willing and able to overcome their addictive habitual attitudes and behaviors, work through change-generated senses of loss and grief, and reverse their natural resistance to change. Fantasize about you and an ever-widening circle of colleagues performing accelerating numbers of PIC teaming exercises concerning self-selected issues of importance. Finally, walk yourself mentally through PIC techniques, transposing words into action images.

Then gather some peers, and begin informal work-related teaming. You now know how to do it. Do not worry about inevitable mistakes. Celebrate them just as you do your child's first stumbling efforts to walk. We learn as much in failure (perhaps even more) as we discover in success. Everything you need to start rests between these covers and in your personal capacity to choose.

Always remember that teaming techniques (including the PIC) attempted without driving philosophy and theory lead to eventual despair and cynicism. Both quality management and project management histories substantiate this truth. Direct, therefore, what is toward what ought to be.

*"See you—'out there!'"*

# Shuster's Laws of Management and Teaming

These evolving laws underlie the ignition theory of management and teaming. Some are more self-evident than others. New insights alter and adapt them.

## DEFINITIONS

1. Management: the *act* of determining the way we do the things we do.
2. Leadership: the *act* of igniting mobilizing visions. Leaders must:
   - Have a vision.
   - Project that vision into the minds of others.
   - Inspire others to adopt (and adapt) that vision as their own.
   - Enable others to act on that vision.
   - Inject awe into others.
   - Lift others over horizons.
   - Prepare others to lead.

Everyone does at least one of these things; therefore, everyone participates in leadership.

Moral leadership: acting in the interest of constituents rather than in one's own self-interest.

3. Commitment to excellence (a private ethical choice) means:
   - fanatical *trust* in peoples' *integrity*
   - obsessive *intolerance* for anything less than full and continuous application of ignition principles and practices.
4. Commitment both creates and emerges from an *enabling environment* that:
   - Liberates intellect.
   - Generates consensus.
   - Empowers people to act.
   - Eliminates fear of failure (failure acceptance prevents disasters).
   - Loves, nurtures, and embraces risk, change, and failure.
   - Celebrates diversity.
   - Cements unity.
   - Inspires joy.
   - Ensures fulfillment.
   - Recognizes dignity.
5. External customer satisfaction depends upon internal customer satisfaction.
   - Internal customers include all organization members.
   - External customers include:
     - Immediate product/service recipients (clients).
     - Extended product/service recipients (clients of clients).
     - Vendors.
     - Professional associations and competitors.
     - The public at large.
6. Empathic service means giving your customers more than they expect by helping them satisfy their customers.
7. Teaming is an act that occurs whenever two or more people communicate with each other, formally or informally, in an enabling environment characterized by individual innovation and collective consensus.

# LAWS

1. The ultimate ends of ignition management are individual material, intellectual, emotional, and moral fulfillment.
2. Every human organization is a system composed of survival interdependent individuals, such that:
   - Each individual influences, and is influenced by, all.
   - The healthiest organizations are those in which individual members are bonded and integrated into an interdependent, accepting, unified *organic community*.
3. People are disposed to resist changing habitual attitudes and behavior.
   - Individual habitual attitudes and behavior are *addictive*.
   - People will not change until they are *psychologically ready to withdraw* from their addictions.
   - Purposeful action is required to enable people to work through and recover from their addictions.
   - *Unlearning* inappropriate behaviors is more difficult than *learning* appropriate counterparts.
4. "Groups do not act ... people do!"
5. No one can change another person's mind, but one can place others in environments that enable them to choose to change their own minds.
6. Obstacles imposed upon us are not a matter of personal choice and accountability, but our responses to imposed obstacles, being self-generated, are a matter of personal choice and accountability.
7. People are creatures of integrity and generally want to:
   - Do a good job.
   - Belong to something bigger than themselves.
   - Experience joy in work.
   - Break bureaucratic chains of alienation.
   - Be:
     - Recognized.
     - Trusted.
     - Treated with dignity.
     - Delegated authority and accountability.

8. Theory is the window to reality.
    - Imagination drives theory.
    - Testable theory is empirical theory.
    - Imagination is more important than knowledge.
9. Perfection is an acceptable standard of performance.
    - Perfection can be approached incrementally.
    - Horizons of perfection grow and expand:
        - As they are approached.
        - With imagination.
        - According to attitudes and events.
        - In unexpected ways.
10. Education is not a function of community; it is the community.
11. Processes are conversion devices (A becomes B) and, as abstractions, are rendered operational only by individual action.
12. No one can delegate involvement.
13. It is not enough to want to change; people must know how to change.
14. Measurement is crucial to management transformation, but:
    - It is vital to know what, why, when, where, and how to measure.
    - Some things cannot be measured, for example:
        - Business lost by customers who never return.
        - Normative assertions, i.e., what one:
            - *Should* or *ought* do
            - *Should not* or *ought not* do.
15. Never try to convince the unconvinceable.
16. Good parts fail in bad systems.
17. We can choose to avoid issues, but we cannot elude consequences.
18. "All experience hath shewn that mankind are more disposed to suffer, while evils are sufferable, than to right themselves by abolishing the forms to which they are accustomed" (The Declaration of Independence).
19. Rework ruins, unless it instructs.
20. *Proactive* error prevention surpasses *reactive* error correction.
21. Continuously cycle visions and results: conceive, design, plan, do, evaluate, then conceive again.

22. If it's "broke," fix it; if it "ain't broke," improve it. But, never leave it alone.
23. Seek surprises, embrace change, and glory in turbulence; chaos and order are compliments.
24. Managers create and control the system within which workers work and must, therefore, view them not as subordinates, but as customers and vendors.
25. New ideas seldom make old sense.
26. If the Devil is in the details, then Hell is in the design.
27. Things worth doing are worth doing poorly—at first.
28. Praise generously; criticize cautiously.
29. Failure is fine; fear of failure is not!
30. The process will set you free!
31. Never take away a person's choice.
32. Techniques serve the process ... the process does not serve the techniques.

# APPENDIX *II*

# System and
# Environment

Organizations that are conducting serious inquiries into quality management seem to share a common fear, seldom voiced aloud prior to their inquiries. Their anxiety comes from the nagging worry that, against all accepted expectations, the company might not survive in an increasingly competitive environment. This raises the terrible specter of unemployment for all, setbacks in professional careers for many, and total loss of earning power for some. Little wonder that they are willing to consider radical changes in the very habits and culture that shape their corporate behavior. A quest for survival, then, provides a common denominator for all organizations—public and private, manufacturing and service, profit and nonprofit. What is it about innovative quality management processes that make them so successful as devices for increasing the chances of competitive survival? The answer is positive adaptation. Positive adaptation is the surest key to competitive survival.

To adapt means to bring an organism into correspondence with the reality of a situation—that is, to creatively adjust, reconcile, and fit. To be adaptable is to be pliable, supple, tractable, and moldable. To positively adapt means to proactively use reality for the direct benefit of the organism. Organizations displaying these qualities survive by finding ways to mobilize their human resources in support of their interests. Innovative quality improvement processes provide that proactive way. They direct and focus collective talents and energies to best exploit and capture individual creative potentials for adaptation, growth, and fulfillment.

## STRESS: RISK, UNCERTAINTY, AND CHANGE

Competitive survival would hardly be a problem for anyone if the future were 100 percent predictable. However, our horizons are quite unpredictable, and our reach is but a guess. For each answer sought, for each question asked, for each alternative contemplated, there stands in our way the risk of failure, the uncertainty of outcome, and the inevitability of change. Together, these three potentially demoralizing agents inject stress into an organization's decision-makers' hearts and minds. Positive adaptation allows them to overcome stress through preparation, attitude adjustment, and direct action. They need not passively endure stressful confrontations and merely hope to emerge from the fray with less than mortal wounds. They can purposefully turn stress around on itself and convert lurking dangers into welcome opportunities.

Therefore, it is important to understand the linkages through which positive adaptation allows individuals (acting collectively) to redirect and overcome stress. Systems analysis provides a useful model for clarifying those linkages—that is, for explaining how the Process for Innovation and Consensus (PIC), for instance, promotes adaptation. The device gained wide popularity in both the physical and social sciences after World War II.

## SYSTEMS ANALYSIS

Systems analysis does not focus on things; it pertains rather to relationships between things. Thus, a systems analyst in an automobile manufacturing plant would not concentrate on physical equipment, such as a clutch or transmission (things). He would instead be interested in how the two units work together (relate) to transmit mechanical energy from the engine to the wheels. The systems analyst thinks about patterns of interactions and interdependencies that form a unified set of actions and behaviors joining the individual parts into an integrated whole.

This idea is not isolated to relationships between inanimate objects; it applies just as directly to relationships between people. It pertains to this study, because it provides useful insights into how organizations can mobilize human resources to adapt to stress.

A system is comprised of any two or more interrelated things; thus, a clutch and a transmission (two things) interrelate to transmit mechanical energy to a driveshaft. They are also part of the larger automobile system that performs to transport people and cargo. Similarly, individual people joining to act in PIC teaming form a system designed to improve performance quality and productivity.

The simplest notion of an operating system is illustrated in Figure AII-1. Whatever kind of system is under consideration, it does not exist in a vacuum. It exists in the world; that is, the world is its environment. For instance, an automobile exists within the world, and the world is its environment—within limits. Those limits circumscribe the areas of the world that will most probably be the car's immediate environment. The probability that a Chevy will be found one hundred feet off of the ground suspended in an Amazon jungle tree is surely less than the probability of its sighting on the Los Angeles Santa Monica Freeway.

Systems are constantly interacting with their environments. Some interactions are stressful; i.e., a seashore climate will more than likely cause rust to corrode the body of a car. Conversely, the protective environment of a garage might shield the car from salt damage. Think of interactions as kinds of transactions between the environment and the system. There are two basic kinds of transactions: inputs and outputs. Inputs are transactions moving from the environment into the system; outputs move from the system into the environment. For instance, a human driver presses down on the accelerator of our Chevy, which represents an input communicating the command to move. The Corvette (we might as well enjoy our fantasy) system processes the command, culminating in the output, wheels turning and car moving. A system, in other words, can be thought of as a processing or conversion device. It processes inputs and converts them into outputs.

## Figure AII-1
### Simple Systems Model

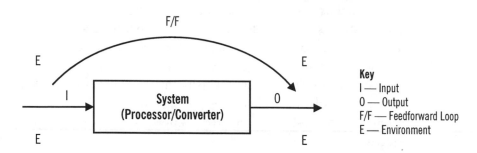

F/F

E                                      E

I          **System**          0
        **(Processor/Converter)**

E                                      E

**Key**
I — Input
0 — Output
F/F — Feedforward Loop
E — Environment

To carry the automobile analogy further, think of an internal combustion engine as a system. It converts chemical energy (air and gasoline) inputs into mechanical energy (shaft torque) output. Similarly, a generator is a system that converts mechanical energy (shaft torque) input into electrical energy (voltage and current) outputs. The car engine and generator perform as a system to charge the battery. The principle is no less applicable to PIC teaming. Participants process input conditions and convert them into output implementing actions, and we have already seen how important the setting or environment is to the health and success of any PIC activity.

Transactions moving in the direction input-system-output are said to be moving in the feedforward direction. Systems are designed to feedforward inputs into outputs. The simplest kinds of systems described in Figure AII-1 are incomplete for our purposes. We seek a model explaining how systems positively adapt to stress and survive because of their adaptability.

Adapting systems are most simply illustrated in Figure AII-2. Systems adapt through the mechanism of feedback. Please note that the direction of feedback information is output-system-input, the reverse of feedforward. Feedback information communicates the character of the system's output response to an input, thereby allowing the initiator to appropriately adjust her requirement (and the input). Assume, for example, that the Chevy's driver wants to accelerate from forty to sixty miles per hour (mph). The speedometer and the driver comprise the system's output converter, because it is through them that the feedback input is communicated to the input (accelerator). The driver desires sixty mph, twenty mph greater than the feedback input. The stimulus input is, therefore, plus twenty mph. The circled X symbol in Figure AII-2 is employed in control systems theory to indicate the mixing of inputs into a combined resultant input. In the example, the mathematical summation is simple algebraic addition. In most behavioral systems, the precise character of the summation network is seldom reducible to unequivocal and precise mathematical formulation.

Seeing the difference between the current and desired speeds, the driver presses the accelerator. That is the mechanism through which stimulus input is input into the system. Assume that the car accelerates to fifty-five mph; then input remains sixty mph, but feedback input is now fifty-five mph (assuming that the speedometer is accurate, and the driver can read and interpret it). Now stimulus input is plus five mph. The pressure on the accelerator must now be eased, adapting to the fact that the current pressure, if continued, will accelerate the vehicle beyond the desired speed of sixty mph. The driver, therefore, is adapting to the actual changing conditions of vehicle acceleration and speed, with respect to the desired speed, through feedback. Imagine the changes in input parameters if the road becomes hilly, and the system must respond to consequent speed variations. Cruise control systems replace the speedometer/driver combination as the output converter element with a computer.

The output converter is the feedback loop processor/converter. It acts on the output in the same way that the feedforward loop input converter acts on the stimulus input. Assuming that the feedback loop is fault-free, then feedback input should be an exact representation or analog of the output. In our car analogy, for example, the actual output is the car accelerating to sixty mph. The output converter is comprised of the speedometer/driver mechanism or a cruise-control device. If the speedometer malfunctions or the driver is unable, for some reason, to see or interpret it, then the feedback input will not correspond to the output.

## Figure AII-2
### Expanded Systems Model

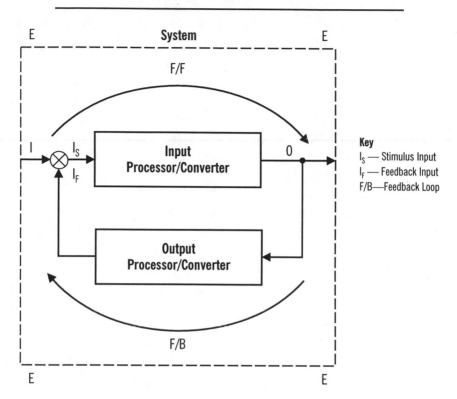

Although the car's velocity reaches sixty mph, for instance, the speedometer might read fifty-five mph, and the driver's perception of the car's speed will be incorrect. He will, therefore, continue to accelerate the auto until feedback input equals sixty mph, at which time the car's actual speed (output) will be greater than the figure.

Extending this concept to the PIC, the reader should recognize this process operating throughout its techniques. The very essence of the PIC is to apply individual creativity and collective consensus making to corporate stresses in the interest of deriving feasible working adaptation resolutions.

The complexity of large organizations sometimes muddies the waters of adaptation analysis, regardless of the model being employed.

It might be trite to repeat the old saying that human behavior is complex, but it is also true, and it is against this background that the real value of the systems model, as a device for clarifying adaptive processes, is illuminated. Figure AII-3 includes input elements in the model that add the perspective needed to cut through some of the complexities of human behavior analysis. The central themes of these additions were introduced by political scientists, such as University of Chicago professor David Easton, in the early 1950s. They were interested in a question very similar to ours: "What is it that makes political systems survive under stress?"

## SYSTEM INPUTS

In the refined model, illustrated in Figure AII-3, the input is seen as a summation of two major tributaries. The first tributary is demands; the second is sustenance or life support. Recall that every system is designed to fulfill the purposes of its customers. The Chevy system, for instance, is designed to fulfill the transportation requirements of its users. Demands are inputs reflecting the wants of users. When the driver of the car presses the accelerator, shifts the gears, presses the brakes, or turns the wheel, she is initiating a demand into the car system from which she expects corresponding outputs.

This principle is no less active in organizations. Individuals and departments are literally bombarded with demands for some new piece of information, immediate action, expanded responsibility, revised documentation, faster service, or other infinitely various outputs over time. In a perfect organization, one might expect that all inputs would represent demands consistent with corporate goals, and that the output responses would exactly correspond to and satisfy those demands. But how familiar are the cries heard about personal conflicts, interdepartmental conflicts, territoriality, special interests, hidden agendas, poor attitudes, indifference, split loyalties, and a basket of other negative factors that demoralize people and cripple performance. These stress forces act quite independently of the demand-process/convert-output function. A question can be legitimately asked about the extent to which human responses in organizations are more a function of the earlier cited debilitating

# Figure AII-3
## Complete Systems Model

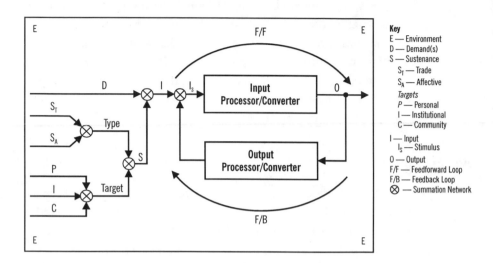

forces and less a function of pure legitimate demands. The systems model suggests that the input is indeed a mixture of demands and other factors, combined in Figure AII-3 as input sustenance.

Sustenance means life support—that is, the energy that enables the system to function. In the car engine, sustenance is provided by air and gasoline. Without these two fuels, the engine could not come to life and function to process inputs into outputs. Even with air and gasoline, engine performance—that is, its ability to accelerate on demand or run smoothly—depends on the character of the air and the gasoline. At high altitudes, for instance, the air might be too thin to sustain expected engine performance. Perhaps the octane rating of the gasoline is less than adequate for the engine's design parameters. If so, then the engine will knock, and performance will degrade. Consequently, when the demand, accelerate, is input, it will mix with the sustenance input, thin air or low octane gasoline, and the delivered output, increased speed, will be degraded in response to the composite input.

Engine status, itself, can affect sustenance. If the air and gasoline are both satisfactory, for instance, but the engine is out of tune, or the carburetor is clogged, then overall engine life support will diminish. Therefore, if sustaining fuels are absent, or if the system is incapable of incorporating available sustenance, its ability to properly accept, process, and convert demands into appropriate outputs will degrade or disappear.

People provide the inputs to human organization systems. The members of the system—employees—perform the bulk of processing/converting in both the feedforward and feedback loops. They also place substantial demands on the organization. But it is the sustenance input that they inject into the system that can be viewed as the key factor determining the health of the corporation—that is, its ability to effectively process and convert in both loops. Vendors (resource suppliers) and customers (output users and sponsors) also have significant roles to play in this process, but the focus here is on the employees as contributors and receivers of stress—all employees, at every level of responsibility.

Consider all of the familiar conflicts and special interests that impose corrosive stress on organizations. This model is supposed to clarify the mechanism of corrosion and show why quality management processes, including the PIC, reverse the sickness and rehabilitate the patient. A complete examination of the sustenance input in Figure AII-3 and Table AII-1 provides the necessary clues to answer these issues.

Consider the sustenance input and all of its subsidiary elements as a composite of all the life support attitude and behavior inputs from each employee and the many subcultures and coalitions that form among pockets of individuals. Broken down into its parts, this composite sustenance would be replaced in Figure AII-3 with a dense crowd of sustenance inputs feeding into the input summation network.

The life support that human beings give to an organization is not chemical, as was the sustenance offered by air and gasoline to the engine. Rather, it comes from behavior. An individual need not be enthusiastic, happy, content, excited, or devoted to a group to sustain it. He need only act in a manner that ultimately supports

**Table AII-1**

## Impact of Sustenance on System Performance

| Sustenance Type | Sustenance Target | | | Positive Impact on Stress Erosion |
|---|---|---|---|---|
| | PERSONAL | INSTITUTION | COMMUNITY | |
| Trade | 1 | 2 | 3 | Low |
| Affective | 4 | 5 | 6 | High |
| | Low | ⟶ | High | |
| | Positive Impact on Stress Erosion | | | |

general progress toward corporate goals. Sometimes the most disenchanted of us plod through the years, miserable or indifferent, all the while contributing part of our skills (that minimal amount necessary to meet some set requirement). To the extent that individual performance is less than would occur with fully motivated incentives, stress has eroded the character, quantity, and content of desired outputs.

All of the complex and various forces, then, that combine to stress an organization can be thought of as culminating in the system input of sustenance. Sustenance can, therefore, provide a measure of the level of stress active in a system. Once measured, actions can be taken to reduce or eliminate the causes, thereby increasing the organization's ability to adapt and survive.

Working backward from S in Figure AII-3, overall sustenance is shown to be a summation of two types, trade sustenance and affective sustenance. Remember that individual human behavior is the mechanism through which life-sustaining energy is transmitted to the organization. Therefore, sustenance flows from the individual to the group. Trade sustenance is contractual in nature, involving little or no emotional or linking features. It involves quid pro quo standards—that is, this for that, something for something, and one for one. An employee might, for example, work overtime for many reasons, one of which is that she is promised extra pay or compensatory time off. She might entertain only the very slightest interest in the work or its outcome, but she works the overtime to receive an explicitly agreed return. The employee's behavior, therefore, sustains the organization. Note that the system output was as much determined by its ability to process/convert the sustenance input factor (work only for explicit return) as it was by its ability to process/convert the demand input. The two inputs were quite independent, and in the purest analytical sense the worker's decision to contribute was not influenced by demand.

By far the most important of the two types for stress reduction, affective sustenance's origin is in the emotional linkages that bind individuals to the organization. Terms such as loyalty, devotion, belonging, patriotism, satisfaction, happiness, and attachment are modifiers and descriptors that come to mind when the subject is broached. Were this type of sustenance flowing from the worker toward the organization, then the overtime would be performed with little or no regard for an explicit return. The binding affection linking the person to the group would guarantee a level of involved performance not contemplated in the earlier case.

The principle conclusion to be drawn from this characterization of the types of sustenance is that:

> organizations cannot adapt sufficiently to survive in a competitive environment if the sustenance offered by its employees is primarily trade sustenance.

Consider the dilemma of the supervisor requesting that one, and only one, of three employees work the overtime, assuming that the three tend to be largely trade-sustenance oriented. Assume that two of the workers have requested overtime (exclusively for the extra income) and that the third person consistently expresses distaste for overtime. There is hardly a satisfactory alternative choice that the supervisor can make. At least one person will be dissatisfied with each overtime selection alternative, and that person's sustenance will diminish all the more, adding to an already overburdened atmosphere of stress. If one of the two who desire extra income is selected, then no retentive sustenance grows from his quarter. He simply trades something for something, bonding no affective linkages to lessen future stress.

Worse yet, the no-overtime worker might have to be selected, in which case the tiny quid pro quo of money for overtime will be overwhelmed by negative feelings (and consequent further erosion of scarce affective sustenance) engendered in all three of the individuals. The fact is that, in organizations where affective sustenance is minimal, almost every decision will tend to erode it further, because in the very act of meeting the needs of one employee, a manager is likely to deny a need to one or more of the other individuals.

However, had the atmosphere been one of high-affective sustenance, the overtime selection would have involved little or no stress factors. People imbued with positive feelings about the organization and their place and worth within it can absorb unwelcome decisions as necessary and functional. They can even reinforce their positive overall orientation toward the organization through the satisfaction of sacrificing a personal interest for the good of all. The principle to be drawn from this characterization of the types of sustenance is that:

> organizations can adapt sufficiently to survive in a competitive environment if the sustenance offered by its employees is primarily affective sustenance.

The two principles of sustenance are illustrated in the forth column of Table AII-1, Positive Impact on Stress Erosion. For the trade type, the impact is low (or even negative); for the affective type, the impact is high. One crucial assessment to be made within an organization, therefore, is the prevailing pattern of sustenance by type. From this single parameter, much can be inferred and correctives estimated.

The other vital parameter of sustenance is its target, that is, the object(s) toward which it is aimed and directed (targeted). Returning to the overtime example, assume that the disenchanted employee displaying only trade sustenance targets his very negative affective orientation toward one person, Joe Smith, the immediate supervisor. In fact, his feelings about the organizational structure, policies, and general procedures are not really so negative, but the specific person in the supervisory position immediately over him poisons the working environment enough to blacken his overall mood and contribution. The employee's target might not be the immediate supervisor, but a manager several steps removed, or more than one manager, or even one or more working peers. The point is that the targets of discontent are individuals—i.e., specific persons. This focus of sustenance toward human individuals (positive or negative) is called the personal target.

If sustenance targeted at the personal level is negative, then the stress it causes can be relieved by a shift in personnel assignments or by accommodations between the individuals involved. Rotations occurring in the normal course of time can often relieve the pressures debilitating personal sustenance and its consequent stress. Positive attitudes aimed toward the other two sustenance targets are sometimes enough to mitigate the impact of their negative counterparts targeted at the personal target. As stressful as personal-targeted negative sustenance can be in an organization, its impact will be less threatening to the overall corporate body than a like occurrence at the other two targets.

The second target of sustenance is institutions, with focus on the organizational structure (roles, policies, procedures, rules, offices, charters, and established patterns of interaction) defining how and where people are to associate within the corporate system boundary. Lack of institutions-targeted positive sustenance is potentially far more stressful than lack of personal-targeted support. The target this time is not a specific person, but a regulated and imposed element of the organization's authority structure. It is no longer true that the worker is unhappy with Joe Smith. He might be delighted with Joe, but the very position of supervisor that Joe currently occupies (the role) is the target of the worker's dismay, along with all the company's arrangements subsumed within that department. Indeed, the worker's discomfort might extend to wider corporate horizons—for example, the total organization chart, policies, and procedures. If his low esteem for these institutions is shared across a sufficiently wide spectrum of people, a quiet but pervasive cloud of stress can drift over the entire assembly. Intruding wisps of performance erosion occur that are at once difficult to perceive, evasive to grasp, impervious to admission of culpability by those whose interests it protects, and resistant to accommodation.

Stress introduced through negative institutions-directed sustenance cannot be eliminated so easily through interpersonal accommodations. This is what W. Edwards Deming (1982) means when he says that good workers cannot perform satisfactorily within inherently poor systems. Institutional arrangements are created and maintained by managers as the arena within which workers must function. Widespread institutions-targeted negative sustenance must therefore be sensed as a legitimate input to the system, and must be responded to through the system loops. Quality management processes are specially useful in improving institutions-targeted negative sustenance, if only because they encourage networking, and because the issues they tend to illuminate bear directly on heretofore taboo issues of entrenched interests and territorial associations. Since institutions-targeted issues reach more deeply into the bowels of an organization than do personal-targeted issues, it follows that successful reduction of negative institutions-targeted sustenance will have a greater and more fundamental positive impact on overall corporate stress than will reduction of its personal-targeted counterpart.

Community-targeted sustenance reaches into the very heart of an organization's reason for being; it gets to the issue of the worth of the enterprise itself. An extreme example of community-targeted negative sustenance would be reflected in a worker's deep concerns about her employer's chemical plant seriously poisoning the environment, or the weapons facility that manufactures death and destruction, or the publishing firm that distributes pornography and/or slanderous yellow journalism. These are, of course, very extreme examples, but they make the point. It is not unusual for people to find themselves caught in employment (from which they have no reasonable or probable hope of escape) that they find meaningless at best and rotten at worst. Their frustration is not directed toward individual people; neither is it aimed at institutions or organizations. More fundamentally, it is targeted at the very taproots of the enterprise and can be cured by nothing less than the worker leaving the company, a reorientation of the worker's basic values, or a complete redirection of the corporate strategic mission and goals. Widely felt stress at this level can be truly fatal to any organization whose personnel suffer significant community-targeted negative sustenance. They are saying, in effect, that "our enterprise should not exist—or, at least, I should not be part of it!"

In summary, community-targeted positive sustenance is created in the act of one's joining an organization. The person accepts a role in the corporate enterprise and thereby absorbs some part of its activity and accountability.

The hierarchy of Positive Impact on Stress Erosion of the sustenance target is shown across the bottom of Table AII-1. The impact is lowest for personal-targeted and highest for community-targeted sustenance. Reversing the perspective, it is obvious that the same low-high relationships hold for potential negative impact on stress accumulation of support targets. As shown, community-targeted negative sustenance is significantly more stressful and threatening to an organization's survival prospect than is its personal-targeted counterpart.

The six cells of Table AII-1 are numbered 1 through 6. The category, Institution, represents trade-type/personal-targeted sustenance. It is based on a contractual-type, something-for-something agreement between parties and carries little or no potential for binding emotional commitments. It is, therefore, the category with the least potential for affecting stress, either positively or negatively. The potential for having such impact increases with the cell (category) numbers. Category 6 has the greatest potential for stress impact because it is Affective Type and community targeted, for all of the reasons given earlier.

One of the first things to assess in a quality-interested organization is its internal status with respect to the categories of sustenance defined in Table AII-1. This is a direct indicator of the levels and insidious penetration of stress pervading the corporate culture. It is, hence, a guidepost illuminating the way toward stress alleviation and increasing adaptation capability and survival potential.

## IMPLICATIONS

Systems analysis suggests that people respond to requests for reasons that might have little to do with the substance of the need (demand) requiring action. They might instead respond to perceived threats to interests deemed important to personal survival and position (sustenance). Do individuals, then:

> survive ... to act in behalf of the organization, or act in behalf of the organization ... to survive?

These are not unlike the questions raised in election studies; i.e., "Do elected officials run for election in order to serve the people, or serve the people in order to be elected?" Which of the two alternatives is the end and which the means? It should be understood that there is nothing inherently evil about acting in one's own interest. The intent here is to understand motives, not to judge them, to fix defects instead of blame.

The foregoing analysis implies that in organizations that suffer high degrees of internal stress, and where trade sustenance dominates affective sustenance, the latter ends-means motive is probable. The focus is less on customer needs and promoting corporate goals then it is on status maintenance. Such conditions are harbingers of limited adaptability to environmental changes and stresses and can be, ultimately, foretellers of corporate demise. But with a reversal of such internal stress conditions, the former alternative is likely. The focus shifts to the customer and promotion of the corporate mission. Such reversals do not just happen; they occur as the result of painstaking, positive, and continuous efforts to accumulate large deposits of affective sustenance as bulwarks against the external stresses so sure to occur in the uncertain and risky competitive environment. They occur because heretofore blocked and broken feedforward and feedback decision loops are rebuilt and opened, allowing the vital fluids of ideas and consensus to nurture the corporate body back to health.

A sense of continuity emerges from this growth, a confidence that one positive act will be followed by another. A perception of integration of interests slowly emerges (affective sustenance), as problems earlier found to be intractable and chronic dissolve in ever-widening circles (clearing loop channels). People begin to perceive just how dependent others really are on their performance (that what they do matters after all) and, logically, how they too depend on others (systemwide interdependence). This sense of mutual inter-dependence of interests and performance grows slowly at first, but at an accelerating rate if and only if it is continuously fed.

The impetus needed to ensure continuous feeding comes from innovative quality management initiatives. As a part of such movements, the PIC inspires every positive element illuminated through systems analysis. Its capacity, for instance, to unlock and unclog feedforward and feedback loops is enormous, but not more so than its ability to link personal interests and generate large accounts of affective sustenance. Drawing its participants from the total organization, individuals suddenly find themselves ensconced in a high-priority action enterprise with people whom they have likely never met and whom they have probably railed against as the ghostly *theys* so often perceived as and blamed for fouling up the works.

The eye-openings crisscrossing the PIC environment produce a shared, enlarged perspective and encourage each individual's nat-ural tendency to confer on their newfound peers a sense of profes-sional dignity impossible to imagine in prior settings. More than any other factor in quality and project management processes, this people-appreciation element is the most important. This in no way minimizes the great value of techniques, measurement, and pro-motion that are also central to such enterprises. But, in the last analysis, only people act, and final accountability must attach to individuals, not to tools, techniques, and devices.

## THE QUALITY-SURVIVAL LADDER

The systems model shows that adaptation to stress is the key to cor-porate survival in competitive environments. The factors creating adaptability were illuminated and shown to be inherent elements of innovative quality management processes, including the PIC. With this established, a ladder of seven logically connected steps, linking individuals directly to overall corporate survival, can be constructed, which views organizations as dependent on mutually bonded individual employees—not on its departments, divisions, other working groups, and formal structures. This difference in viewpoint is neither merely semantic nor a play on words. Rather, the perceived split between individuals versus organizational structures, as vital determinants of corporate strength, creates fundamentally different attitudes and behaviors. This is not a new idea; Alexander Hamilton called it the fundamental flaw of the Articles of Confederation and the central virtue of the proposed Constitution of 1787:

> The great and radical vice in the construction of the existing Confederation is in the principle of LEGISLATION for STATES or GOVERNMENTS, in their CORPORATE or COLLECTIVE CAPACITIES, and as contradistinguished from the INDIVIDUALS of whom they consist. Though this principle does not run through all the powers delegated to the Union, yet it pervades and governs those on which the efficacy of the rest depends. ... we must resolve to incorporate into our plan those ingredients which may be considered as forming the characteristic difference between a league and a government; we must extend the authority of the Union to the persons of the citizens-the only proper objects of government. (1788)

Advance the clock two hundred years, and shift your focus from effective governance of a political community to effective governance of a business organization; the principle slips not a notch. It remains universal for any collection of people intent on constructing a collective that is at once secure for the public and nurturing to the individual. Working backward down the ladder from survival to people, the seven steps interact as follows:

1. Survival ... comes from ... competitive position.
2. Competitive position ... comes from ... effectiveness.
3. Effectiveness ... comes from ... continuous performance improvement.

4. Continuous performance improvement ... comes from ... quality/project management processes.
5. Quality/project management processes ... come from ... knowledge, skill, and application.
6. Knowledge, skill and application ... come from ... commitment.
7. Commitment ... comes from ... individual character.

The intermediate milestones of the ladder are familiar as integral elements of the PIC. The ladder is a culmination of quality/project management and PIC principles.

## COMING FULL CIRCLE, FROM PEOPLE TO PEOPLE

Effective positive adaptation implies the capability of producing desired results. This does not suggest that everyone always does produce desired results. It simply means that they possess a potential to do so. The character of an organization's competitive position, therefore, is dependent on the degree to which its people act on their potential. Acting on potential is the key to effectiveness and derives, as this essay suggests, from the continuous application of quality/project management processes that have been shown to possess those highest virtues of systems that maximize the ability to adapt to stressful environmental conditions. The terms knowledge, skill, and application, taken together, mean that it is not enough to simply possess these virtues. It is also necessary that they be applied—that is, used—in determined ways. Where does determination come from? It can only come from one trait: human commitment—i.e., single-minded, obsessive intolerance for anything less than quality attitudes and behavior.

Committed people do whatever it takes to continuously improve and settle only for perfection, with respect to that obligation. To be committed is an ethical choice that each individual must make within her own mind and heart. The PIC emphasizes that quality-mindedness, at bottom, is a personal commitment—i.e., a human characteristic residing in the deepest values shaping each employee's sense of professional integrity. It is, at heart, an ethical prescription, driving what should (or should not) be done in specified circumstances.

This same theme was stressed in the systems model. Demands come from people. Sustenance, positive and negative, is felt (and targeted) by people. Feedback and feedforward loops are created, nurtured, maintained, or destroyed by people. Outputs are generated by people. Thus, the quality-survival ladder leans on personal values and integrity, and, in the end, services emanating from that level of quality performance (so cherished in this and similar essays) are motivated, initiated, and delivered for the benefit of—people.

# Profound Loss and Five Stages of Grief: Elisabeth Kübler-Ross

> We read the world wrong and say that it deceives us.
> Tagore, *Stray Birds*, LXXV

Elisabeth Kübler-Ross' five stages of grief confirm that people grieve similarly in times of great or profound loss. Although she examines recovery from loss of loved ones, her healing process enables us to see parallels in losses accompanying radical life changes, including those at work. Losing workplace security, familiarity, and comfort attacks our sense of self-worth, leaving us vulnerable to emotional stresses that may be healed through the same five stages described by Dr. Kübler-Ross. I have noted (over long experience) significant grief-like reactions to such losses. Full recovery seldom happens. Loss survivors simply embark on a never-ending "recovering" journey. Some individuals find more peace, closure, and acceptance than other people find.

Easing people's journey through the stages requires, as Kübler-Ross explains, substantial empathy and understanding by significant others. Like it or not, those managers and peers with whom we spend the majority of our workdays are significant others. We mutually affect each other in deeply personal ways. This study suggests what we know about the loss-grieving process, our roles in it, and what we can do to help sufferers through the recovering process.

Consider what we have learned about resistance to change, culturally ingrained habitual addictive attitudes and behaviors, and the sense of loss and pain associated with withdrawing from addictive work-related rules, roles, ego-building expectations, and associations. What we do and how we do it contributes greatly to our self-esteem, confidence, worth, and image. Losing what we do assails our sense of who we are. We lose ourselves, close loved ones indeed, thereby triggering alienation of the worst sort: self-alienation!

Imagine, for example, the:

- concert pianist losing a finger
- amputee dancer
- overage athlete
- blinded painter
- downsized employee summarily laid off
- senior functional line manager with P&L authority who, after years of controlling events, must accede to an array of project/program managers "intruding in my house."

Picture the sleepless hours, physical and mental impairments, and countless other stresses suffered by such victims. These events create profound loss—and consequent grief. How, then, do we deal with it?

## THE FIVE STAGES OF GRIEF

Kübler-Ross, a physician, psychiatrist, and internationally renowned thanatologist (terminal illness specialist), described five stages of death and dying—i.e., 1) denial and isolation, 2) anger, 3) bargaining, 4) depression, and 5) acceptance, in her 1969/1997 bestseller; On Death and Dying. Her subtitle, What the Dying Have to Teach Doctors, Nurses, Clergy, and Their Own Families, tells us that:

- Those surrounding terminal patients must listen to them if they wish to help.
- Professional healers have much to learn from their terminal patients.
- Family members, friends, and significant others (anyone closely associated with the patient) can help. Compassion, empathy, love, and assistance require no professional credentials or licenses.

■ Virtually all patients can reach substantial peace with and acceptance of their conditions if those close to them learn the process, act empathetically, and deal with their own grief.

The following outline of the stages identifies their primary characteristics and behavior patterns.

## Stage One: Denial and Isolation

■ Experienced, at least partially, by all patients.
■ Unexpected shocking news causes temporary numbness.
■ Initial statements such as "No, not me, it cannot be true," "The X-rays were mixed up," and "I'm getting other opinions."
■ Might avoid (block) reminders of the condition.
■ Might fail to do things that could relieve pain and extend life.
■ Functions as a buffer after receiving unexpected shocking news.
■ Allows one time to collect oneself, and mobilize other, less radical defenses.
■ Dialogue about condition helps, but only when the patient is ready and ending when he resumes denial (can no longer face facts).
■ Usually a temporary defense, replaced by some acceptance.
■ Intensity proportional to how one is told, how much time is left to reach acceptance and stress-coping skills.

## Stage Two: Anger

■ Very few people can deny indefinitely.
■ Indicated by questions such as, "Why me?" or "Why couldn't it have been him?"
■ Difficult for healers and family, because patient displaces anger toward them.
■ When others respond with grief and guilt, the patient's discomfort and anger increase.
■ Others find it difficult to place themselves in the patient's position and understand lashing out at those who continue to enjoy what is denied to them. The circle of hostility feeds back on itself if others choose to take angry responses personally.

- Patients who are respected and understood will soon lower voices and reduce angry demands.
- Patients used to being in control of all situations react with rage to new helplessness. Others must find ways to let them make as many daily decisions as they can.

## Stage Three: Bargaining

- Less well known, but briefly helpful to patients.
- Manifested by thought that "maybe we can succeed in entering into some sort of agreement that may postpone the inevitable happening" or "since God did not respond to my anger, He may be more favorable if I ask nicely." The root bargain is always postponement.
- Like a child who figures that parents will allow something "if only I voluntarily do something around the house I seldom or never do."
- The reward sought is always an extension of life or temporary pain relief.
- Most bargains are made in secret with God, e.g., a life of service in return for extension. Promises might be guilt related; therefore, they should not be brushed aside. Listen to them, and respond empathetically.

## Stage Four: Depression

A sense of great loss replaces anger as patient becomes weaker, thinner, and symptomatic.

- Increasing worry over financial burdens and possible job loss.
- Two kinds of depression:
  - ◆ Reactive—caused by past losses. Others can try to cheer patient.
  - ◆ Preparatory—caused by sense of impending losses. i.e., a tool to prepare for the coming loss of all love objects and to facilitate eventual acceptance. Others cannot try to cheer patient; they must listen and understand and give non-verbal assurances, e.g., hold hands and share quiet

moments. This stage is necessary for the patient to reach acceptance. The patient must be allowed to share sorrow over impending loss of everything she loves without being told, "Do not feel sad." Shared sadness reduces anguish and encourages acceptance.

### Stage Five: Acceptance

Given time and help working through stages, the patient will eventually lose anger and depression over his coming fate, and will contemplate the coming end with some degree of quiet expectation.

A tired and weak person will doze, but not in avoidance or depression. Sleep periods increase in opposite direction of newborn children.

- Acceptance is not a happy stage. One is almost void of feelings and wants to be left alone and is not stirred by outside world events. Circles of interest diminish.
- Knowing she is not forgotten when nothing else can be done is comforting.
- Few patients fight to the end, which only impedes acceptance process.
- Patients are usually grateful to those acknowledging their need to detach from the world.

## ORGANIZATIONAL CHANGE AS A HEALING PROCESS

Time and again, as colleague and consultant, I watch peers and client personnel react as patients grieving over irreversible losses in their work lives. They find themselves involuntarily torn from a familiar environment to which they will never return—and sense this as a form of dying. Symptoms evident in all of the above stages emerge and demand the same healing balms from managers, peers, family members, and significant others.

The pace of transformation and teaming successes is directly proportional to the rate of progress working through the stages (to final acceptance) that significant numbers of employees experience. Nothing I have witnessed over the years is quite as sad as watching those locked in the early and middle grief stages for excessively prolonged periods of time. We have heard that managers and leaders must become coaches, counselors, and facilitators instead of hierarchical commanders. Now they are called to healing, major (but unfamiliar) players in their organization's journey from dysfunctional to functional community.

Do not doubt for a moment that we are capable of doing what we must do. Kübler-Ross makes it clear that it is a matter of choice, not schooling. Capacities for compassion, sensitivity, empathy, and caring reside in all of us. Does training help? Of course! Think of this book, in fact, as a sensitizing and healing training manual. Easing people's journey through profound loss grief stages and helping them get through the pain of withdrawing from habitual addictive behaviors—in the interest of creating (competitive and fulfilling) transforming and projectized cultures—is a worthy calling. Philosophically and theoretically grounded, the Process for Innovation and Consensus is one powerful, tested, and certain tool for accomplishing those ends.

# Achieving 100 Percent Satisficing Consensus

> We've done it all, yet we don't take credit for it.
>
> Ray Bradbury

> Give a little, take a little!
>
> Unknown

The term satisficing, coined by James G. March and Herbert Simon (*Organizations*, 1958, 1993, 2d ed.) refers to collective decision-making under conditions when less than optimal choices are available to participants. We shall address satisficing consensus as a virtue to be devoutly sought. Teaming philosophy demands commitment to an organic community promoting universal belief that 1) members are survival interdependent, i.e., E Pluribus Unum! ("Many as one"), 2) "We rise or fall together," and 3) all collective decisions must produce win-win outcomes.

## VOCABULARY

The Process for Innovation and Consensus (PIC) satisficing technique uses the following specialized vocabulary.

**Individual Interest:** Personal needs, wants, desires and satisfactions, i.e., independence at the cost of belonging.

**Collective Interest:** Social needs, wants, desires and satisfactions, i.e., belonging at the cost of independence.

**Individual (Personal) Payoff:** Amount of individual interest satisfaction gained through association with others.

**Collective (Social) Payoff:** Amount of collective interest satisfaction gained through association with others.

**Consensus:** Collective agreement.

**100 Percent Optimizing Consensus:** Collective agreement of all participants on the basis of each individual demanding 100 percent personal payoff (optimization) regardless of amount of collective payoff (virtually unobtainable).

**100 Percent Satisficing Consensus:** Collective agreement of all participants on the basis of all individuals accepting less than 100 percent personal payoff in the interest of achieving balanced personal and collective payoffs (quite obtainable as demonstrated in Chapter 6, Section 1.2.5).

## COMPETING INDIVIDUAL AND COLLECTIVE INTERESTS IN GROUP DECISION-MAKING

People have competing individual and collective interests (tradeoffs). Satisfying one interest requires sacrificing, in some proportion, the other. For example:

- agreeing to participate in a boring activity (*individual interest sacrifice*) in order to be with one's friends (*collective interest payoff*).

- foregoing the boring activity (*individual interest payoff*) but losing companionship (*collective interest sacrifice*).

## PROCESS FOR INNOVATION AND CONSENSUS VOTING OUTCOMES

PIC voting participants (see Chapter 6, Section 1.2.5) must identify and rank, for themselves, which few of many alternative statements they most prefer during voting sessions. When the voting session ends, they must search within themselves to ascertain in which of three, and only three, states of mind they find themselves, with respect to the voting outcome (see Table AIV-1).

# Table AIV-1
## Three Possible Process for Innovation and Consensus Voting Outcomes

| | |
|---|---|
| **1. Satisfaction (Optimized)** | 100% individual payoff voting outcome. Optimizing-minded people raise personal payoff (their own very highest preferred choices being similarly chosen and ranked by voting peers) above all else; i.e., winning means "my way (I win or we all lose)." Unacceptable for win-win purposes. Virtually unobtainable outcome and antithetical to quality/project management win-win teaming philosophy. |
| **2. Dissatisfaction** | High collective payoff with zero individual payoff. Unacceptable for win-win purposes. Sometimes intimidates individuals to "go along to get along," a clear lose-win outcome, similar to that obtained in majority voting. |
| **3. Satisficing** | High collective payoff with significant (but less than 100%) individual payoff. Acceptable and prized for win-win purposes. Achieves Deming's system optimization and quality/project management survival interdependence, so characteristic of organic win-win communities. PIC convergence tools, culminating in three voting techniques (*multivoting, nominal group technique,* and *discrete summation*) are specifically designed to produce satisficing win-win consensus (Chapter 6, Section 1.2.5). |
| **Satisficing Consensus Decision Rule** | Employ only those decision mechanisms that promote a 100% satisficing consensus. |

## PRINCIPLE TO PRACTICE

We have come full circle from teaming and transforming management philosophy and theory to effective implementing technology. Abstract and transcendent principles remain impractical and pie-in-the-sky only so long as we choose to make them so. Made manifest by concrete theory-faithful tools and techniques, and placed in the context of critical organizational priorities, they become powerful decision-making drivers.

Like any disciplined enterprise, teaming success depends upon individual participants' willingness and ability to do what is both necessary and right. Commitment is the measure of one's willingness. But willingness alone transforms nothing and no one. Teaming innovation and consensus realization requires the kind of philosophy and theory-based implementing techniques described here (review Figure 2.2). Although willingness and ability are different human attributes, both their individual and collective processes are intimately related.

## SATISFICING'S INSPIRATION

Watching and experiencing satisficing attitudes and behaviors blast through ingrained command/obedience prejudices makes people realize that no one can command values and attitude changes in others. Tyrants alone resist undeniable and repeated satisficing demonstrations.

People are fundamentally creatures of deep professional integrity (S/L #7, Appendix I). Given a platform of clear perspective, they can be trusted to make good decisions. Each individual's decision to adopt a transforming perspective and alter habitual behavior patterns is an intensely personal ethical choice. It rests upon each person's deepest sense of what social norms are ultimately good, right, and proper. Such decisions are made in corners of privacy that each of us occupies in privately chosen times and circumstances. That is why transformation is inherently a management philosophy. It demands that we reconsider our ultimate beliefs concerning what is real, true, and right (review Table 1.1), with respect to complex human relationships. It insists that we reevaluate the ends toward which we are striving, and compels us to act in accordance with that revaluation. This helps explain the deep sense of warm satisfaction that accompanies us on the transforming journey—over and above the very tangible rewards of economic and corporate achievement. We become more aware of our core ethical principles and feel good about the correspondence of our behavior to them.

We do not, therefore, command attitude changes in others. Quite the contrary, we liberate and enable people to change their own attitudes, according to demonstrated evidence that such changes are both ethically and instrumentally appropriate. People, then, act in accordance with a mutually newfound trust in each other. They see in bold new terms that "a house divided against itself cannot stand" and that "a house unified within itself will not fall."

Nothing brings this home to teaming newcomers more forcefully than experiencing satisficing consensus, the queen of teaming technology.

# A Universal Employee Bill of Rights

> Necessity is the plea for every infringement of human freedom. It is the argument of tyrants; it is the creed of slaves.
>
> William Pitt

One evening a few years ago, while writing a conference keynote paper about organic communities and enabling environments, I wondered aloud to my wife, Suzanne, about what guarantees and limits employees could legitimately expect in a truly fulfilling workplace. She just happened to be finishing a paper for one of her master's leadership courses in organizational development. Her topic, taken directly from contemporary headlines, concerned what she called unalienable employee rights. Marking the obvious link to the Declaration of Independence, I asked her if she meant the same quality of rights as Jefferson. She replied that she did indeed.

Suzanne had, in fact, taken the analogy further and constructed a universal employee bill of rights, modeled on colonial Virginia's bill, our federal Constitution's first ten amendments, and Eleanor Roosevelt's United Nation's declaration of human rights. Suzanne's bill immediately captured my imagination. She had somehow tapped the essence of my feelings on the ambiance pervading a fulfilling, organic, enabling, respectful, and humanizing professional community. She touched its soul, so much so that I want to share it with you. Here, then, are some human relations *oughts* that every quality/project management transforming-minded leader would do well to ponder.

# A UNIVERSAL EMPLOYEE BILL OF RIGHTS

## Preamble

We the people of (company name), in order to form a just and mutually prosperous organization, ensure standards of ethical conduct, promote a tranquil corporate community, proportionately serve our economic, social, cultural, and environmental values, and secure universal unalienable material and spiritual blessings of life, for ourselves, and our posterity, do ordain and establish this Universal Employee Bill of Rights.

Note: Articles 1–4 are taken directly from the Universal Declaration of Human Rights, Article 23.

### ARTICLE 1

Everyone has the right to work, to free choice of employment, to just and favorable conditions of work, and to protection against unemployment.

### ARTICLE 2

Everyone, without any discrimination, has the right to equal pay for equal work.

### ARTICLE 3

Everyone who works has the right to just and favorable remuneration ensuring for himself {herself} and his {her} family an existence worthy of human dignity, and supplemented, if necessary, by other means of social protection.

### ARTICLE 4

Everyone has the right to form and join trade unions for the protection of his {her} interest.

### ARTICLE 5

Everyone has the right to self-respect and dignity. No one has the right to prevent another person's freedom of opportunity or pursuit of self-respect.

### ARTICLE 6

Corporations shall make no policy regarding any person's religion, faith, belief, or spiritual values; or abridging constitutionally protected political freedoms of speech, assembly, and press.

### ARTICLE 7

Corporations shall not violate any individual's right to be secure in their persons, houses, effects, and work stations against unreasonable searches and seizures. Employees shall not violate the corporation's right to reasonable searches and seizures.

### ARTICLE 8

No person shall be compelled to be a witness against him or herself, nor be deprived of any rights herein specified without due process of constitutional law or appropriate corporate policies and procedures.

### ARTICLE 9

No one shall impair any person's right to just compensation and comparable worth.

### ARTICLE 10

No one shall have the right to abuse or intimidate others.

### ARTICLE 11

In all prosecutions of alleged misbehavior, the accused has the right to the presumption of innocence unless and until the facts of the case prove otherwise beyond a reasonable doubt and to a moral certainty. All such proceedings shall be conducted under due process of constitutional law and appropriate corporate policies. The accused shall have the right to be immediately informed of the nature and cause of the accusation, to be confronted with all witnesses against him or her, to have compulsory process for obtaining witnesses in his or her favor, and to have defense assistance sufficient to balance the weight of the accusers.

### ARTICLE 12

All persons have a right to protection from (and no one shall impose) cruel and unusual punishment, personal retribution, witch hunting or sanctions out of proportion with an offense.

## ARTICLE 13

The enumeration of rights herein specified shall not be construed or interpreted to deny, disparage or, in any way, demote other rights retained by people.

## ARTICLE 14

No corporation shall deny to any person within its jurisdiction equal protection under corporate policies or constitutional guarantees. No corporation shall discriminate against any person on the basis of background, gender, race, ethnicity, condition of birth, age, religion, nationality, or any other factor pertaining to origin or characteristics of nature.

## ARTICLE 15

No persons shall be denied the right to be informed about matters for which they are held accountable.

## ARTICLE 16

No corporation shall institute policies of procedures harmful to the health, safety, or environment of employees. No person shall be denied the right to be immediately informed of potential risks to health, safety, or environment.

## ARTICLE 17

No one shall deny employees the right to peacefully associate for the promotion of their own interests.

## ARTICLE 18

No one shall be denied right on the basis of their position, station, or function within the organization.

## ARTICLE 19

Corporate hiring and termination policies and practices shall not violate either explicit or implicit rights guaranteed by this document. Employees shall be given a copy of this document on the first day of their employment and shall not be denied the right to meaningfully inquire about it with an official who is competent to discuss and clarify its intent and specifications. Updates and changes shall be distributed to all employees with all due haste.

## ARTICLE 20

Agreed elements of material compensation, (e.g., wages, bonuses, commissions, or benefits) shall not be abridged, eliminated, or denied to employees without due process under the articles of this document.

## ARTICLE 21

Employees shall be guaranteed necessary and sufficient education, resources, processes, and support to achieve reasonable performance expectations.

## ARTICLE 22

Corporations shall not impose arbitrary coercive power.

## ARTICLE 23

No one shall deny any person's free and immediate access to his {her} own personnel file or to any documentation pertaining, or referring, to his {her} personal interests or employment history and performance (known or unknown by him {her} to exist).

## ARTICLE 24

No one shall deny a person's right to know any and all conditions of probationary employment.

## ARTICLE 25

All employees shall have the right too pursue real or perceived grievances without intimidation, threat, or alienation.

# Bibliography

## SELECTED REFERENCES

### Books

Bennis, Warren, and Burt Nanus. 1985. *Leaders: The Strategies for Taking Charge*. New York: Harper & Row, Publishers, Inc.

Clawson, James G. 1999. *Level Three Leadership: Getting Below the Surface*. Upper Saddle River, NJ: Prentice-Hall, Inc.

Cohen, Jack, and Ian Stewart. 1994. *The Collapse of Chaos: Discovering Simplicity in a Complex World*. New York: The Penguin Group.

Cornford, Francis M. (tr.) 1963. *The Republic of Plato*. New York: Oxford UP.

Covey, Stephen R. 1991. *Principle-Centered Leadership*. New York: Simon & Schuster.

Davidson, Gerald C., and John M. Neale. 1994. *Abnormal Psychology*, 6th ed. New York: John Wiley & Sons, Inc.

Deal, Terrence E., and Allen A. Kennedy. 1982. *Corporate Cultures: The Rites and Rituals of Corporate Life*. Reading, MA: Addison-Wesley Publishing Company, Inc.

Deutsch, Karl. 1963. *The Nerves of Government*. London: The Free Press of Glencoe.

Dewey, John. 1929. *The Quest for Certainty: A Study of the Relation of Knowledge and Action*. New York: Minton, Balch and Co.

Downs, Anthony. 1957. *An Economic Theory of Democracy*. New York: Harper & Row.

Drucker, Peter. 1967. *The Effective Executive*. New York: Harper & Row.

Duncan, W. Jack. 1973. *Decision Making and Social Issues*. Hinsdale, IL: Dryden Press.

Easton, David. 1965. *A Systems Analysis of Political Life*. New York: John Wiley & Sons, Inc.

Etzioni, Amitai, ed. 1969. *A Sociological Reader on Complex Organizations*, 2d ed. New York: Holt, Rinehart and Winston.

Gibran, Kahlil. 1982. *The Prophet*. New York: Alfred A. Knoph, Publisher.

Gleik, James. 1988. *Chaos: Making A New Science*. New York: The Penguin Group.

————. 1992. *Genius: The Life and Science of Richard Feynman*. New York: Pantheon Books.

Harris, Philip R., and Robert T. Moran. 1990. *Managing Cultural Differences: High-Performance Strategies for a New World of Business*, 3d ed. Houston: Gulf Publishing Company.

Jones, Roger S. 1992. *Physics for the Rest of Us: Ten Basic Ideas of Twentieth-Century Physics that Everyone Should Know … and How They Have Shaped Our Culture and Consciousness*. Chicago, IL: Contemporary Books, Inc.

Jowett, B. (tr.) 1953. *The Dialogues of Plato, Vols 11 & IV*. New York: Random House.

Kepner, Charles, and Benjamin S. Tregoe. 1963. *The Rational Manager*. New York: McGraw-Hill.

Kübler-Ross, Elisabeth, M. D. 1993. *On Death and Dying: What the Dying Have to Teach Doctors, Nurses, Clergy and Their Own Families*. New York: Simon & Schuster.

Machiavelli, Niccolo. 1908. *The Prince*. London and New York: Dent and Dutton. Translated by W. K. Marriott.

March, James G., and Herbert A. Simon. 1958. *Organizations*. New York: Wiley.

McGregor, Douglas. 1963. *The Human Side of Enterprise*. New York: McGraw-Hill.

Monte, Christopher F. 1991. *Beneath the Mask: An Introduction to Theories of Personality*, 4th ed. Fort Worth, TX: Harcourt Brace College Publishers.

Parsons, Talcott, and Edward A. Shils, eds. 1951. *Toward A General Theory of Action*. New York: Harper & Row.

Peck, M. Scott, M. D. 1987. *The Different Drum: Community Making and Peace*. New York: Simon & Schuster.

Powell, James N. 1982. *The Tao of Symbols: How to Transcend the Limits of Our Symbolism*. New York: Quill.

Riker, William, H. 1962. *The Theory of Political Coalitions*. New Haven: Yale UP.

Rossiter, Clinton. 1961. *The Federalist Papers*. New York: The New Amercian Library.

Sabine, George H. 1962. *A History of Political Theory*. New York: Holt, Rinehart & Winston.

Seiler, John A., ed. 1967. *Systems Analysis in Organizational Behavior*. Homewood, IL: Richard D. Irwin and Dorsey Press.

Sherif, Muzafer, et al. 1961. *Intergroup Conflict and Cooperation: The Robbers Cave Experiment*. Norman, OK: University Book Exchange.

Smith, Adam. 1937. *Wealth of Nations*. New York: Modern Library.

Stephan, Cookie White, and Walter G. Stephan. 1990. *Two Social Psychologies*, 2d ed. Belmont, CA: Wadsworth Publishing Company.

Stubberud, Allen R., Joseph J. Distefano III, and Ivan J. Williams. 1967. *Theory and Problems of Feedback and Control Systems*. New York: McGraw-Hill Book Co., Schaum's Outline Series.

Thibaut, John W., and Harold H. Kelly. 1959. *The Social Psychology of Groups*. New York: Wiley.

Turnbull, Colin M. 1983. *The Human Cycle*. New York: Simon & Schuster.

Yalom, Irvin D. 1985. *The Theory and Practice of Group Psychotherapy*, 3d ed. New York: Basic Books, Inc., Publishers.

Young, Stanley. 1968. *Management: A Systems Analysis*. Glenview, IL: Scott Foresman.

Yukl, Gary. 1998. *Leadership In Organizations*, 4th ed. Upper Saddle River, NJ: Prentice-Hall, Inc.

Weinberg, Steven. 1992. *Dreams of a Final Theory*. New York: Pantheon Books.

Weintraub, Sandra. 1998. *The Hidden Intelligence: Innovation Through Intuition*. Boston: Butterworth Heinemann.

Wheatley, Margaret J. 1994. *Leadership and the New Science: Learning about Organization from an Orderly Universe*. San Francisco: Berrett-Koehler Publishers, Inc.

## Articles

Boulding, Kenneth E. 1966. The Ethics of Rational Decision. *Management Science* 12 (February): B-161–B-189.

Bower, Joseph L. 1965. The Role of Conflict in Economic Decision-Making Groups: Some Empirical Results. *Quarterly Journal of Economics* (May): 263–77.

Contant, Michael. 1970. Systems Analysis in the Appellate Decision-Making Process. *Rutgers Law Review* 24: 293–322.

Crutchfield, Richard S. 1955. Conformity and Character. *American Psychologist* 10: 191–98.

Erickson, Richard F. 1969. The Impact of Cybernetic Information Technology on Management Value Systems. *Management Science* (October): B-40–B-60.

Faust, W. L. 1959. Group Versus Individual Problem-Solving. *Journal of Abnormal and Social Psychology* 59: 68–72.

Guetzkow, Harold, and John Gyr. 1954. An Analysis of Conflict in Decision-Making Groups. *Human Relations* 7: 367–82.

Huber, George P., and Andre Delbecq. 1972. Guidelines for Combining the Judgments of Individual Members in Decision Conferences. *Academy of Management Journal* 15 (June): 161–74.

Lewin, Kurt. 1947. Frontiers in Group Dynamics. *Human Relations* 1: 5–41, 141–53.

Maslow, A. H. 1943. A Theory of Human Motivation. *Psychological Review* 50: 370–96.

Shuster, H. David. 1969. Greek and Medieval Thought and a Modern Problem of Social Obedience. Unpublished paper, University of Rochester.

Shuster, M. Suzanne. 1994. Human Chaos and Corporate Order: A Perspective on Margaret Wheatley. Unpublished paper, Santa Barbara, CA, Antioch University.

————. 1993. Radicalism and Community: A Comparison of Alinsky and Peck. Unpublished paper, Santa Barbara, CA, Antioch University.

Simon, Herbert A. 1965. Administrative Decision Making. *Public Administration Review* (March): 31–37.

————. 1955. A Behavioral Model of Rational Choice. *Quarterly Journal of Economics* (February): 99–118.

Wiest, W. M., L. W. Porter, and E. E. Ghiselli. 1961. Relationship Between Individual Proficiency and Team Performance and Efficiency. *Journal of Applied Psychology* 45: 435–40.

# QUALITY AND PROJECT MANAGEMENT REFERENCES

Adams, John R., and Miguel E. Caldentey. 1997. A Project-Management Model. In *Field Guide to Project Management*, edited by David I. Cleland. New York: Van Nostrand Reinhold, pp. 48–60.

Amsden, Davida M., Howard E. Butler, and Robert T. Amsden. 1991. *SPC Simplified for Services: Practical Tools for Continuous Quality Improvement*. New York: Quality Resources.

Anderson, Douglas N. The Quality Evolution. Unpublished, 3M.

Angus, Robert B., and Norman A. Gundersen. 1997. *Planning, Performing, and Controlling Projects: Principles and Applications*. Upper Saddle River, NJ: Prentice Hall.

Barra, Ralph. 1983. *Putting Quality Circles to Work*. New York: McGraw-Hill Book Co.

Betker, Harry A. 1985. Storyboarding: It's No Mickey Mouse Technique. *The Juran Report* 5 (Summer): 25–30.

Bothe, Davis R. 1986. Quantifying the Defects. *Quality* 25 (February): 71–72.

Champy, James. 1995. *Reengineering Management: The Mandate for New Leadership*. New York: HarperCollins Publishers.

Crocker, Olga L., Syril Charney, and Johnny Sik Leung Chiu. 1984. *Quality Circles: A Guide to Participation and Productivity*. New York: New American Library.

Crosby, Philip B. 1979. *Quality Is Free*. New York: McGraw-Hill Book Co.

Deming, W. Edwards. 1986. *Out of the Crisis*. Boston: MIT Press.

————. 1982. *Quality, Productivity and Competitive Position*. MIT: Center for Advanced Engineering Study.

Dmytrow, Eric D. 1985. Process Capability in the Service Sector. *The Juran Report* 5 (Summer): 31–37.

Feigenbaum, Arman V. 1986. Quality: The Strategic Business Imperative. *Quality Progress* (February): 27–30.

————. 1986. Total Quality Leadership. *Quality* 25 (April): 18–22.

Fine, Charles H., and David H. Bridge. 1985. Managing Quality Improvement. Unpublished paper, MIT.

Garvin, David A. What Does "Product Quality" Really Mean? Unpublished paper, Harvard University.

Grenier, Robert. 1986. Total Quality Assurance, Part IV. *Quality* 25 (February): 54–56.

————. 1986. Total Quality Assurance, Part V. *Quality* 25 (April): 38–41.

Halpin, James, F. 1966. *Zero Defects*. New York: McGraw-Hill Book Co.

Holmes, Donald S., and A. Erhan Mergen. 1986. Chi-Square vs. X & R Chart. *Quality* 25 (February): 60–61.

Hoogstoel, Robert E. 1985. A Life Cycle for Quality Circles? *The Juran Report* 5 (Summer): 23–24.

Ishikawa, Kauro. 1976. *Guide to Quality Control*. Tokyo: Asian Productivity Organization.

Juran, Joseph. 1964. *Managerial Breakthrough*. New York: McGraw-Hill Book Co.

————. 1979. *Quality Control Handbook*. New York: McGraw-Hill Book Co.

————. 1980. *Quality Planning & Analysis*. New York: McGraw-Hill Book Co.

————. 1981. Product Quality: A Prescription for the West. *Management Review* (June/July), reprint.

Karabatsos, Nancy A. 1986. World Class Quality. *Quality* 25 (January): 14–18.

Kepner, Charles H., and Benjamin B. Tregoe. 1981. *The New Rational Manager*. Princeton, NJ: Princeton Research Press.

Laford, Richard. 1986. Don't Settle for More Inspectors. *Quality* 25 (January): 46.

Liebman, Murray E. 1986. New Global Competitors. *Quality Progress* (February): 58–60.

Making Quality a Part of the Woodwork. *Quality* 25 (March): 58–60.

McDonald, James F. 1986. Global Quality Manufacturing Strategy. *Quality Progress* (February): 36–38.

McGrath, James. 1985. The Common Threads of Quality Improvement. *Quality* (October).

O'brien, Walter J. 1986. The Customer: A Global Profile. *Quality Progress* (February): 24–25.

Olsen, James E. 1986. The Quality Challenge. *Quality Progress* (February): 12–14.

Peters, Tom, and Nancy Austin. 1985. *A Passion for Excellence: The Leadership Difference*. New York: Random House, Inc.

Peters, Tom, Nancy Austin, and Robert H. Waterman Jr. 1982. *In Search of Excellence: Lessons from America's Best-Run Companies*. New York: Warner Books, Inc.

Shuster, H. David. 1990. *Teaming for Quality Improvement: A Process for Innovation and Consensus*. Englewood Cliffs, NJ: Prentice-Hall, Inc.

Sullivan, L.P. 1986. Japanese Quality Thinking at Ford. *Quality Progress* 25 (April): 32–34.

Taguchi, Genichi. 1986. *Introduction to Quality Engineering: Designing Quality into Products and Processes*.

# Index

245

# Upgrade Your Project Management Knowledge with First-Class Publications from PMI

### THE ENTERPRIZE ORGANIZATION

Every day project leaders are approached with haunting questions like: *What is the primary reason why projects fail? How technical should managers be? What are the duties of a project management office?* These haunting questions, along with many more, are just a few of the question and answers Whitten discusses in his latest book, *EnterPrize Organization*. This book is for seasoned employees as well as those just entering the workforce. From beginning to end, you will recognize familiar ways to define the key project roles and responsibilities and discover some new ideas in organizing a software project.
ISBN: 1880410796 (paperback)

### A FRAMEWORK FOR PROJECT MANAGEMENT

This complete project management seminar course provides experienced project managers with an easy-to-use set of educational tools to help them deliver a seminar on basic project management concepts, tools and techniques. *A Framework for Project Management* was developed and designed for seminar leaders by a team of experts within the PMI® membership and reviewed extensively during its development and piloting stage by a team of PMPs. It serves as a first step for individual attendees who wish to obtain their Project Management Professional (PMP®) certification.
ISBN: 1-880410-82-6 (Facilitator's Manual Set)
ISBN: 1-880410-80-X (Participant's Manual Set)

### THE PMI PROJECT MANAGEMENT FACT BOOK

A comprehensive resource of information about PMI and the profession it serves. Professionals working in project management require information and resources to function in today's global business environment. Knowledge along with data collection and interpretation are often key to determining success in the marketplace. The Project Management Institute (PMI®) anticipates the needs of the profession with *The PMI Project Management Fact Book*.
ISBN: 1-880410-62-1 (paperback)

## PROJECT MANAGEMENT SOFTWARE SURVEY

The PMI® *Project Management Software Survey* offers an efficient way to compare and contrast the capabilities of a wide variety of project management tools. More than two hundred software tools are listed with comprehensive information on systems features, how they perform time analysis, resource analysis, cost analysis, performance analysis, and cost reporting, and how they handle multiple projects, project tracking, charting, and much more. The survey is a valuable tool to help narrow the field when selecting the best project management tools.
ISBN: 1-880410-52-4 (paperback); ISBN: 1-880410-59-1 (CD-ROM)

## THE JUGGLER'S GUIDE TO MANAGING MULTIPLE PROJECTS

This comprehensive book introduces and explains task-oriented, independent, and interdependent levels of project portfolios. It says that you must first have a strong foundation in time management and priority setting, then introduces the concept of Portfolio Management to timeline multiple projects, determine their resource requirements, and handle emergencies, putting you in charge for possibly the first time in your life!
ISBN: 1-880410-65-6 (paperback)

## RECIPES FOR PROJECT SUCCESS

This book is destined to become "the" reference book for beginning project managers, particularly those who like to cook! Practical, logically developed project management concepts are offered in easily understood terms in a lighthearted manner. They are applied to the everyday task of cooking—from simple, single dishes, such as homemade tomato sauce for pasta, made from the bottom up, to increasingly complex dishes or meals for groups that in turn require an understanding of more complex project management terms and techniques. The transition between cooking and project management discussions is smooth, and tidbits of information provided with the recipes are interesting and humorous.
ISBN: 1-880410-58-3 (paperback)

## TOOLS AND TIPS FOR TODAY'S PROJECT MANAGER

This guide book is valuable for understanding project management and performing to quality standards. Includes project management concepts and terms—old and new—that are not only defined but also are explained in much greater detail than you would find in a typical glossary. Also included are tips on handling such seemingly simple everyday tasks as how to say "No" and how to avoid telephone tag. It's a reference you'll want to keep close at hand.
ISBN: 1-880410-61-3 (paperback)

## THE FUTURE OF PROJECT MANAGEMENT

The project management profession is going through tremendous change—both evolutionary and revolutionary. Some of these changes are internally driven while many are externally driven. Here, for the first time, is a composite view of some major trends occurring throughout the world and the implication of them on the profession of project management and on the Project Management Institute. Read the views of the 1998 PMI Research Program Team, a well-respected futurist firm, and other authors. This book represents the beginning of a journey and, through inputs from readers and others, it will continue as a work in progress.
ISBN: 1-880410-71-0 (paperback)

## New Resources for PMP Candidates

The following publications are resources that certification candidates can use to gain information on project management theory, principles, techniques, and procedures.

## PMP Resource Package

*Earned Value Project Management* by Quentin W. Fleming and Joel M. Koppelman

*Effective Project Management: How to Plan, Manage, and Deliver Projects on Time and Within Budget* by Robert K. Wysocki, et al.

*A Guide to the Project Management Body of Knowledge (PMBOK® Guide)* by the PMI Standards Committee

*Human Resource Skills for the Project Manager* by Vijay K. Verma

*The New Project Management* by J. Davidson Frame

*Organizing Projects for Success* by Vijay K. Verma

*Principles of Project Management* by John Adams, et al.

*Project & Program Risk Management* by R. Max Wideman, Editor

*Project Management Casebook* edited by David I. Cleland, et al.

*Project Management: A Managerial Approach, Third Edition* by Jack R. Meredith and Samuel J. Mantel Jr.

*Project Management: A Systems Approach to Planning, Scheduling, and Controlling, Sixth Edition* by Harold Kerzner

## A Guide to the Project Management Body of Knowledge (PMBOK® Guide)

The basic management reference for everyone who works on projects. Serves as a tool for learning about the generally accepted knowledge and practices of the profession. As "management by projects" becomes more and more a recommended business practice worldwide, the *PMBOK® Guide* becomes an essential source of information that should be on every manager's bookshelf. Available in hardcover or paperback, the *PMBOK® Guide* is an official standards document of the Project Management Institute. ISBN: 1-880410-12-5 (paperback), ISBN: 1-880410-13-3 (hardcover)

## Interactive PMBOK® Guide

This CD-ROM makes it easy for you to access the valuable information in PMI's *PMBOK® Guide*. Features hypertext links for easy reference—simply click on underlined words in the text, and the software will take you to that particular section in the *PMBOK® Guide*. Minimum system requirements: 486 PC; 8MB RAM; 10MB free disk space; CD-ROM drive, mouse, or other pointing device; and Windows 3.1 or greater.

## Managing Projects Step-by-Step ™

Follow the steps, standards, and procedures used and proven by thousands of professional project managers and leading corporations. This interactive multimedia CD-ROM based on PMI's *PMBOK® Guide* will enable you to customize, standardize, and distribute your project plan standards, procedures, and methodology across your entire organization. Multimedia illustrations using 3-D animations and audio make this perfect for both self-paced training or for use by a facilitator.

## PMBOK® Q&A

Use this handy pocket-sized question-and-answer study guide to learn more about the key themes and concepts presented in PMI's international standard, *PMBOK® Guide*. More than 160 multiple-choice questions with answers (referenced to the *PMBOK® Guide*) help you with the breadth of knowledge needed to understand key project management concepts.

ISBN: 1-880410-21-4 (paperback)

## PMI PROCEEDINGS LIBRARY CD-ROM

This interactive guide to PMI's annual Seminars & Symposium proceedings offers a powerful new option to the traditional methods of document storage and retrieval, research, training, and technical writing. Contains complete paper presentations from PMI '92–PMI '97 with full-text search capability, convenient onscreen readability, and PC/Mac compatibility.

## PMI PUBLICATIONS LIBRARY CD-ROM

Using state-of-the-art technology, PMI offers complete articles and information from its major publications on one CD-ROM, including *PM Network* (1990–97), *Project Management Journal* (1990–97), and *A Guide to the Project Management Body of Knowledge*. Offers full-text search capability and indexing by *PMBOK® Guide* knowledge areas. Electronic indexing schemes and sophisticated search engines help to find and retrieve articles quickly that are relevant to your topic or research area.

## Also Available from PMI

**Project Management for Managers**
Mihály Görög, Nigel J. Smith
ISBN: 1-880410-54-0 (paperback)

**Project Leadership: From Theory to Practice**
Jeffery K. Pinto, Peg Thoms, Jeffrey Trailer, Todd Palmer, Michele Govekar
ISBN: 1-880410-10-9 (paperback)

**Annotated Bibliography of Project and Team Management**
David I. Cleland, Gary Rafe, Jeffrey Mosher
ISBN: 1-880410-47-8 (paperback)
ISBN: 1-880410-57-5 (CD-ROM)

**How to Turn Computer Problems into Competitive Advantage**
Tom Ingram
ISBN: 1-880410-08-7 (paperback)

**Achieving the Promise of Information Technology**
Ralph B. Sackman
ISBN: 1-880410-03-6 (paperback)

**Leadership Skills for Project Managers**
Editors' Choice Series
Edited by Jeffrey K. Pinto, Jeffrey W. Trailer
ISBN: 1-880410-49-4 (paperback)

**The Virtual Edge**
Margery Mayer
ISBN: 1-880410-16-8 (paperback)

**ABCs of DPC**
Edited by PMI's Design-Procurement-Construction Specific Interest Group
ISBN: 1-880410-07-9 (paperback)

**Project Management Casebook**
Edited by David I. Cleland, Karen M. Bursic, Richard Puerzer, A. Yaroslav Vlasak
ISBN: 1-880410-45-1 (paperback)

**Project Management Casebook Instructor's Manual**
Edited by David I. Cleland, Karen M. Bursic, Richard Puerzer, A. Yaroslav Vlasak
ISBN: 1-880410-18-4 (paperback)

**PMI Book of Project Management Forms**
ISBN: 1-880410-31-1 (paperback)
ISBN: 1-880410-50-8 (diskette version 1.0)

**Principles of Project Management**
John Adams et al.
ISBN: 1-880410-30-3 (paperback)

**Organizing Projects for Success**
Human Aspects of Project Management Series,
Volume 1
Vijay K. Verma
ISBN: 1-880410-40-0 (paperback)

**Human Resource Skills for the
Project Manager**
Human Aspects of Project Management Series,
Volume 2, Vijay K. Verma
ISBN: 1-880410-41-9 (paperback)

**Managing the Project Team**
Human Aspects of Project Management Series,
Volume 3, Vijay K. Verma
ISBN: 1-880410-42-7 (paperback)

**Earned Value Project Management**
Quentin W. Fleming, Joel M. Koppelman
ISBN: 1-880410-38-9 (paperback)

**Value Management Practice**
Michel Thiry
ISBN: 1-880410-14-1 (paperback)

**Decision Analysis in Projects**
John R. Schuyler
ISBN: 1-880410-39-7 (paperback)

**The World's Greatest Project**
Russell W. Darnall
ISBN: 1-880410-46-X (paperback)

**Power & Politics in Project Management**
Jeffrey K. Pinto
ISBN: 1-880410-43-5 (paperback)

**Best Practices of Project Management
Groups in Large Functional Organizations**
Frank Toney, Ray Powers
ISBN: 1-880410-05-2 (paperback)

**Project Management in Russia**
Vladimir I. Voropajev
ISBN: 1-880410-02-8 (paperback)

**A Framework for Project and Program
Management Integration**
R. Max Wideman
ISBN: 1-880410-01-X (paperback)

**Quality Management for Projects
& Programs**
Lewis R. Ireland
ISBN: 1-880410-11-7 (paperback)

**Project & Program Risk Management**
Edited by R. Max Wideman
ISBN: 1-880410-06-0 (paperback)

# ORDER ONLINE AT WWW.PMIBOOKSTORE.ORG

Book Ordering Information
Phone: 412.741.6206
Fax: 412.741.0609
Email: pmiorders@abdintl.com
Mail: PMI Publications Fulfillment Center
    PO Box 1020
    Sewickley, Pennsylvania 15143-1020 USA